JOY & COMPASSION

Very occasionally in our lives we find a book that can literally transform us. This is such a book. It is a book of love. It is a book of compassion. It is a book of prayer. And it is a book of contemplation. It is a spiritual guide to each one of us who embraces the many insights it has to offer. Without question, this book is a God-inspired gift to us all.

Professor R. Quentin Grafton,
Australian National University

Susan Joy's tribute to her children as 'my greatest accomplishment' says everything about the spirit with which she offers the beautiful thoughts within this collection of reflections. Her *kenosis* mirrors that of her master, who became the great servant of all, a friend – and now, as it had been in life – her constant companion. These stories and prayers take us to the very heart of the diaconal vocation, whose spirit permeates the volume. Here also we discover a faith expressed with great clarity, cheerfulness and insight. Her openness is palpable in this *Festschrift* to Life. It teaches us with unapologetic and unmistakable directness that in the practice of perfect love there can be no fear.

The Rev'd Nikolai Blaskow
Associate Chaplain, Head of Religious and Values Education,
Gippsland Grammar School

I encourage you to read this book daily at private worship, along with the suggested Bible passage. Susan Joy turns the reader's attention to how they know, where they are, with God, Jesus. This will help in any spiritual journey. George MacLeod, founder of the Iona Community, says in the book *Only One Way Left*, 'It is the primacy of God as Now that we must recover in Christian mysticism, as the starting point of the new holiness'. I commend this book to you.

Chris Polhill,
Member Iona Community,
Early woman priest in the Church of England, poet, and writer

These writings reveal a ministry of care that is profound and deep, offering a presence to assure anyone that they are not alone, and that confidence can be found in Jesus. Susan Joy lived up to her name in a joyous approach to the world around her, an enjoyment of God's creation which transcends mere appreciation. She lived up to the creative *imago Dei* in which she was formed, taking what had been fashioned by God and weaving a new work.

Bishop Matt Brain
Bishop of Bendigo

We see Susan Joy as a person of colour and creativity, with a pastoral heart, humility, and a wonderful sense of liturgy and ritual. Written in a down-to-earth style, this book of reflections and observations on faith life, encapsulated in prayers, is a treasure. Dip into it, sit with it, share it, be entranced by it.

The Very Rev'd Susanna Pain
Dean, St Paul's Anglican Cathedral, Sale
Spiritual director, pastoral supervisor, InterPlay facilitator

Susan Joy brings her life to these reflections on faith. In life, she was a sign of liberation, a picture of joy. In life, she loved with a heart never defeated by fear or prejudice. In life, she walked alongside, bringing comfort and courage. In life, she taught, always taught, usually in story, always with colour. In her dying, Susan Joy kept living and teaching: love wins, life wins, and in all things, there is a place for joy. In dying, she assaulted our thrall with death. In this exquisite collection, Susan Joy still teaches.

The Rev'd Richard Browning
Director of Mission, Anglican Schools Commission

These reflections and prayers offer clues, encouragement and support, as we consider the question 'how then shall we live?'. Susan Joy draws from her experience and strong faith to share insights, compassion and wisdom, for our contemplation and meditation, and to prompt discussion and action.

Beattie Hatfield
Retired primary school principal

STORIES & PRAYERS
FOR A LIFE OF FAITH

JOY & COMPASSION

SUSAN JOY NEVILE

COVENTRY
PRESS

Published in Australia by
Coventry Press
33 Scoresby Road
Bayswater VIC 3153

ISBN 9780648982210

Copyright © the Estate of Susan Joy Nevile 2021

All rights reserved. Other than for the purposes and subject to the conditions prescribed under the *Copyright Act*, no part of this publication may be reproduced, stored in a retrieval system, or transmitted in any form or by any means, electronic, mechanical, photocopying, recording or otherwise, without the prior permission of the publisher.

Scripture is from the *Holy Bible, New International Version* ®, *Niv* ® Copyright © 1973, 1978, 1984, 2011 by Biblica, Inc.® Used by permission. All rights reserved worldwide.

New International Reader's Version (NIrV) Copyright © 1996, 1998 by Biblica.

The Message. Copyright © 1993, 1994, 1995, 1996, 2000, 2001, 2002. Used by permission of NavPress Publishing Group.

Good News Translation® (Today's English Version, Second Edition)

Copyright © 1992 American Bible Society. All rights reserved.

Catalogue-in-Publication entry is available from the National Library of Australia http://catologue.nla.gov.au

Cover design by Ian James – www.jgd.com.au
Watercolour painting by the author, photo by Rebecca Worth
Text design by Coventry Press
Set in Fontin 11pt

Printed in Australia

To my children
Bethany, Joel, and Tobias

my greatest accomplishment

Table of Contents

Foreword
The Ven. Anne Ranse, Archdeacon Emeritus, OAM 6

Acknowledgments 10

Introduction
Maurice Nevile 12

1   We are, we can be   27

Called 29

Known 33

Child 36

Friend 40

Open 46

Wise 50

Great 54

Humble 57

Vulnerable 61

Secure 64

Acceptable 69

Care-full 72

Generous 76

Thankful 79

2 With us — 83

- The way 85
- Welcomed 88
- Love 91
- Hope 94
- Peace 99
- Light 102
- Belonging 106
- Promises 109
- Grace 113
- Father 117
- King 121
- Kingdom 124
- Authority 128
- Power 134
- Rules? 137
- Riches 141
- Abundance 145
- Miracles 149
- Not alone 153
- Sacrifice 156
- New ways 160
- God's eyes 163
- God's vision (all about Mary) 166

3 Along the way 173

Committing: saying 'yes' 175
Doubting, believing, following 178
Seeing Jesus,
listening to Jesus 182
Welcoming Jesus 186
Growing 190
Bearing fruit 193
Understanding 197
Risking faith 201
Loving 205
Taking a journey 208
Searching 212
Trusting 217
Praying 220
Accepting gifts 225
Waiting 229
Choosing 232
Deciding 236
Forgiving 239
Standing, kneeling 243
Resting 246
Rejoicing! 249

4 Encountering troubles — 253

Starting over 255
Bound 258
Tempted 262
Lost, found 267
Confused 272
Tumbled and tossed 276
Failing to act 281
Facing giants 284
Reaching out 287
Shouting out! 291
The scream 294
Burdened 299
Scarred 302
Separated 307

5 We change, we become — 311

Getting ready 313
Invited 316
Beginning 320
Knowing yourself 324
Wearing armour 328
Leader 332
Servant 335

Sorry, reconciled	342
Getting excited!	346
Reshaped	349
Transformed	353
Living with faith	357
Finding true life	362
I am	366
Sources	373

Foreword

A life of joy and compassion:
Susan Joy Nevile

It is a privilege and an honour to be able to introduce Susan Joy through her writing. Many readers will be blessed to have such a book as this to read, to be enlightened and inspired for their own journey on the pathway of life, wherever they are up to with God. Susan Joy's writings are God-gifted and Spirit-filled. All those who read them will be blessed and will go back to its pages over and over again. What a gift she has left us.

More than ever before, I think people are searching for a deeper relationship with God. Many people have no problem recognising the hand of God in the bright hues of the rainbow, the magnificent mantle of the starry night sky, the breathtaking sunrises, and sunsets, but many of these seekers are hoping for more. They are searching for God's presence in the routine moments and stories of their everyday lives, and they wonder.

Susan Joy was the 24th deacon ordained into the permanent diaconate of the diocese of Canberra and Goulburn. She was ordained on 28 November 2009 in St Saviour's Cathedral in Goulburn, at a time when I was the Head of the Household of Deacons. I saw her journey through the discernment process to her ordination. Therefore, as a deacon myself, I feel I am qualified to comment on these writings.

Others, like the clergy and the people of her parish church of Holy Covenant, Jamison, her family, and many who knew her, saw in her something special, something different. There was humility about her and something 'Godly', and people affirmed and supported her journey in lay ministry and ordination.

Susan Joy saw ministry as a calling by God to go out to love and serve the Lord, to reach the vulnerable, or those on the margins, on the edge of the community and faith. She talks of her call as not a one-off call, because Jesus invites us every day to follow him. In her reflection on 'Servant', Susan Joy says 'I cannot sit back as if it's done... There is more to this process of following'. She had earlier noted that:

> The idea of being a servant often does not sit well in our individualistic hedonistic success-driven commercialised culture. We often have a cringe reaction... Maybe the word raises too many connotations of subservience, of having to obey and act without question, and of being exploited. But the idea of servant is essential to the story of Christ's ministry and message.

She expands on this, quoting the words of Stuart Barrie from the poem 'Follow, follow' (in Ruth Burgess, *Bare Feet and Buttercups*, Wild Goose Publications, 2008):

> Never once, did he say,
> 'Worship me I am the One.'
> Adoration was not sought
> or ever needed by the Son.
>
> All he wanted was the heart,
> no chant or hollow plea.

The gift he asked? ... 'Release your grasp.
Relax, and follow me.'

And Susan Joy did. The clarity of expounding scripture can only come from one who is connected deeply with Christ. Susan Joy has an exceptional ability to link the historic scriptures with our lives today. In these writings, the clear message of seeing ourselves in the solution, the purpose of the story and the daily application, is profound yet easy to read, short and succinct enough to hold engagement, and enough to be able to see and recall the story that packs a punch and adds a hook in the tail.

This book is an excellent resource for personal reflection, for church resources, for group study, for people of any age and for those wondering and seeking faith in the invisible God. The writings are a wonderful resource for the diaconate and those seeking personal spiritual growth. Each reflection captures an aspect of faith life and takes you into the relevant story(ies) with brilliant clarity. Stories from the Bible and beyond are brought to life, giving the reader a view into what happens when God enters both the great and small detail.

Susan Joy takes life experience and wraps it around stories for faith. As readers, we are in no doubt that these reflections come from a Godly life, lived with Christ and in Christ. Here are beautiful words from a deep, spiritual heart. Words of daily life flow in and out of the stories and we can feel her passions for justice and care. Those fortunate to have known Susan Joy will certainly hear her voice in these words and will sense the Spirit working through her.

In her ministry, Susan Joy nurtured and sustained many. Her ministry was in schools as a chaplain, as a family and children's minister at her local church, and for ten years in hospice and hospital pastoral care, supporting patients, families and staff through their experiences and bringing them love and hope. She was the deacon of the Eucharist and was gifted in creating liturgical settings for the various seasons of the church year. She has let God fill her with good things like patience, love, and wisdom.

I will draw on wordings of the Diaconate Ordination Ritual: she taught what she believed, she lived what she believed, she preached what she believed, she did all she was called to do.

As you read these reflections, enjoy and be moved by them to the very depth of your soul. You will come out a changed person, a person who has felt the warmth of the words and appreciated their application for a life of faith. I found my heart on fire and, like any good read, I could not put the text down. I kept turning the pages to see what gems the next reflection held.

So, read this book and be blessed as you discover and have affirmed the depths of God's love for you, and his commitment to be with you through all the moments of your life.

Thank you, Susan Joy.

The Venerable Anne Ranse, Archdeacon Emeritus OAM

Deacon in the Household of Deacons
Canberra and Goulburn Diocese
Director and Chaplain to
the Holistic Care Nursing Ministries
Holy Covenant Anglican Church, Canberra.

Acknowledgments

I am grateful to Coventry Press, and especially to editor Hugh McGinlay, for seeing the value of this book and for the faith and commitment to publish with more than the usual challenges and risks. I thank Coventry Press staff for their fine work to produce it.

I thank The Ven. Anne Ranse OAM for writing such a beautiful and fitting foreword, as someone who knew Susan Joy well, as person and deacon.

As I shared thirty-three years with Susan Joy, I know many of the people who were part of her rich and varied life, through family and friendship, education and work, ministry and church, or creative and other activities. To them, and to others I do not know, on her behalf I acknowledge their significant influences on her, and for how she understood and realised her faith. I hope that they will see their connection to her within this book. I know that Susan Joy was immensely grateful for the opportunities and experiences of her work in hospice and hospital pastoral care, school chaplaincy, family/child ministry, and telephone crisis counselling. She was also encouraged and affirmed in her studies at St Mark's National Theological Centre, Canberra, and throughout her preparation for ordination as a deacon. She deeply valued the role of the permanent diaconate and her calling to serve God in the world, coming alongside people where they were.

I am grateful to the family and friends who supported or otherwise reached out to me throughout the two years I

Acknowledgments

worked on this book and began to recover and restart my life after losing Susan Joy. Perhaps this was to meet for coffee, to walk together, to gift or share a meal, to invite me over or drop in to visit, or just regularly to make contact to check how I was going. Through their concern, care, and company, they valued both me and Susan Joy. I thank them for being with me in those ways at such a time of profound sadness.

Our children, Bethany, Joel, and Tobias gave me much strength, while dealing themselves with the shock and pain of losing their mother as young adults. They looked after me, and each other, and I know that Susan Joy would be hugely proud of them. I thank them for their understanding, patience, and love.

From Susan Joy I received more than thirty years of friendship, forgiveness, belief, kindness, and unconditional love. She influenced and blessed me with her humility, courage, quiet wisdom, gentle spirit, open heart, and resolute faith. She inspired me with her passion and gift for colour and creativity, expressed most clearly in her many beautiful quilts. She brought into my life everything now most precious to me. One day in early 1985, Susan Joy first reached for my hand as we set out together for a walk. She holds my hand still. She chose me. She was light for me. She was Christ to me.

Maurice Nevile

Introduction: A voice, on how to live as a person of faith

Maurice Nevile

'For we live by faith, not by sight.' (2 Corinthians 5:7, NIV)

Living by faith

How can we live as people of faith in this world? What does it mean to believe, to belong, to trust, to risk, to serve, or to find true life? How can faith sustain us at times of trouble, and how is God with us, guiding us on the way? How can we hope, search, pray, or love, and become the people God knows we can be? And as we 'live by faith' (2 Corinthians 5:7), how can we create a life of joy and compassion?

A life of faith brings us closer to God. We are invited and welcomed, we are strengthened and forgiven, we are listened to and accepted, we are held and cared for, we can find peace and rejoice, and we can transform ourselves, and the world around us. At times, we can feel sure and secure in our faith life, that we know where we are going, how to get there, and who is with us. But through experiences, our faith may also become unclear, or may be shaken, especially at moments

Introduction

of great change, challenge, or pain. We can wonder what is happening or how we should act. We can hesitate or be overwhelmed. We can wonder what to believe or who we should be. We can feel let down or alone. We can make poor choices or fail. We can become weary or give up. We can lose the light and find ourselves in darkness.

This book offers a collection of eighty-six story-focused reflections, and accompanying prayers, to support your life of faith. Each reflection focuses on a specific aspect of faith life. The reflections show how 'story' is an immensely powerful means for understanding ourselves, our life experiences, and our relationship with God, as we live in faith and seek to be as Christ to others. This book will encourage and enable you to connect to stories and to engage with the stories you encounter and create for yourself, in and for your own faith life.

Stories are drawn from the Bible and also from a highly diverse range of other sources, including literature (especially children's literature), movies, art, sport, politics, and the ordinary moments and events of life, for example losing your keys, catching the wrong bus, getting hurt, being in the dark, standing at the back of a crowd, being invited (or not), or waiting at hospital.

Some stories from the Bible might be familiar, like an ark loaded with animals, a brave boy's battle with a giant, a baby born under a star, the wind and flames of Pentecost, and a king killed on a cross. Other Bible stories might be less well known, including a funeral procession as a widow prepares to bury her only son, or a captured slave girl advising a general. Bible stories are rich with characters and their actions. For example, you will read about the Bible's 'big names'– Jesus and his disciples, Mary and Joseph, Abraham and Sarah, David, Jonah, Elizabeth, James, Martha, Peter, Stephen and others. You will read too about a rich young man, a lost son, a Canaanite woman, an Ethiopian official, a generous widow, a wicked tenant, a tax collector, a paralysed man, a thief, a woman bent over, angels, banquet guests, vineyard workers, and many more.

And well beyond the Bible, you will read about figures of life and literature, including boxer Muhammad Ali, John Newton, Maria of Ravensbrück, Mother Teresa, St Francis of Assisi, and also Indiana Jones, Mary Poppins, Charlie Brown and friends, characters of the Harry Potter, Narnia, and The Lord of the Rings books, among many others. And you will encounter an angry dog, a shoemaker, a girl who likes herself, a first friend, a fourth wise man, a grateful student, a helpful bus driver, an accountant who becomes an artist, an Afghani man who turns bomb shells into flower plots, and a sparrow who shares bread with a homeless man.

Stories are also rich with objects that help to tell stories of faith. For example, from the Bible you will read about jars of wine, a clean slate, Caesar's coin, a cloak, a bronze snake, a young boy's lunch, bread and a cup shared between friends, a crown of thorns, and a stone rolled away. Beyond the Bible, you will read too about a pea, cricket pads, balloons, show bags, candles, junk mail, a guilt detector, a broken vase, a magic tape measure, a brick in a backpack, a security blanket, a chocolate fudge banana cake, and others. And there is also a nest in scraggly hair, a menorah that strengthens a community, a game that reveals who we are, and a roulette wheel where a scream changes destiny.

The fundamental message of this book is that a life of faith

Introduction

is one of joy and compassion, as gifts from God for how we can live, and live with others. By reflecting on various forms of story, the book shows us how God is always alongside us. A faith life will have struggle and stumbles, but because God is there to sustain us, we can then sustain others. So, while we may not always be happy, with faith we can dare to rejoice by looking for God's love to transform our experience of the present and so lead truly fulfilling joyous lives. And while we can sometimes think compassion is reserved for people whose job it is to help those in need, God calls us all to care for others, the vulnerable, the broken, the outsiders, the poor, the troubled, and anyone whom God gives us, as an integral part of our faith life.

These reflections will help you in your faith life, for example to:

- recognise and experience small and quiet miracles
- give to others and appreciate what God gives you
- distinguish between what burdens or helps you
- understand the impacts of your choices
- find reconciliation through forgiveness
- change direction if you lose your way
- know how to follow, and lead
- trust, and wait in confidence
- hope, and be transformed
- see the world as God does

- ☐ see Jesus around you
- ☐ find peace and rest
- ☐ know God's love
- ☐ rejoice

You might embrace this book early in your faith life journey, readying yourself as you begin and interested in what is involved. Or you might be well on the way, perhaps seeking to energise your progress, clarify your understanding or direction, find support, or to return to familiar ground. Reflections do not assume a well-established biblical understanding or commitment to Christian belief, but instead gently introduce and contextualise stories and concepts, or the thoughts of theologians and others, such as Ana Maria Bidegain, Walter Brueggemann, John Goldingay, C. S. Lewis, Henri Nouwen, Rachel Naomi Remen, Bishop Desmond Tutu, and Joy Carroll Wallis. Prayers are written directly from the reflections in ordinary and inclusive language, and in an interactive and accessible style.

Reading these reflections

The reflections are organised into five sections representing broadly the constitution of a life of faith. Reflections are written as stand-alone texts, so you can read them in any order, though there is also a sense of flow within and across the five sections.

The first section, WE ARE, WE CAN BE, has fourteen reflections about *us*, the people undertaking faith life, as God

Introduction

knows us, and knows how we can be. For example, we are 'Called', 'Known', 'Child', 'Friend', and 'Humble'.

In the second section, WITH US, there are twenty-three reflections about the nature and character of *God, Jesus*, and *Spirit*, alongside us, for example as 'The way', 'Hope', 'Peace', 'Light', 'Grace', 'Father', and 'Abundance'.

In the third section, ALONG THE WAY, there are twenty-one reflections about *what we do*, and *what happens*, as we create and experience a life of faith, for example 'Committing', 'Doubting', 'Growing', 'Searching', 'Praying', and 'Rejoicing!'.

The fourth section concerns ENCOUNTERING TROUBLES, and has fourteen reflections about *the difficulties we face* as we create our faith lives, for example 'Starting over', 'Bound', 'Tempted', 'Facing giants', 'The scream', and 'Scarred'.

The fifth and final section, WE CHANGE, WE BECOME, offers fourteen reflections highlighting how a life of faith *can impact and form us*, as we engage with the world and find who we are with God, for example 'Getting ready', 'Knowing yourself', 'Wearing armour', 'Transformed', 'Finding true life', and 'I am'.

According to your preference or interests, you could jump right in to read about being 'Known', then consider 'Hope' and 'Grace' before thinking about 'New ways' and 'Risking faith'. Or you might choose to settle on one section and move through or between its reflections for a while, perhaps to explore the kinds of troubles one can encounter in a life of faith. Alternatively, you can work your way through from start to finish, to begin by reflecting on yourself as a person of faith, and end by reflecting on how faith life can change you. Although each prayer is written directly from and for its accompanying reflection, you can also read the prayers independently.

17

Reflections have a common structure. Each reflection has:

- a title indicating the aspect of faith life in focus
- the Bible passage(s) and/or other sources referred to, or relevant
- a summarising and guiding headline
- the reflection itself
- one or two prompting questions (or comments, actions)
- a prayer arising directly from the reflection

Susan Joy Nevile, and this book's origins

I came to write this introductory chapter, and to bring this book into being, as the author's husband of nearly thirty years. Susan Joy Nevile died in late August 2018, aged 55.

In mid-August 2017, Susan Joy and I began a seven-week trip to Europe, beginning with her attendance at a European conference for pastoral carers, held in Finland at Järvenpää just north of Helsinki. She had worked as a hospice and hospital pastoral carer for ten years, supporting patients and their families, and also staff, through the demands and traumas of medical need and care. This was her first major international conference, and something of a dream come true to meet with like-minded colleagues, and at a beautiful lakeside venue. She was also keen to progress her early thoughts for beginning a PhD.

After that conference we flew to London for some tourist days, and then caught a train to Edinburgh, on our way to a week's retreat at Iona Abbey, on the Isle of Iona off Scotland's west coast. As Susan Joy left the Edinburgh train, she first noticed symptoms of the illness which within a year would cut short her life. We completed the Iona retreat, and despite feeling increasingly worse throughout the week, she was able to attend mealtimes, worship services in the abbey twice daily, and also do some limited activities. With some initial medical attention, Susan Joy improved greatly on the last day and took a leading role in the farewell service. For many years, she had wished to visit Iona. She had long appreciated traditions of Celtic spirituality and worship, and she had used and valued many resource books by Wild Goose Publications of the Iona Community. So, I will always think of that last Iona day as a miracle. We resumed travel but within days her condition deteriorated seriously, she was hospitalised, and there, in regional west coast Scotland, we were told of her terminal diagnosis.

Susan Joy described these writings as, 'my voice – on faith and how to live as a person of faith in this world'. She had written that as a note taped inside a ring binder containing some paper copies, and another note, taped to the front cover, said that our youngest son had wanted them. Some copies were typed, but most were handwritten and showed revising. This book has its origins in my discovery of that ring binder. Susan Joy had written throughout her more than twenty years' experience as a school chaplain, family/children's minister, and then as a hospice/hospital pastoral carer. She had written too for her ministry studies and during her preparation for ordination as a deacon. She was able to draw on her extensive background in leading worship across many settings, and in teaching from early childhood, through primary and high school and up to university.

In the subsequent weeks, I found many more writings, including some as digital files, and I gradually realised just how much material there was. As I looked more closely, I realised too how remarkably consistent the writings were. Most significantly, they were all *oriented around stories*, typically weaving between Bible and other forms of story. This orientation reflects Susan Joy's educational and professional background, but also her personal nature. Since childhood she had always been an avid reader, and described her interest in story like this: 'I am someone who is attuned to narrative, always looking for what is happening in a story, what it means, and I am always seeking to pick the ending of a movie' (see 'The scream').

Her writings had many other features in common: they were written as reflections, each focused on a specific aspect of faith life; their relevant stories were mostly introduced and explained; they were concise, and mostly similar in structure and length; they shared a personal, interactive, inclusive, and accessible style; they did not assume a firmly established Christian understanding or commitment; they were clearly written; and their impact was to guide, encourage, prompt, support, and sometimes challenge. I realised that given their great number, and with minimal repetition across the texts, together they covered a wide range of aspects of faith life.

I decided that many more people than our youngest son might value and benefit from Susan Joy's insights on how to live as a person of faith, and so the idea was born to gather and publish her reflections as a book. As an academic in the social sciences, and also an experienced academic editor and copyeditor, I was glad to have the knowledge, skills, and confidence to take on such a large task, and also the

Introduction

strength to persevere, especially with the heartache of those first months as I discovered and began to work through her texts. I wished so dearly to discuss the texts with her, to tell her how much I valued them, and how they were inspiring and impacting me.

I collected, typed up, edited, and formatted Susan Joy's reflections into a coherent whole. Many reflections were near-complete, but others needed some fleshing out and finishing for clarity and continuity, and especially to ensure that stories and sources were sufficiently introduced and contextualised. A couple of reflections, for example on 'Fear' and 'Dry bones', were mainly notes, and so I had to abandon them. I was deeply sad to lose 'Dry bones' because I knew Susan Joy loved that passage from the book of Ezekiel 37, with its stunning image of God breathing the bones into life, conveying the extraordinary power of God's Spirit. For each reflection, I identified or refined the title, according to its focus, and wrote a summarising headline. I organised the reflections according to a broad framework of 'a life of faith'. I found and completed details for all Bible passages and other quoted sources. To end each reflection, I formulated one or more questions or comments to prompt further thought, discussion, or action. I added cross references to link some reflections.

I made simple line drawings by tracing over watercolour paintings that Susan Joy completed in her final few months, and these appear on the section title pages. Detail of one painting also appears on this book's cover. Susan Joy was especially keen to paint trees. In her journal writing she described trees as 'a place of sanctuary for me'. She recalled how as a child she would hide in her tree house and listen to people as they passed by in the street below. She noted too that she valued trees because, like the kingdom, they grow to give shelter (Luke 13:18-19).

For each reflection, I also wrote an accompanying prayer. I indicate joint authorship for the prayers because I wrote directly from the reflections and so relied on Susan Joy's own thoughts and wordings. I was also influenced by Susan Joy's voice and usual style. When writing prayers, she preferred to use brief and familiar language, simple and repeating structures, corporate forms (i.e. we, us, our), and she often began with a descriptive address term, reflecting the prayer's focus (e.g. 'Generous God'). I had for reference an earlier collection of Susan Joy's prayers, 'Prayers of light, life, and love', which I had previously compiled and produced. For example, and most relevant to this book, here are her prayers titled 'Stories' and 'Faith'.

Stories

Jesus
you told great stories
they helped people to make sense of their lives
they revealed God in ordinary things
they encouraged people
they changed people

help us to be changed by your stories
help us to take up your challenge
to live as your people

Amen

Introduction

Faith

Loving God
sometimes we are amazed by what can happen
when people have faith...
seas can part
walls can fall
battles can be won

help us to see the faith miracles
which we can sometimes overlook...
friendships that are saved
challenges and problems that are shared
days that are brightened by kindness or a smile

help us to find new ways to live our faith
at home and wherever we go
Amen

    I knew too that Susan Joy appreciated Michael Leunig's prayers and poems. I am delighted that Susan Joy and I have effectively collaborated to create the prayers.

    But it is fitting that I elaborate on 'joy' and 'compassion', the words of this book's title. These two words capture Susan Joy's sense of what it is to live as a person of faith. So significant were they to her that for her funeral she asked for them to be written, one word each side, on the large sheet of fabric draped over her coffin. She also requested that we play a favourite song of hers, '(I've been given) Two Wings' by Australian a cappella gospel choir *Café of the Gate of Salvation*. It has these lyrics:

Lord I've been given two wings
to fly to Heaven's gate
Two wings so wonderful
that even the angels celebrate

One wing is compassion
kindness for every living thing
one wing is joy
seeing glory in every living thing
oh Lord please let me use these wings

Lord let me use
lord, lord, lord, lord
let me use these wings

(song lyrics by Tony Backhouse. Used in full with permission)

In her life, Susan Joy flew with those two wonderful wings: compassion, and joy. She was a person of kindness, and she was a person always to see God's glory in the world around her, and particularly in the people whom God had given her. She also loved the idea of angels celebrating! In her reflection on 'Miracles', she writes that 'when people change, to try to live in God's ways, to be as God wants and knows they can be, God throws a party in heaven ... God is really a party God. God knows how important it is to feel joy, and to share life's joyous moments'. Susan Joy tells us also that Psalm 23 was special and significant to her (see 'Secure'). Even in her last months, she was certain of her invitation to God's banquet, and that her cup overflowed.

As I was not previously aware of most of Susan Joy's reflections, I was the book's first reader. I came to them at a time of substantial loss, grieving the person at the core of my life, the person who most closely and fully shared my past, present, and anticipated future. And just a month before Susan Joy's illness appeared, I had had to let go of my 30-year university/research career. So, the two years over which I worked on this book were my life's darkest and most difficult. At such distressing and life-changing events, personal faith can be significantly shaken, questioned, or even given up. However, as I read and worked through Susan Joy's reflections, I found my own faith to be clarified, affirmed, and encouraged. Through her words I found wisdom, inspiration, comfort, and healing, enabling me to get up and move forward. I found myself returning to truths. I was reminded of how my life story, and hers, related to others' stories, to Christ's story, and to God's great story for the world.

Susan Joy noted that these reflections are her 'voice', and I am sure that you will hear her clearly. She might have been too humble to think of collecting and publishing her writings in this way, and I would guess that she had no idea just how much she had written over so many years. Anyway, her calling and gift was not to publish but to be present with people, to listen, and to care. But I know that she would understand why I was compelled to create this book on her behalf, and I know that in spirit she has been with me throughout. As Susan Joy considers across this book, from suffering can come compassion, from despair can come joy, from loss something can be found, and from death can come life. From her loss, this book was found. From her death, this book comes into our lives.

I will risk a metaphor. Susan Joy asked for everyone attending her funeral to receive a packet of flower seeds to take home for their garden. At a time of death and ending, Susan Joy gave people seeds to remind of life and beginning. The seeds would grow and in time reveal their potential by showing bright colours of God's creation. She was passionate about exploring with colour, especially in her quilting, and in her last months through her watercolour paintings. She held close to a quote attributed to Dutch artist Petrus Van der Velden (1837-1913): 'colour is light, light is love, love is God'. Perhaps then, like those seeds, to grow and one day burst into colour, these reflections are Susan Joy's gift to us as we grow and realise the potential of our faith lives. What then will we show to the world of ourselves, and of God?

In her final months, Susan Joy wrote that her dream for relationships was to 'keep on loving, seeing the positive, seeing the gift in each person', and that to her 'success' meant 'coming alongside someone'. I know that through this book you will sense her loving positive presence coming alongside as you see and draw on your own gifts and create your life of faith. She would hope for your faith life to be one of joy and compassion. But this is her book, and so to Susan Joy I leave the last words, from her reflection 'Finding true life':

> we are being offered an alternative model of being, shown in Jesus' death on the cross, giving his life for us. That is where true life is found. Only when we can say who Jesus is, as the one who suffers and dies on the cross, can we begin to understand that. Only then, when we live our lives as the people of the cross, following that same road and giving of ourselves for the people around us, do we find the life to which Jesus calls us.

1 We are, we can be

Called

Jonah

WE ARE CALLED TO LOVE OTHERS

You have got a call! Well, we all do. How do we respond to the chances and challenges that come our way? As a school chaplain and teacher, I used to feel that there was something special about a new school year. As I looked out at the familiar faces, and some new ones, I saw hope, anticipation, even confidence, about what might come, but also often doubt or worry about what is ahead. And I can understand why so many people make new year make resolutions: I will eat well, I will exercise more, I will be better organised, I will not be late, I will control my temper. The start of a year is a great time to think about the person we want to become, and the challenges we will encounter, or set ourselves, to make it happen. This is also true of a major change, or new endeavour or journey.

Here we will follow the story of someone who was given a challenge. It is the story of Jonah. God asked Jonah to do a job. We can say Jonah was 'called by God'. To be called means that we discover, come to know, what God particularly wants us to do in the world. Well, Jonah had it spelled out for him. God commands him to go to the city of Nineveh to prophesy against it, because the people had fallen into wickedness and God wanted them to change their ways. But Jonah does not do this. Jonah runs away – from God – and boards a boat bound for another city, called Tarshish. At sea, there is an extraordinary storm, which he sleeps through, and he is blamed and eventually thrown overboard. He is swallowed by a great fish and spends three days in its belly before praying to God and is then vomited out. God *again* commands Jonah to go to Nineveh, and this time he does go, telling the residents that in forty days the city will be overthrown. Led by the king, the people repent, and God spares the city. But Jonah gets angry at God for his compassion, and leaves the city, and God teaches him a lesson about pity.

This story is easy to love. There is humour when Jonah is asleep in the storm, action when Jonah admits fault and is tossed overboard to be swallowed by the fish, and human drama as Jonah confronts the city of Nineveh, only to get angry when they do change their ways. No wonder it is a favourite Bible story, but sometimes it is too easy to think of it as only about the guy and the big fish, or to point our finger at Jonah and judge him a fool for not doing what God asked him to do. We can say to ourselves 'I would never be like that. If I got a call from God I would respond to the challenge, *not* run in the opposite direction!' And we can say that feeling quite safe in our hearts that God really would not call *us* as he called Jonah...

Maybe we feel safe because when we think of people being *called* by God we bring to mind the 'big important' people, the Bible celebrities, like Paul who went out to start many churches, or maybe Moses who had to tell the Pharaoh to let God's people go free. Or maybe we think of more recent people, like Martin Luther King Jr or Mother Teresa, who were driven to seek large scale social change, and had huge impacts on thousands or even millions of people. We might consider too a priest or a nun, as people who spend all their time on 'special God stuff'. But we tend *not* to think of *ordinary people*, who do *ordinary jobs* like a bus driver, a builder, a nurse, a florist, a public servant, a teacher, or even a student, as people who are called by God.

And here is a problem, or let us say, challenge – God calls everyone. God does not care what work we do, how experienced we are, how 'important' we are, or whatever our age or gender – God gives everyone a call. It is a call to love, just as Jonah's call was. Because at the heart of the book of Jonah is a love story. God wants Jonah to understand and share his love for the people of Nineveh, to know that God loves all people, even when they have turned their backs on him.

God wants *us* to do the same thing, to follow and know that we are loved, and to share that love with others. Sometimes that can grow to something that affects people all around the world, as it did for Mother Teresa. And sometimes it grows to something that affects the people around us, in our family, in our work and school, in our neighbourhood and wider community. So, our influence might extend to whomever is right next to us, or in the next room, house, or suburb. And that is still important. We all have the call to think about the person we want to become, and about how to live and to love others. We are called to think about how we will respond to the situations we find ourselves in, and the chances and challenges that God gives us. And *that* call is *not* just at the beginning of the year.

> HOW ARE YOU CALLED?
> HOW DO YOU RESPOND?

God
you call us to follow you
through life's chances and challenges
you call us to understand
you call us to act
you call us to be

when we pretend that we cannot hear
or run away to hide
or do not respond
because we are tired, afraid, or busy
you call us again, and again

thank you for never giving up on us
and for finding us
and guiding us on both where to go
and how to get there

Amen

Susan Joy Nevile and Maurice Nevile

Known

John 13:31-38 (NIV)

WE WILL BE KNOWN FOR HOW WE LOVE OTHERS

How do others know us, as people, and as people of faith who follow Christ? I confess that during one Olympics, I watched quite a lot of the TV coverage. One of my lasting memories of those many spent hours was that in the background there was a repetitive sound. It went like this: 'Aussie Aussie Aussie... Oi Oi Oi'. When I heard this, I knew immediately that the people chanting, incessantly, were Australians. They were cheering on the athletes whom they perceived to be their heroes, the ones they wanted to win, or at least to perform well. I could tell, even without looking at the TV, what country they were following and supporting. Similarly, if someone wears some clothing, even just a cap, with a sporting team's name or logo on it, others can form some ideas about the sport that person follows, and the team to which they give their allegiance. And we might be able to 'work out' something more about the person. Perhaps they read media stories about their team, or talk with friends about the team's performances, or even go to games to directly experience the highs and lows of being a committed fan.

Now it is often much harder to work out information about people. Sometimes we need to watch them closely, to see what they do. We might see how they spend their time, to see what activities they do. We might see whom they spend their time with. We might notice what they choose to spend their money on, or what they eat, or what they are interested in, what they care about, what gets them excited. From all these we might get some idea about them as a person.

But how can we know if someone is a follower of Jesus Christ? People don't usually wear 'Jesus caps', and we don't hear them chanting loudly 'Jesus Jesus Jesus... Oi Oi Oi '! In the text here, Jesus gives us an answer to that question (v. 35): 'By this everyone will know that you are my disciples, if you love one another'. It is not by what we wear. And it is not by what we say. It is how we act that gives us away as Jesus' followers. It is how we love others. If you know the 'Harry Potter' books/movies, I think it is like when Dumbledore tells Harry that it is the choices we make that show who we truly are. As we choose how to act, who we are, and who we follow will be revealed. That is how people will know us. Do we act with love? And not just any 'love'. Jesus says, 'As I have loved you, so you must love one another' (v. 34). So, it is not a weak and warm fuzzy feeling kind of love. Jesus shows us very clearly the love he is talking about. Before he was arrested, Jesus shared a meal with his disciples, at what we call 'the last supper' (Mark 14:22-24):

> While they were eating, Jesus took bread, and when he had given thanks, he broke it and gave it to his disciples, saying, 'Take it; this is my body'. Then he took a cup, and when he had given thanks, he gave it to them, and they all drank from it. 'This is my blood of the covenant, which is poured out for many', he said to them.

This is the kind of love that took Jesus to the cross, and the love which brought him out of the tomb. And Jesus challenges us. If we want to be known as his followers, we are to love one another, as he loved us. It is a very substantial challenge, and sometimes, or often, or maybe even many times, we do not make it. But God always gives us the chance to say sorry for those times, and the chance to try again. As Jesus' followers, we stumble, and we fall, but God is always there to help us to get up, and to continue. God knows us for who we are, and for who we can and will be.

> **WHAT IS YOUR CHANT?**
> **HOW DO YOUR CHOICES**
> **SHOW WHO YOU ARE?**

Knowing God
help us to follow in your ways
so that others will know us
for how we act with love
to one another
just as you love us

Amen

Susan Joy Nevile and Maurice Nevile

Child

Luke 15:11-32 (NIV)

Henri J. M. Nouwen (1994) *The Return of the Prodigal Son: A Story of Homecoming*. Darton, Longman, and Todd. London.

IF WE TURN TO GOD, WE ARE WELCOMED HOME

For a child, what does it mean to 'leave home', and to come home? Here our reflection is prompted by some thoughts from Henri Nouwen's book *The Return of the Prodigal Son* in which he describes how an encounter with the Rembrandt painting of that name, and his reflections on the story told in Luke, deeply influenced his own spiritual path (see 'Father'). I encourage you first to look at the painting, perhaps at its Wikipedia page. The painting shows both the younger son, who left home and family for a life of foolish and selfish indulgence, and the older son, who remained home to work and dutifully support his father. What do the painting and story tell us about being a child, about home, about leaving, and about coming home?

The younger son is shown receiving a blessing from his father, who welcomes him back. We know where the son has been, and what he has done, wastefully spending his inheritance. We know that this loving embrace only comes after the son had left, having said to his father, in effect, 'I wish you were dead', having denied who he was at home, and sought to find what he wanted in a faraway land. He left in public and spectacular ways, becoming lost in his visible and wayward actions.

Nouwen puts at the base of all leavings our denial of the spiritual reality that we belong to God, a denial of the voice which says, 'you are my beloved child'. He describes it as a very soft and gentle voice, which does not force itself on us. It is unlike the many loud voices around us that dominate our attention and energy, full of promise, that say 'go out and prove that you are worth something', 'show us that you are worth loving' (p. 40). With our ears ringing with those voices we become deaf to the quiet voice of unconditional love, and we 'leave home' to look for it elsewhere, even somewhere far away, in a spiritual if not physical sense. Nouwen (p. 42) notes that if we spend our time asking the world, 'Do you love me? Do you really love me?', we can become defined by the world's response, when it answers: 'I love you if you are good-looking, intelligent, and wealthy. I love you if you have a good education, a good job, and good connections. I love you if you produce much, sell much, and buy much'.

Our yearning for the voice of love can pull us further away from home to where it cannot be satisfied. How can we tell that we are being pulled into distant places?: when we find ourselves full of anger, resentment, jealousy, revenge, lust, greed, and rivalries; and when we find ourselves brooding on why someone rejected us, hurt us, or is more successful, or more socially accepted. Nouwen comments (p. 42) that:

> Often I am like a small boat on the ocean, completely at the mercy of its waves. All the time and energy I spend in keeping some kind of balance and preventing myself from being tipped over and drowning shows that my life is mostly

a struggle for survival: not a holy struggle, but an anxious struggle resulting from the mistaken idea that it is the world that defines me.

Perhaps the younger son is easier for us to understand, and sympathise with, because we can see his path away from home, and its cost, in his mistakes and misery, and his asking for forgiveness. When we look at him, we can see our own leavings. Maybe ours are not as public and spectacular, but we 'leave home' in more subtle ways, when we do what we know can separate us from God. How can we hear the quiet voice calling us home, as a beloved child?

There is also the older son. Perhaps he is harder to identify with. He was dutiful, law-abiding, responsible, hardworking. People respected him, admired him, and praised him. He was the model of a good son. Yet when faced with his father's joy at the return of the younger son, what does he do? He refuses to enter into it. His response is to be angry, resentful, bitter, proud, unkind, selfish: 'Look! All these years I've been slaving for you and never disobeyed your orders. Yet you never gave me even a young goat so I could celebrate with my friends'. Perhaps we can see ourselves in him when we wave our finger and focus on the faults of others, feeling superior to them.

As Nouwen notes, the father has really lost both sons. From where has the older son's response come? It is closely wedded to the desire to be good, to do the right thing, to be likeable, and acceptable. He has made a conscious effort to avoid temptations, to be different from others. Nouwen expresses this as a deeper complaint, coming from a heart that feels it never received what was its due. The complaint is both self-righteous and self-rejecting. He seems emotionally distant from his father. Both sons have 'left home': one has gone to seek love, affirmation, and acceptance in other places; one has stayed home to earn these and measure them out.

We do not know how the story ends. We do not know how the younger son accepted the household's celebration for his return, or whether the elder son ever reconciled himself with his brother, his father, or himself. What we do know with certainty is the heart of the father that longs to meet his child with joy, blessings, forgiveness, and mercy. We know that God longs for the return of all children, for all of us to receive a blessing. As a child of God, we need only to turn to him, and the blessing is there. He will lean over us, put his arms on our shoulders, embrace us, and welcome us home, where he has kept our place.

> HOW HAVE YOU 'LEFT HOME'?
> HOW HAVE YOU BEEN WELCOMED BACK?

God
we are your children

forgive us when we stay home
feeling rejected and self-righteous
forgive us when we leave home
to find our worth in the world

thank you for always being there
to welcome our return with blessing
and your loving embrace

Amen

Susan Joy Nevile and Maurice Nevile

Friend

John 15:9-17; Luke 5:17-39 (NIV)

Charles M. Schulz (1964) *I Need All the Friends I Can Get.* Determined Productions.

A REAL FRIENDSHIP HAS A LOVE THAT GIVES ITS ALL, AND TRANSFORMS PEOPLE

A true and strong friendship can enrich our lives and support us through times of trouble. The story here, according to John, is known as the 'farewell discourse' because it is part of the final things Jesus wanted to say to his friends before his arrest, ahead of his crucifixion. He was helping them to think about what love is, and how much he cared for them. It was important because he knew they would be confused by what was going to happen the next day, and they needed to know the strength of their friendship with Jesus.

Do you remember your first friend? I can remember mine – Suzanne, from kindergarten class. We were friends right up to year six, and I can remember my first ever sleepover at her house. The walls of her bedroom were a light green, the curtains over the window were white and pale yellow. Her bed was under the window, and mine was against the wall. I can remember lying awake in the strange room, in the strange bed, telling myself to be brave, and that it would be OK because my friend was just over there. It is curious what can start a friendship. I do not remember what brought me and Suzanne together, but for many years my daughter had a very close friend, ever since they were in the first year of school. It started when the teacher was marking the class roll on the first day and called out 'Bethany'. The two girls both said 'yes'. They have had their ups and downs, but they began with something important in common, and their friendship lasted many years and into adulthood.

When I have talked with children about friendship, we have thought how sometimes it is difficult to know if someone is really your friend. We decided it would be good to have a way to measure, like a ruler, how much someone cared for you, to see what kind of a friend the person was. Unfortunately, we don't have such a measure – we need to work these things out for ourselves as we go along, using the means that we have: other people's words and actions, what they say, and what they do. We must see if their words and actions match up. To do this we need to understand what real friendship is all about.

If we think about our own friends, close by or maybe more distant, recent, or long term, what is it that makes them a friend? Is it how they talk to us, or maybe how they listen to us? Is it what they share with us, or allow us to share with them? Is it what they give us, and allow us to give to them? Is it how they care for us, or allow us to care for them? Is it just being together, knowing one another? For some, friendship is about meeting needs, having someone around who can be there to help, or who can make them feel good about themselves. For others, it is about someone to be with, to enjoy experiences and good times together. Still others see a goal of friendship is to find someone who understands you or shares how you look at the world. The writer C. S. Lewis talked about how making a friend is like discovering a fellow traveller and journeying together on a secret path.

In a book of 'Peanuts' cartoons, by Charles M. Schulz, Charlie Brown was confused about the nature of friendship. Here are some of the answers he found: 'A friend is someone who's willing to watch the program you want to watch'; 'A friend is someone who will hold a place in line for you'; 'A friend is someone who sticks up for you when you're not there'. I find such cartoons helpful because visually they can highlight and prompt thinking about what it means to be a friend. When I have used them in class with children it seems that individuals find that a particular cartoon stands out, resonating with their own understanding. For me, two stood out: 'A friend is someone who takes off the leash!' and 'A friend is someone who will share his home with you'. In the first cartoon, Charlie Brown has removed Snoopy's leash, and Snoopy dances with joy in his new freedom. In the second, Snoopy and Woodstock hug on top of Snoopy's kennel.

Well, Jesus did not want *his* friends to be confused, he wanted there to be no doubt about why their friendship had happened, and what it was all about – Jesus says, 'I chose you'. He wants them to be certain of how much he cares for them, no matter what will happen. He spells out that, for him, a friendship is about love. Not a soppy kind of love – a real friendship has a love that gives its all. That is what Jesus offers to everyone who is willing to be his friend. On his last night with his friends, the night before he died on the cross, Jesus was helping them think about just what love is. Jesus loved us so much that he stretched out his arms on the cross. It was not just words. Jesus died for his friends. As our friend, he died for us.

The Bible has many examples of friendship, of who friends are, and what they do, but our story here really stays in the mind. As a school chaplain, when I used to talk to the youngest children about Bible stories that they knew, they often remembered this next one. Jesus was teaching, and the crowd included teachers of the law and people from many places. Some men came carrying a paralysed man on a mat and wished to lay him before Jesus, but the size of the crowd prevented them from getting into the house. So, they went up on the roof, moved some tiles, and lowered the man, on his mat, into the middle of the crowd, right in front of Jesus! Jesus recognised their faith, and said, 'Friend, your sins are forgiven' (Luke 5:20). Maybe children remember the story so well because they are intrigued by the idea of making a hole in the roof of a house. If you are visualising this, note that it is a flat roof, but even so, it must have been quite an effort for the friends to get the man up there, and for the others quite a shock to be listening to Jesus and suddenly see a man on a mat being lowered down. It makes for a dramatic and memorable scene.

What did they feel then, in the house? – surely shock, but also surprise, and wonder, and awe. We have an idea about some of them. We know that the Pharisees and teachers and officials were outraged: 'Who is this fellow who speaks blasphemy? Who can forgive sins but God alone?' (Luke 5:21). We also have an idea what Jesus felt because he looked up at the friends and saw how much faith they had, even before he spoke to the man. In the story, we do not hear about the man's friends and their reactions, but I will focus on them.

If I try to pick some words to describe the friends, two spring to mind: *desperate* and *confident*. I would usually not put those two together to describe someone, but when we think about what they did, they must have really wanted their friend to be healed, and they had the strength of mind to act. Let us think in practical terms. When they heard Jesus was coming to town, their concern was not to get front row seats. They thought of their friend. They went to get him, literally carrying him down the road to bring him there, and when faced with the problem of the crowd they did not give up, but carried him up onto the roof, and found a way in. They were so confident that Jesus could help their friend that they were desperate to bring the two together. These are thoughtful, kind, courageous, persistent, and awesome friends. After responding to the Pharisees, Jesus tells the man to get up, take his mat and go home, and the man leaves praising God. The people in the house believed that they had seen something remarkable that day, and surely they had.

The story here, with a man on a mat needing healing, gives us a fantastic example of friendship, of being a friend. The man was healed, and his life was transformed, not only because of God's love and power but also because of his friends, of their care and commitment to him. *We* are called to be *that* kind of friend. Sometimes we want to be, but we are not sure how, or we succeed for a while but fall short, perhaps because it is too hard, or too painful. Yet we *can* always do what the friends did in the story, we can take our friends to Jesus by talking to God about them, knowing that God is listening with love.

> HOW ARE YOU A FRIEND?
> HOW DO YOU KNOW
> WHO YOUR FRIENDS ARE?

God, our dear friend
you set us free
and you welcome us home

thank you for the friends
who accept us as we are
who encourage and support us
who help us to laugh at ourselves
who help us to laugh at life
who see what we need
who believe in us
who value us
who love us

Amen

Susan Joy Nevile and Maurice Nevile

Open

Acts 8:26-40 (NIV)

HOW OPEN ARE WE TO THE OPPORTUNITIES GOD GIVES US?

God gives us moments and opportunities, to act, and to change. The story here is not so well known. We find it early in the book of Acts, amongst the first stories of Jesus' followers after the ascension and the coming of the Spirit which is celebrated at Pentecost. The story sits alongside Peter's healing of the lame man at the temple, Stephen's stoning, and Saul's persecution of the church and subsequent conversion. It is the story of Philip and the Ethiopian official. Philip is one of the twelve, we hear about his calling in the book of John. We do not know much about him, but he says to his friend Nathanael, 'We have found the one Moses wrote about in the Law, and about whom the prophets also wrote – Jesus of Nazareth, the son of Joseph' (John 1:45, NIV). Nathanael replies: 'Nazareth! Can anything good come from there?' (v. 46). Philip is one of the people early on in Jesus' ministry to see who he really is.

In our focus text here, Philip is told by an angel to go south to the road to Gaza. On the journey he met an important Ethiopian official, who had been to Jerusalem and was heading home. He was reading from the book of the prophet Isaiah, and the Spirit prompted Philip to go over and listen (vv. 32-33):

> He was led like a sheep to the slaughter,
> and as a lamb before its shearer is silent,
> so he did not open his mouth.
> In his humiliation he was deprived of justice.
> Who can speak of his descendants?
> For his life was taken from the earth.

There had been a history of Ethiopian Jews since King Solomon's time, so it is not as unusual as we may think to find that one of the queen's high officials had been in Jerusalem to visit the temple. At the time of the early church, the kingdom – or we should really say 'queendom', as one only hears of the queens of this country – covered the western third of what is now Sudan. So that is all of Eritrea, Yemen, and Ethiopia, and most of Somalia. It was an exotic place – Ethiopia exported luxury items like gold, incense, and ivory. In many ways it was vastly different from the Judean towns, and the official was very different to the people with whom Philip was used to speaking. Even though we are told that the man was a 'believer', he was culturally a long way from those born into the Jewish faith in Judea. And because of this, it was likely that he was not allowed into the full worship at the Temple in Jerusalem. Yet when these two unlikely companions met on the road and travelled together, they found common understanding.

Philip asks the Ethiopian if he understands what he is reading, and the Ethiopian replies that he cannot unless someone explains it to him. This is not really a story of conversion. Philip has not converted or changed the Ethiopian's faith. Rather, it is a story of *inclusion*. The official turns to Philip and asks, 'What is to keep me from being baptised?' Philip can see no reason why this man cannot become part of God's family and baptises him. The Ethiopian continues on his way, full of joy. It is a great story and gives us insight into the growth of the early church. But to me it does more than this.

As I reflect on this story, again and again what comes to me is the idea of openness. We have Philip's openness to God: he responded to God's prompting, he did not say, 'I don't want to go to Gaza, why should I?' He got up and he went. And on the road, he took the opportunity that God gave him to connect with someone else. In turn, the Ethiopian official is open to Philip's question and so receives help in understanding the scriptures. Through this exchange would develop one of the earliest Christian churches, which grew and continues to this day. The Coptic Orthodox Church traces its origins to that Ethiopian official baptised by Philip.

It makes me wonder about how open we are. How often do we miss or even ignore the chances that God gives us, chances to connect with people that we come across, in ways that can be enriching for both? Sadly, I think many of us can live closed lives. As early as the school playground, children can be isolated and excluded, and in our adult lives we see this at work, in the community, even church, with how we can categorise and label people. We see it when we judge people by what they wear, by their weight or appearance, by how old or healthy they are, by where they live, or by their car or career. It seems that we often need definite lines or boundaries: we want to know who is in and who is out, who is with us and who is not. Closing ourselves to others can make us feel secure.

Unfortunately for us, for our typical ways, the example God gives us is one of open boundaries; God's example is of radical inclusion. God does not say, 'you have to be this kind of person to be part of my family'. Everybody is welcome.

Everybody is included. God is like a parent eagerly waiting for all the family to be gathered around the table for a huge celebration. And I do not think we are just meant to sit there, waiting to be served – we also need to be open to include, we need to make sure there is room for everyone. And we do this by becoming more like Christ, our light and God's great example.

> WHAT MOMENT OR OPPORTUNITY
> DO YOU HAVE TO ACT, OR CHANGE?

God
help us to be open
to moments of chance
to risk
to connect
to include
to welcome
to be enriched by opportunities

because at your great celebration
there is room for everyone

Amen

Susan Joy Nevile and Maurice Nevile

Wise

1 Kings 3:3-14 (NIV)

**BY DRAWING CLOSE TO GOD
WE CAN BETTER UNDERSTAND OUR OWN WISDOM**

What does it mean to be 'wise', and what can we do to become wise? We would hope that wisdom was something to be sought and valued, to empower us to learn about the people and features of the world around us, to be aware of what is happening in our lives, and within ourselves, and to make good and right decisions. The Bible gives us some stories of wise people, and perhaps one of the best known is Solomon. Let us start with Solomon's response in the text here, when God appears to him and says: 'Ask for whatever you want me to give you' (v. 5). What would *you* have asked for? Wealth? A long life? Triumph over your enemies? World peace?

Solomon asked for 'a discerning heart to govern your people and to distinguish between right and wrong. For who is able to govern this great people of yours?' (v. 9). God was pleased: 'I will do what you have asked. I will give you a wise and discerning heart, so that there will never have been anyone like you, nor will there ever be' (v. 12). Indeed, God gave much more than Solomon asked, including both wealth and honour, so that in his lifetime he would have no equal among kings. God also promised that if Solomon walked in obedience and kept God's decrees and commands, then he would have a long life.

Well, God definitely came through on Solomon's wish. Solomon is renowned for his wisdom. The classic story of Solomon is when he decides between two women both claiming to be the mother of a baby boy (1 Kings 3:16-28). There was no DNA testing in those days, so what is Solomon to do? He orders the baby to be cut in half. One woman says, effectively, 'OK, so neither of us will have him'. The other woman says no, to give the baby to the first woman, because she loves the child and cannot let him be injured. So, Solomon gives the baby to the second woman – as the true mother. There are stories still told in Africa of Solomon's wisdom and of his meeting with the Queen of Sheba. Yes, Solomon certainly counts as wise.

What comes to your mind with the word 'wise'? Some people might think instantly of those three wise men who travelled far to visit the Christ child. Others might recall the great minds of European history, perhaps philosophers or scientists. Or still others could think of the ancient or mystics from cultures beyond Europe, or elders in indigenous communities. It is worth considering what we think of as a wise person. What are they like? How would we know if we found one? (Let alone three!) More importantly, how can we become wise ourselves? And what is it that makes someone wise? Is it life experience? Is it age? If age brings wisdom, there is little point worrying about it – wisdom will come to all, in time! But sadly, that seems not to be true. Maybe wisdom is found in seeking and accumulating knowledge, in what and how much we learn, like the ability to quote Shakespeare, or to understand $E=mc^2$. So, is the pursuit of education the sure path to wisdom? If not, could wisdom instead be to reflect, appreciate, and examine the world, and our part in it? Well then, where is the bottom line? On what basis can we assess life around us? How do we know what to value, what is good or bad, right or wrong, beautiful or ugly, what is worth keeping and what is worth losing?

We can have one answer in Psalm 111:10 – if you really want to become wise, you must begin by having respect for the Lord (NIRV), or, in a more traditional translation, the fear of the Lord is the beginning of wisdom (NIV). What did Solomon do before the dream? He went up to the high places and drew close to God, because in seeing God clearly he could also see himself, as he was – not the mighty king of a great nation, but, as we hear him describe himself – I am only a little child (1 Kings 3:7). Solomon could also see what was needed: a ruler with understanding, and a discerning heart.

To me, Solomon seems quite wise, even before he is gifted by God, because some wisdom lies in knowing we can turn to God to better understand ourselves, and in responding to what is needed – not just in identifying a problem, or an issue, but by becoming involved in its solution. For example, the wise men of the Christmas story did not just observe the star, they were moved by it, and they embarked on a long journey (two years) to become a part of what the star meant. Let us hope that we too may travel a path of wisdom and be part of a wonderful, healing, transforming miracle.

> **WHAT IS YOUR PATH OF WISDOM?**

God
by turning to you
by being close to you
by seeing you clearly
we ask for a discerning heart
to live with wisdom
to be part of your transforming miracle

Amen

Susan Joy Nevile and Maurice Nevile

Great

Mark 9 (NIV)

TO BE GREAT WE MUST GIVE OF OURSELVES

Boxer Muhammad Ali was affectionately known as 'the Greatest' after he famously declared 'I am the greatest'. He was also well known for self-promotion. In the book of Mark, we get a different sense of greatness. In the first eight chapters we hear of Jesus' teachings, healings, and then things heat up. Jesus predicts his death at the end of Mark chapter 8, and the disciples do not understand (see 'The way', 'Peace'), and in chapter 9 there is the transfiguration (see 'Seeing Jesus'), some dramatic healing, then Jesus takes the disciples aside to teach them. Again, Jesus predicts his death, and again his followers do not understand. They then travel to Capernaum and apparently along the way the disciples argue about who was the greatest, because on their arrival Jesus asks them, 'What were you arguing about on the road?' (v. 33). It must have been embarrassing for the disciples. No wonder they were quiet. Likely they looked at one another, or out the window. Who would answer? How would they explain that they had been fighting over who was 'number one', to the very person who just a few hours earlier had explained to them that he was to be betrayed, would die, and would then be resurrected? It would seem rather petty.

What saddens me is that we still have that same old petty argument – who is 'number one', who is the first? For example, in school, it could be pushing to be first in line or to be picked for a team, or to get special roles, and wanting the best exam results. In the workplace, it might be battling for recognition and promotion, or just competing to speak in meetings, or to be heard. It is sad too when people think and behave as if they were 'better' than everyone else, entitled, as if rules only applied to others, like driving and on the road: 'that Stop sign isn't for me', 'I can drive faster than the speed limits', 'I can park where I want'. Or, we see it when people do not respect or listen to others, or are greedy, or think their own time is more valuable than anyone else's, or that they are somehow more important, perhaps because of what they do or own.

So, what does Jesus say to the disciples' argument? He does not say, as in some senses he is quite able, 'Well, actually, I'm the most important person that has ever been born'. He does not say, 'Well, Peter was the disciple I called first, so he's the most important'. And he does not say, 'Okay, Judas looks after the money – that's a significant job – so that makes him the most important'. No. Does Jesus name the oldest, the biggest, the best looking, or even the richest or most successful? Again, no. Instead, Jesus sits down, calls them together, and gives that wonderful upside-down answer: 'Anyone who wants to be first must be the very last, and the servant of all' (v. 35). And to prove the point, he takes a child and places the child among them. Children today might think they have a tough life – they must go to school and do what their parents and teachers tell them. But in Jesus' time, children were among the most unimportant people in the community. They had no rights, and mostly nobody considered their needs at all. Jesus' action shows God's perspective: he draws the child in, from the outside of the group – to the very centre. Jesus is saying that in God's eyes, the least, the unnoticed, the forgotten, the marginalised, the humble, and the powerless, *they* are the ones who matter.

God looks at things so very differently to us. The Messiah, the chosen one, the Son of God, is not going to be a powerful leader who throws out the Romans. No, he is going to suffer, be rejected, be condemned, die, and then rise again. If you want to be first, and important, well then, you must be 'the servant of all'. In other words, greatness in God's eyes is not about what we achieve and get for ourselves, it is about who we are, and how we give of ourselves.

> **WHERE DO YOU ARGUE ABOUT GREATNESS?**

God
we are sorry that we often argue over greatness
help us to see differently and to be great
not by what we achieve
but by who we are
and by giving of ourselves

Amen

Susan Joy Nevile and Maurice Nevile

Humble

Luke 18:9-14 (NIV)

IN BEING HUMBLE WE ARE EXALTED

Our attitudes can greatly affect who we are and how we live, and how we impact other people. Here we will reflect on one of the simplest stories, or parables, that Christ told. In fact, there are only two characters in it – a Pharisee and a tax collector.

You may well know the term 'Pharisee', but what does it really mean? It means 'separated one'. A Pharisee was one who was separated from others. The Jewish scribes and rabbis, beginning with the Ten Commandments, had added, and added, to the Jewish law, until it included tens of thousands of regulations covering all of life. Pharisees considered following these regulations to be of the utmost importance. They were not just content to observe the Old Testament law, they added interpretations and sub-laws. For example, they said you had to wash your hands in a certain style before you ate, or you had committed a great sin. According to their formula, you had to allow water to wash over your fingers while rubbing your hand with your fist, letting the water drip off your wrist. When this was done, you turned your hand over and repeated the process. If you did not do it *exactly* in that fashion, you would be in violation of their law and no longer be allowed in fellowship with them.

As we can imagine, their rules made it difficult for them to function in daily life, so they separated themselves and set up their own little group and would not associate with the commoners. Tax collectors or 'publicans' were hired by the Roman government to collect taxes from their own people and turn it over to the despised Romans. They were seen to be traitors, living the high life off the labour of their own people. The Jews hated these tax collectors so much that they were not allowed into the temple, not allowed into the synagogues, and they could not give testimony in the Jewish courts of law.

Now that we have an idea about the characters, let us think about the story. It is one of those upside-down stories. The mere idea of bringing together a Pharisee and a tax collector in the same story was a wild thing to do. And the ending was truly radical! If Jesus had asked for a phone vote on 'who went home right with God?', nobody would have picked the tax collector – all his listeners would have got right behind the Pharisee. So, Jesus tells this story to shake them up a bit – you think you know about God, and what pleases God, well think about this! And it is worth understanding more by getting to the heart of what Jesus was saying.

Different writers have varying views. Some go into detail about what each character said in their *prayer*. Others say that the words in the prayers are unimportant, but what really matters was the manner of speech – in other words this is a story about *attitude*, and our attitude affects all that we do. We can see the Pharisees' attitude right from the start. When I was young, there was a common term of abuse for people who thought they were better than others: they were 'posers'. The Pharisee is a poser, a show-off. It is all about him. He has not come to God to ask for help, or to tell God how much he loves him, or to say sorry: he has come to talk about himself.

The Pharisee thanks God for three sins that he does *not* commit, 'God, I thank you that I am not like other people – robbers, evildoers, adulterers – or even like this tax collector' (v. 11). He thanks God for one man with whom he cannot be compared, 'or even like this tax collector' (v. 11). And he thanks God for two good deeds that he continues to do, 'I fast twice a week and give a tenth of all I get' (v. 12). In keeping all the laws in their most extreme form (Jewish law asked you to fast once a year), he had come to rely on himself. In trying so hard to be holy, to be right with God, he had lost the very thing he was striving for. He did not need God, he could do it by himself, in his own strength, and he wanted everyone else to know that.

In contrast, the tax collector lurks quietly in the shadows. Somehow this tax collector has slipped past the guards at the door of the temple. He has come only to pray. He does not want anyone to notice that he is there, or he could be in serious trouble. As one of the most despised people in all Israel, his life could even be in danger. Yet his being there shows how much he wants to be close to God. And he says his simple prayer 'God, have mercy on me, a sinner' (v. 13). In this prayer, we have a quite different attitude. The tax collector realises that nothing he can do can make him right with God, it is only God's mercy, God's love that can do this. He comes to God humbly, asking for forgiveness.

The story can prompt us to think about our own attitude. Do we fall into the very traps that caught the Pharisee? Are we ready to judge and see faults in others, but not in ourselves? Do we focus on what we do well, avoiding where we need improvement? Jesus reminds us to be humble, and in God's mercy we will be exalted.

> GOD, HAVE MERCY ON ME, A SINNER ...

God
we are afraid to see ourselves honestly
we are afraid to appear weak or wrong
even to ourselves
we avoid the challenge of changing who we are
and how we treat others

we think we can do it all alone

help us to be brave enough
to be humble
to turn to you
to ask for your help
to accept your help
and so be exalted in your mercy

Amen

Susan Joy Nevile and Maurice Nevile

Vulnerable

Matthew 16:21-28 (NIV)

Terry Tempest Williams (2000) *Leap*. Pantheon Books, New York.

FROM VULNERABILITY TRANSFORMATION CAN OCCUR

We try to be strong, but at times in life we must acknowledge our vulnerability and grow from it. I remember having coffee with two friends, both women of faith, and both having faced great difficulties in their lives. These included loss of close family members, threatened sense of self identity, chronic physical problems, and ongoing mental health concerns. Together we talked about the invitation in this passage from Matthew to 'take up your cross' (vv. 24-26), in the light of their significant struggle and pain.

> Then Jesus said to his disciples, 'Whoever wants to be my disciple must deny themselves and take up their cross and follow me. For whoever wants to save their life will lose it, but whoever loses their life for me will find it. What good will it be for someone to gain the whole world, yet forfeit their soul? Or what can anyone give in exchange for their soul?'

As we talked further, it became clear that both women had carried, and still carried, many burdens, many crosses. Two words surfaced for us: vulnerability and transformation. We spoke of Jesus' vulnerability in taking up the cross, exposing himself to what was to come, opening himself to God's will. The experiences of my two friends, and of many people I have seen in my hospice and hospital pastoral care work, is one of being broken, powerless, and vulnerable. They understood well what Jesus was talking about, but they were aware too that this is not the end of the story. Their experiences of brokenness opened their hearts and lives to others. As Terry Tempest Williams notes, 'Life is a process of being broken open', and Joanna Macy hints at the potential for this openness: 'the heart that breaks open can contain the whole universe' (https://www.joannamacy.net/main). From these words, I recall how Jesus teaches us that 'unless a kernel of wheat falls to the ground and dies, it remains only a single seed. But if it dies, it produces many seeds' (John 12:24).

Christ's words, the words of modern writers, and the experiences of my friends, all express the hope that it is from a position of vulnerability that transformation can occur. Jesus did not just die, he rose again, and he lives. The cross holds suffering, but also life, hope and healing. We are called to be open to brokenness, but we are also called to be agents of transformation. We can find ways to be open to allow our hearts to be stretched to include those whom God gives us. How are we to be so? For each of us it will be different, but with God's help, for each of us it *will* be possible.

> **WHERE ARE YOU VULNERABLE?**
> **WHERE CAN YOU GROW?**

Caring God
we struggle
we feel pain
we lose hope
we are afraid
we are broken

heal us
strengthen us
stretch our heart
so that in our brokenness
in our vulnerability
we are transformed
and can open our lives
to others

Amen

Susan Joy Nevile and Maurice Nevile

Secure

Matthew 7:24-27

Charles M. Schulz (1963) *Security is a Thumb and a Blanket*. Paul Hamlyn, London.

GOD'S LOVE IS SECURE, THE ROCK
ON WHICH WE CAN BUILD OUR LIVES

If, like me, you are a little too old and sophisticated to play in sandpits, you might at least have experience with a child building a sandcastle or two. It is a common enough activity for young families living at the coast, or on a beach holiday. I remember one summer I made a huge sandcastle with my youngest. After some time of our cooperative and diligent building, it had a moat and turrets, and we decorated it with shells and seaweed. We also added flag poles, and small round pieces of seaweed became people inside the castle. We then sat and watched as the tide came in, wave by wave, at first slowly, and then quite quickly, destroying our castle.

That is the image I have when I hear this reading from the book of Matthew: a house in a place that looks great, with wonderful water views, but that is built on ground that is easily washed away when the rains come. Jesus tells us that this is how a foolish person hears but does not follow his teaching. In contrast, anyone who hears Jesus' teaching and *does* follow it, puts Jesus' words into action in their own life, is like someone who builds a house on rock so that it is stable and does not wash away with rain and wind. Sometimes, we see distressing TV coverage of mudslides, of overflowing rivers, where a building shifts and then slides away, perhaps leaving just a wall or two teetering on the brink. I think this is what Jesus had in mind, houses with foundations that are not secure and are unable to withstand damaging forces. So, if you have ever built a house or done extensions, you will know how important it is for holes and trenches to be filled with concrete and reinforcing to form a base. But Jesus was not talking as a building inspector, he does not care about concrete and reinforcing! Jesus cares about how we establish the foundations of our lives.

What are our foundations, what makes us feel safe and secure? We all have things that help. American cartoonist Charles M. Schulz makes some suggestions with his 'Peanuts' characters. Maybe, you are like the pianist Schroeder, who feels secure when he has the music in front of him. I am. When I speak in public, maybe to give a sermon, I prefer to have the words before me, knowing that I don't have to face the risk of losing my thoughts – it is all set out on paper before me, just in case. Once I did leave the sermon in my office and preached from memory, feeling sick in my stomach but having to continue, to let go of what had been my security. Or maybe you are like Charlie Brown's little sister, feeling secure and in control if you can touch the bottom when swimming, having your feet firmly grounded, for example in life circumstances and events that are neat and predictable. Maybe you feel secure in your natural talents, like Frieda and her naturally curly hair, relying on what you are good at.

Maybe you are secure like Snoopy, who has accumulated a stack of bones by his kennel, or Patty with her jewellery in a box with a lid, or Charlie Brown knowing that there is some more pie left for later. Maybe, like Linus, you are secure in a group of friends, where you do not stand out, with people who accept you and will be there when you need them. Or maybe you share Linus' security in hearing others in your home, a reminder that you are surrounded by familiar people, and you are not alone. And Linus, like my daughter, also had the security of a blanket! Sometimes, objects give us comfort and make us feel safe. If you pause to think on it, right now, what gives you a sense of security?... What makes you feel safe?

Unfortunately, in many ways these things are just like the sand to which Jesus refers. They can be swept away. Life circumstances quickly change, for example at work or home; we can have family breakdown, friends can disappoint or leave us, we can lose what we own, and we can have accidents, illnesses and tragedies. Or, change can come more slowly, and we are worn out over time, only later realising that what we have previously relied on has been weakened or lost. These are the winds and rains of life that wear away our foundations, that make us feel like that sandcastle destroyed by waves of the incoming tide, or the building on TV slipping away into mud or raging waters. Jesus says that if we have a secure base, we will withstand these winds and rains. The base, the rock of foundation, is the love of God.

Jesus is telling us about the nature of God's love: it is not damaged and does not wear out; nothing can separate us from it; it has no use-by date; it is not replaced by a newer version; it is not partial and conditional; we can trust and rely on it; and it is *always* there. God's love is the rock on which we can build our lives. The Bible is full of stories and pictures of God's love, and the security it offers. One of the most well-known is that of a shepherd looking after sheep, so I will finish with Psalm 23 (GNT), which is special and significant to me, and to many others.

Secure

The Lord is my shepherd;
   I have everything I need.
He lets me rest in fields of green grass
   and leads me to quiet pools of fresh water.
He gives me new strength.
He guides me in the right paths,
   as he has promised.
Even if I go through the deepest darkness,
   I will not be afraid, Lord,
     for you are with me.
Your shepherd's rod and staff protect me.

You prepare a banquet for me,
   where all my enemies can see me;
you welcome me as an honoured guest
   and fill my cup to the brim.
I know that your goodness and love will be with me all my life;
   and your house will be my home as long as I live.

> **WHAT MAKES YOU FEEL SAFE AND SECURE?**
> **HOW RELIABLE IS IT REALLY?**

God
you make us secure
as the ground beneath us
as the blanket covering us
as the music laid before us
as the familiar voice around us
as the shepherd guiding us in right paths

your goodness and love will be with us
your house will be our home
your banquet will be ready
for all our lives

Amen

Susan Joy Nevile and Maurice Nevile

Acceptable

Mark 7:1-23 (NIV); James 1

IT IS WHAT COMES FROM OUR HEART, WHAT WE SAY AND DO, THAT REALLY MATTERS

Mark tells us the story of the Pharisees and teachers of the law challenging Jesus when they saw the disciples eating with unclean hands, that is, hands that had not been ceremonially washed. This passage does not give us an excuse to eat without washing our hands – it is not talking about germs, and it is not an excuse to break the rules. Rather, from the story we can understand which rules are important and should be kept, and which rules should not be kept. Jesus responds: 'Nothing outside a person can defile them by going into them. Rather, it is what comes out of a person that defiles them' (Mark 7:15-16). We can understand from Jesus what really makes a person 'clean', acceptable, and so helps us to draw closer to God.

There is an irony here because many of the laws that the Pharisees created were based on a desire to draw closer to God, by staying pure, by staying clean, and the washing represented washing away of sin and unworthiness. The problem was that Jesus saw the commandment of God being replaced by the tradition of the elders. This is something that Jesus had ongoing arguments with the Pharisees about – you may know the stories of when Jesus healed someone on the Sabbath, or when Jesus and his friends picked grains to eat on a Sabbath. Jesus even included these ideas in a parable, the good Samaritan. The Priest and the Levite who pass the injured man by, who do not stop to help him, do this because if they got his blood on them they would become 'unclean' and would have to spend both time and money to become ritually clean again. In Jesus' story, the Priest and the Levite had confused what was essential and what was non-essential. So, what is the difference between the two?

Jesus tells us that it is what comes *out* of a person, *from the heart*, in what we say and do, that makes us clean or unclean, and acceptable to God. That is what is essential. What is non-essential are the external things that go into a person, like certain foods. So being clean and closer to God is not a matter of strictly following traditions and conventions, but a matter of the way we live. The book of James, thought to be written by James the brother of Jesus, is clear about this. Being clean is in the way we treat each other. It is not enough simply to do no harm to others – we must actively help others. James talks about two kinds of generosity of the Spirit: being quick to listen, and slow to anger; and generosity of effort. Feed the hungry, welcome the stranger, comfort the sorrowful, counsel the doubtful, forgive all injuries, bear wrongs patiently, tend the sick, visit those in prison, instruct the ignorant. In these ways, from what comes from our heart, we are 'clean', pure, worthy, acceptable, in God's eyes. If we are to follow rules, then these seem to be good ones to live by.

> **WHAT COMES OUT OF YOU,
> FROM YOUR HEART?**

God
we want to be clean
in our words
in our actions
in our hearts
to treat each other with kindness
with generosity
with patience
to be acceptable to you
because that is what really matters

Amen

Susan Joy Nevile and Maurice Nevile

Care-full

Matthew 15:21-28 (NIV)

Nathaniel Lachenmeyer (2005) *Broken Beaks*. Michelle Anderson Publishing.

> THERE CAN BE JOY IF WE CARE, AND LISTEN
> TO THOSE WHO FIND IT HARD TO BE HEARD

Who gets heard? Who gets cared for? If I am honest, this passage of the Canaanite woman is not one that preachers much look forward to. It is a struggle. In this passage, Jesus, whom we often think of as a warm and kind person who could be counted on to teach, heal, and say 'bless you', basically says to the woman 'no, what I have is not for you'. In this instance, Jesus seems to accept the very cultural boundaries that so often he overturns, like using the despised Samaritan as the example of the good neighbour, choosing a child from the crowd as an example of who is the greatest in God's eyes, or having dinner with the local tax collector.

So, what is happening in this story? Jesus had earlier discussed with his friends about holiness, and as I reflect on this story, I find that earlier discussion colours my thoughts. Jesus was arguing that it is what comes out of you, what flows from your heart, especially in what you say, that shows what kind of person you are (see 'Acceptable', 'Knowing yourself'). And so, for me, the story of the Canaanite woman becomes a story about voices. The story has a dramatic reality, with a desperate mother trying to save her daughter from demons. She is calling out to one who held her hopes, with the embarrassed men pushing her to one side. It is a warning about whose voices get heard.

We have the Canaanite woman on one hand, and the disciples on the other. Jesus let the woman come to him, he let her follow them, he let her call out, and the disciples tried to get him to turn her away, to keep her quiet, to ignore her requests for help. But she was allowed to stay. And in the time and space that she was given, her voice expressing both need and faith was heard. In this case, it was the voice of the outsider that carried with it the wisdom 'Even the dogs eat the crumbs that fall from their master's table'. It was the outsider, a non-Jew, who showed what it was to have faith in the Messiah, and in so doing taught the disciples what their job was.

The passage, therefore, prompts me to wonder: what can we learn from those who are pushed to the edges of our community, who do not get heard? I want to share another story from outsiders. It is the picture book *Broken Beaks* by Nathaniel Lachenmeyer, which I used to read to school classes. It tells of the relationship between a small sparrow and a kind homeless man. One day, the sparrow wakes to discover that his beak has broken, for no reason. He is sad, frightened, and finds that he is no longer able to have his pick of the best crumbs. His friends do not help, and eventually he becomes thin and weak, and his friends ignore him. He did not look like them anymore. One evening, he meets and shares a meal, a giant piece of fresh bread, with a 'thin and dirty' stranger who talks to himself. The sparrow could tell the man was different, and from his voice that he too was sad and lonely. They become friends, and the sparrow makes a nest and home in the man's long scraggly hair.

Once, when I practised reading this at home, by chance both my young sons were listening, and as I finished, they commented on the story, pretty much simultaneously. One son said, 'Oh that's so sad', and the other said 'Oh how beautiful'. Sad, beautiful, they were both right. The plight of the sparrow, and the Canaanite woman, is sad. Too often we are just like the other sparrows, the friends, the disciples, who don't want to know what it is like for those on the outside, and who don't want to take the responsibility for solving the problem. And it is also beautiful. When I asked my son why the story was 'beautiful', he said because they had made a connection. They had found each other. In *Broken Beaks*, it is an outsider who shows the wisdom and compassion that is needed. And from that there is joy.

In the story, we have a glimpse of the beauty that comes from being care-full – full of care for others. It is a glimpse perhaps of a time with no strangers, with no barriers of distance, with no hatred between people: of a time with no broken beaks. It will be a time when we all share life-giving bread.

> **IS THERE BREAD THAT YOU CAN SHARE?**

God
help us to be like a sparrow
sharing bread
to care for others
to bring joy
to give hope
to offer fellowship

help us to share the bread of life

Amen

Susan Joy Nevile and Maurice Nevile

Generous

Genesis 22:1-19; Psalm 13 (NIV); Romans 6:1-14

JUST AS GOD IS GENEROUS TO US,
WE ARE TO BE GENEROUS TO OTHERS

Here I reflect on generosity. The Genesis passage is one of the most difficult for us to hear. It is the story of God asking Abraham to sacrifice on a mountain his son Isaac, whom he loves. This story of God's testing is deeply uncomfortable, and many writers disagree on what we are to make of it. Some theologians focus on the testing of Abraham's faith, and this can make God seem harsh. Others see in the story a hint of the Israelites' exile, and being brought back from the very edge by a loving and compassionate God. Psalm 13 gives us a cry from the heart (vv. 1-2):

> How long, Lord? Will you forget me forever?
>   How long will you hide your face from me?
> How long must I wrestle with my thoughts
>   and day after day have sorrow in my heart?
> How long will my enemy triumph over me?

It is a cry that could have come from Abraham's son, a young boy on a long, strange, confusing and frightening journey with his father. And it is a cry I have experienced in many hospital wards. It says, 'I just want to be free of this place, I want to be home, Lord, how long must I endure?'. But like the story of Abraham and his son on the mountain, the psalm does not end in pain, or loss, or sorrow, or despair – it ends in joy! (vv. 5-6). The psalmist trusted in God's generosity.

> But I trust in your unfailing love;
> my heart rejoices in your salvation.
> I will sing the Lord's praise,
> for he has been good to me.

Just as Isaac was bound for sacrifice, we too are bound by our acts that separate us from God: our selfish and harmful ways, our hardness of heart, and our closed ears to the cries of others. In the third passage here, from Romans, we are told that 'the wages of sin is death' (v. 23), but like Isaac, we too are set free by a loving father. The gift from God is eternal life in Christ. Again, the message is one of God's amazing generosity.

So, with this understanding we can think again on the Genesis passage, and now we can hear the story with a quieter heart and draw closer to Abraham as he names that mountain (v. 14) 'The Lord will provide'. He does not name it as a place of testing and fear, or in memory of a harsh God, but with the name of a loving God. For Abraham, this story that we find so hard to hear is really about God's generous provision, no matter what. God receives Abraham's trust, and Abraham receives God's mercy. It is a story about giving and receiving. And this is echoed in the gospel, in the life of Christ. Having received from God, we too are called to give generously, and to welcome those who come our way, even the little ones, the outsiders, the vulnerable, and those who are different. We are called to be generous, just as we trust in God's generosity to us.

The verses in Romans conclude Jesus' instructions to the twelve disciples as he sends them out to teach, to spread his message of God's love. These verses offered the disciples comfort that they would be provided for on their journey.

For us, today, there is also that comfort, but so too is it a challenge.

> **WHAT IS YOUR CRY?**
> **HOW DOES GOD GIVE TO YOU?**

Generous God
we are deeply grateful for your gifts
of mercy
of freedom
of eternal life
help us to give generously to others
just as you give to us

Amen

Susan Joy Nevile and Maurice Nevile

Thankful

Luke 17:11-19 (NIV)

IN THIS DAY WE CAN BE THANKFUL

'Thank you'. They are two simple words. Throughout my work in school, in church, in hospice and hospital, I tell some stories that Christ told, and he told them for particular reasons – to get new ideas about God across to ordinary people. Some stories are of events that happened *about* Jesus, of things that he *did* rather than said. The story here tells us that on his travels Jesus entered a village and was met by ten men who had leprosy. To have this disease would make these men outcasts from their community. They follow Jesus' instruction to go to the priests and as they went, they were cleansed. One of the ten, a Samaritan, a foreigner, turned and came back when he saw that he was healed, and threw himself at Jesus' feet, praising God and thanking Jesus. It is a beautiful moment.

When we hear this story, the message is so straightforward: ten men were outcasts, ten men were cleansed, in effect given their lives back, and only one returned to say thank you. That one man got even more than he bargained for. Jesus saves him. It is easy for us to hear the story and to disapprove of those ungrateful nine men. Yet it is even easier to be like them! We fall into the same trap so readily. We receive all the time; however, somehow we do not get around to the 'thank you'. How does that happen? Well, sometimes we can be overwhelmed by the joy of what we have. We see this at a young child's birthday – the paper is torn off the gift in excitement to reveal what they had been wanting and waiting so long for, and they are immediately off to play with it. In the excitement, the words 'thank you' do not appear. We can see that in the men as they seemingly rush off to the priest to confirm that they have been healed. They are overjoyed that they can return to be part of the community again.

Other times, it is just the opposite, that what we have been given is not what we wanted, and it is disappointment that washes away any sense of gratitude. Perhaps you know this feeling, that sense of being let down, of things not being what you had hoped for. Or even worse, we can feel that because we have so little, there is nothing to be thankful for. My guess is that is exactly how the ten men felt after they had been sent out from the village. I would think none of them felt grateful for the things they had received at that point. The compassion of strangers who gave them food or money, the friendship of the others, the very fact that they were still alive, these gifts could not compare with what they wanted – to be fully healthy again.

It can be easy to not even notice the gifts that we have – we see them day after day, use them, enjoy them, but rarely or never stop to really recognise and appreciate them *as* gifts. We take them for granted. I wonder if this was true for the men *before* they had leprosy, if every day they were really thankful for their families, for the people they lived next to, for their work, for the fact that they could then move around freely, as an accepted part of the community. Singer-songwriter Joni Mitchell was right when she said, 'You don't know what you've got. Till it's gone'. Once these things were taken from the men, they realised how important they were. The nine men, as they rushed back to the village to see the priest, felt as if they had got everything they wanted, but the one who returned got even more. He was not only healed but saved. In returning to thank Christ, he was able start a relationship with Jesus, which was worth far more than his health.

For us, the challenge is to move on from both judging the nine as ungrateful *and* from identifying with them, seeing the times in our lives when we forget to be grateful, to say thanks. Our challenge is to move towards being like the man who came back to Jesus. How can we remember to have an attitude of being thankful? How can we see beyond the gift, to the giver, and so become close to God? One way is to practise saying 'thank you', by saying it to the people around us, not only when it is easy, but when it is hard, when we do not feel like it. We can notice when someone gives to us, of their time, of their selves. It could be friends, family, a colleague, a teacher, even a stranger.

I recall well a very young student who at the end of *every* lesson came up to me to say quietly, 'Thank you for teaching us today, Mrs Nevile'. Her gentle gratitude was a gift to me. Another way is to avoid that disgruntled let-down feeling which stops us from enjoying what we have, by being careful about what it is that we are really hoping for. If we spend lots of time wanting more, thinking that we are entitled to more, then we are more likely to miss seeing and valuing what we already do have. Instead, we can ask ourselves what we really need, and what is really important, what nourishes us, what enriches us, what makes us strong, and what makes us grow.

Finally, we can build an attitude of thankfulness into our day, to find a time to pause and reflect on what happened, and on the good things that were part of it. Each day can be beautiful, and it is up to us to make the effort not to miss it and let it get away.

> **FOR WHAT, THIS DAY, IN THIS PLACE,
> IN THIS VERY MOMENT,
> CAN YOU BE THANKFUL?**

God creator
of earth and everyone
of light and life
thank you
for what we can know
for what we can do
for what we can see
for what we feel
for people close to us
for peace, strength, and hope

hold us gently, always
as we go forward in life

Amen

Susan Joy Nevile and Maurice Nevile

2 With us

The way

John 14, 15 (NIV)

JESUS IS THE WAY, THE WAY OF LOVE

'Love one another...' There was stunned silence. Jesus announces that he must leave them, and none of his friends had a clue. We must feel sorry for the disciples; we can really see them struggling with what Jesus was saying. At the beginning of that week, there was Jesus' dramatic entry to Jerusalem that we call Palm Sunday. Then all week Jesus was up at the temple teaching, explaining God's way of living. The whole city of Jerusalem was in ferment, uproar. Everyone was talking about Jesus, who he is, and what he might do. And then Jesus says he is going, and they cannot follow. No wonder they are stunned and upset.

So, Jesus comforts his disciples, assuring them that his Father's house has many rooms and there will be a place for each of them. He says they know the way to get to him. Thomas however is still unclear, 'Lord, we don't know where you are going, so how can we know the way?' (John 14:5). We can get the sense that the rug has just been pulled out from under their feet. The disciples are feeling confused, perhaps even afraid. And we sometimes get that same feeling: things happen in our lives, in the lives of our friends and family, or in the wider world around us, that make us wonder, 'hang on, what is happening here, God?... this isn't right, this doesn't make sense'. Something happens, often unexpected, and our lives are not as we had imagined, hoped, and even planned. Everything is disturbed and turned all around.

Jesus gives that giant of a response: 'I am the way and the truth and the life. No one comes to the Father except through me. If you really know me, you will know my Father as well. From now on, you do know him and have seen him' (vv. 6-7). Jesus uses the image of *the way*, or in some translations *the road*, to describe himself and explain his work on earth. Jesus is the way to know God. He clearly says that if we look at him, if we know what he did, if we know why he did it, we will understand, and we will know God. What lies at the heart of Jesus' ministry? Or, if we are using the image of the road, what is its base? Jesus spelled it out earlier, in John 13: 'Let me give you a new command: Love one another. In the same way I have loved you, you love one another' (John 13:34-35, MSG).

If, like Thomas, we want to know how to live to follow Jesus, or how to make it right, we need to choose Jesus' way, the way of love. Unfortunately, this way of living is not always easy. It can lead to some hard choices. For how we relate to others, it may mean that we choose to forgive someone who has hurt us, to comfort or care for someone, to stand up for someone who is vulnerable, to reach out to someone whom others ignore, to put ourselves behind others, to put ourselves last. Jesus' way is to serve and to love others.

I would like to end by sharing a story which to me is a great example of the way of love. In Billings, Montana, USA, a five-year-old boy placed a menorah, a special candelabra used by Jewish people, in his bedroom window. Later, some members of a hate group saw it and threw a brick through the boy's window, almost injuring him and his mother. Christians in the town wanted to show their support and care for the boy, to say 'we are with you', so they went out and bought menorahs and put them in their own windows. This simple action brought the town's community together, it challenged and diminished hate, fear and violence. It was the way of love.

> **SPEAK UP, TO SHOW OTHERS THE WAY OF LOVE**

God
when you say 'love one another'
we will not be silent
we will speak up
to say that we are with you
to say that we will follow you
to say to others that your way is love
we will, we will, we will

Amen

Susan Joy Nevile and Maurice Nevile

Welcomed

Luke 19:28-44 (NIV)

WE WELCOME A KING WHO SAVES, NOT ON A THRONE BUT A CROSS

Welcoming is a recurring theme in stories across the Bible. Think of the welcoming father who ran down the steps with his arms outstretched in love to greet his lost son (Luke 15:11-32) (see 'Child', 'Father'). I remember when my youngest son went to a school camp for the first time. It was only two full days and one night, but he felt like he was going away for a long time, so for his return we did what our family does when someone has been away. We made a sign for the front door saying, 'Welcome home!', we bought some special treats for afternoon tea, and he got to do most of the talking at dinner that night (a treat for a youngest child). Those were three practical ways that showed how happy we were to have him back with us – that he was welcomed home.

We hear of Jesus' welcome into Jerusalem in the Palm Sunday story. And what a welcome that was! Luke describes people ripping off their cloaks and placing them on the ground for Jesus to ride over – the equivalent of rolling out the red carpet. It really did give Jesus celebrity superstar or royal status. And the city would have been packed. Jews from all the smaller towns would have come to town to celebrate the Passover, everyone would have been out there to catch a glimpse of Jesus. Stories of his amazing powers and actions had rippled through the community – no wonder the Jewish authorities were worried, no wonder they asked Jesus to try and quieten down his followers – it's a rabble, it's a mob, there is going to be trouble, the Roman rulers won't like this! (v. 39).

Jesus' answer is amazing. He does not toe the line with 'yes sir we don't want trouble with the Romans'. He does not speak of his death (as he does elsewhere) and say, 'Yes, it will all end in tears, there will be trouble, not for you but for me'. Instead, he says, in effect, you cannot stop this, that if all the people were quiet the stones themselves would cry out (Luke 19:40). What does Jesus mean by this? One possibility is that it could be an insult to the Pharisees – *'you* may not be able to recognise who I am, but the dull brainless stones can'. Or Jesus' answer could be an acknowledgment that this was all part of God's plan. For who else but God would be able to make rocks and stones cry out? It is a way for Jesus to say, 'I am the one, the king'. It does not matter what the crowds say, because the earth itself knows Jesus' mission, that he is God's chosen one. Jesus that day had taken steps to show this.

Maybe it is not so obvious to us, but to the crowd then there were clear *signs* – entering Jerusalem on a colt was to fulfil the prophesies about the coming king. Jesus rides a colt that had not yet been ridden by anyone, showing that no one else could do what Jesus is about to do. Jesus, like we do now, knew what was coming. He knew that in a few days the crowds would have turned from their enthusiastic welcome – that they would be calling not for his coronation but his crucifixion. He knew what God's plan entailed, and that he was a king. But he knew too that he was a king who came to save, not on a throne but on a cross. As we are welcomed on our own journey of Christian life, we are to welcome Jesus, as a different kind of king, into our hearts and lives.

> **HOW CAN YOU WELCOME
> CHRIST THE KING?**

God
you sent a king for us
a different king
a surprising king
an amazing king
an unstoppable king
the one king
the earth's king
for whom stones could cry out

we welcome him
our king on a cross
into our hearts
and into our lives
with thanks of joy
and tears

Amen

Susan Joy Nevile and Maurice Nevile

Love

Matthew 1:23-25

IN JESUS, GOD PROVES HIS ENDURING LOVE FOR US

In other reflections we think about seeing and believing (see 'Doubting, believing, following', 'Seeing Jesus', 'God's eyes'), and the signs that help us to see God's kingdom getting closer. These signs happen around us, in the world, and in people that we know as well as within ourselves, as we grow into the people that God knows we can be. Sometimes, these signs are easy to see, but sometimes they need to be believed to be seen. Here I focus on something that is difficult to see, and that is love. Love is tricky, we all believe that it is there, that it exists – but how do we know? How do we prove love? We cannot catch it with a net and pin it down like an insect. We cannot measure it with a tape measure to see if it has grown. And yet most people would agree that love is there, and it does grow.

If we think of our own relationships, or of couples, families, and friendships we know of, how can we see that they love one another? Perhaps we can develop a set of proofs, some statements that we can agree and depend on. We can see love when people: want to be together – there is *understanding*; share with one another – there is *experience*; give to each other – there is *generosity*; give up for each other – there is *sacrifice*. That is a small start. Can we apply our ideas about 'proving love' in another situation? What about how God shows love to us?

Maybe to keep it simple, let us focus on Christ, and our small focus passage from Matthew. What is in a name? Christ was called many different things (prince of peace, son of man, son of God) but two names are mentioned here. When we read the Bible, we find that the names people have can tell us something about them. Immanuel means 'God with us', and Jesus is a Greek translation of a Hebrew name we know well – Joshua. Joshua means 'God saves'. In these two names, we can see reminders of essential ideas of God's love. As Immanuel 'God with us', we see the ultimate example of wanting to be with someone and sharing their experience. As it says in John's Gospel (1:14), God loved people so much that the word of God became flesh. In Jesus, God knows and understands from experience what it is like to be human. God knows our hopes and our joys, God knows our difficulties and our disappointments, God knows our temptations and our pains. What about the idea of giving to, and giving up something, for love? What about sacrifice? The name Jesus, 'God saves', takes us to the cross and to Jesus' giving everything he had. He gave up his life in order to give life to us, to give us the chance of becoming forever closer to God. Jesus is the perfect demonstration, the proof, of God's enduring love for us.

Love

> **HOW COULD YOU PROVE THE LOVE
> IN YOUR LIFE, AND THAT IT GROWS?**

God
we know there is love
in understanding, when we are together
in experience, when we share
in generosity, when we give
in sacrifice, when we give up
and in Jesus, when you became flesh
to live with us
to die for us
to save us

we know there is love
there is
we are certain of it

Amen

Susan Joy Nevile and Maurice Nevile

Hope

Jeremiah (NIV); Isaiah

Gary Haugen (1999) *Good News about Injustice: A Witness of Courage in a Hurting World*. World Vision, USA

HOPE SITS WITH US, AS A SPARK OF LIGHT

When we see pain in the world, not just see but feel it, we can struggle with a sense of sorrow, of lament. The news media remind us constantly of the despair of those who are experiencing or trapped in dire situations. But I think sometimes it is not easy for those of us who live in relative happiness and security to understand the depth of longing for rescue of those who do not. I go to bed each night in a comfortable bed, in a safe house, with a full stomach, and with people that I love around me. But that is not the reality for many millions of people. I am especially reminded each year at the start of Advent with its cry from the heart, a cry of longing for things to change, for God to break through.

This is certainly true both for Isaiah's people, and for the time when Jesus was born. Isaiah wrote during a time of political upheaval and threatened invasion. Jesus was born into a time of political unrest, with an occupying army in control. In both times, there was a yearning for things to be made right.

We too live in a time of upheavals, for example of technological change, of challenged social structures and relationships, or of political and economic uncertainties. No matter where we are, there are people around us who are waiting, longing, aching, hoping, for things to be made right. Now we all have hopes. Some of these we often keep quiet and tucked away near to our hearts. Those might be hopes about ourselves, maybe they relate to our dreams, our battles, or our fears and failures. So maybe we do not share them, or we share them only with those closest to us. But we have hopes also for our family, our friends, our community, our work, our region, our country, or the wider world, and maybe we are more comfortable with sharing these hopes with others. As we act for change, in whatever the situation, hope sits with us, keeping us going – like a spark of light. Without hope we are lost in the darkness. So, our hopes can become our prayers, bringing them to God, and bringing light to our lives, and to the lives of others, just as a candle overcomes the darkness.

We all need hope especially on those grey days when we feel overwhelmed. Sometimes, we are overwhelmed about what is happening *within* us, affected by our feelings about ourselves, and the circumstances and changes of our lives, or in the lives of others close to us. And sometimes we are overwhelmed about what is happening *around* us in the world, maybe from what we notice in the media, the stories and images of war, of disaster, of poverty, like the huge number of children every day who die from diseases associated with a lack of access to safe drinking water and adequate sanitation. How do we respond to such dire knowledge? My husband says it makes him feel like the knight in the movie *Monty Python and the Holy Grail*, who has had all his arms and legs cut off in one-to-one combat with another knight. He is still alive, and now burning with rage and willing to fight, but actually he is unable to do anything. An American writer, Gary Haugen (p. 45), describes it this way:

in our hearts we feel like deer frozen by headlights. The very information that should move us is so overwhelming that it actually paralyses... Instead of energizing us for action, the overwhelming injustice in our world actually makes us feel numb. We sense our hearts melting and our feet sinking into concrete.

The feeling is that combination of longing for something out of the depths of your heart and yet feeling absolutely powerless to achieve it. Jeremiah really knew that feeling. He was a prophet, and his job was to listen to God and then let the people know what God was saying to them. Now the book of Jeremiah is not a happy read. Much of it contains some really tough messages, like God's judgment spoken against Judah, the southern kingdom. In chapter 4, God says:

> Announce in Judah and proclaim in Jerusalem and say – sound the trumpet throughout the land, cry aloud and say 'Gather together let us flee to the fortified cities. Raise the signal to go to Zion! flee for safety without delay! for I am bringing disaster from the north, even terrible destruction. A lion has come out of his lair; a destroyer of nations has set out. He has left his place to lay waste your land. Your towns will lie in ruins without inhabitant.

Talk about tough love! By chapter 33, the Babylonians have just levelled Jerusalem, and those who have survived the attack must have believed that God had abandoned them. But Jeremiah then speaks of God's continuing promise to the people, of healing, health, and security, bringing a message of hope into otherwise gloomy tidings. God will keep the covenant with the people, despite their betrayal. There is hope, they are not abandoned, but they must wait – for God's timing. What are you like at waiting? How do you cope? It is not easy, especially when it looks like what we are waiting for may never arrive, when all around us other people have what we seek, or the opposite of what we seek seems to be happening.

How do we keep going, how do we maintain hope? First, hope needs to be built on something real, it needs a solid base from which to grow. So, if our hope is based on one of God's promises, it helps to remember that God keeps his promises: the one who promised to send his son, did so, and the righteous branch did sprout from David's line. And God promises that there will come a day when all injustice, and its consequent suffering, will be overcome.

Secondly, hope needs to be sustained. A man called Steve Bradbury, as director of an Australian aid organisation, was asked how he kept going in the face of so much suffering. His answer was that he very consciously looked for any examples he could find of love in action – whether contemporary or historical. By reflecting on them, he allowed himself to be challenged and inspired by people's stories. In other words, we can search out other perspectives. Bad news sells in the media, and misery makes for good TV ratings, but hope needs to be sustained with signs of love. Sometimes we can be so bound up in longing for things that we miss the signs, and our hope withers through lack of sustenance.

Lastly, we keep going by acting, by exercising hope, by changing, responding, doing whatever we can, no matter how small the action is, to bring about that which we long for. If we are longing for friendship, what kind of friend are we to others? If we want success and accomplishment, what decisions and sacrifices do we make, and how much effort do we put in? If we wish that fewer people lived in poverty, how can we find out how to support the poor? If we wish to help someone distressed, what comfort can we offer?

> **WHERE DO YOU HEAR A CRY FOR HOPE?**

(for this prayer you can light a candle)
God
you give us hope
as a light in the darkness around us

we will build it with promises
we will sustain it with love
we will exercise it with action
we will use it with confidence
to bring change
Amen

Susan Joy Nevile and Maurice Nevile

Peace

John 14:23-29 (NIV), John 20:19-29 (NIV)

JESUS' PEACE COMES FROM WITHIN

Jesus promises peace. In anticipation of his death, Jesus gives the disciples instructions about how to live, and how to treat each other. Then he tries to prepare them for what is going to happen. Jesus knows what is coming, but the disciples do not yet understand. Jesus can see his death, and the results it will have on his friends. He can see the denials, the fear, the confusion, the despair that they will go through over the next few days.

And then Jesus promises them two things. The first promise is for a 'helper', sent from the Father, which is what they need, someone to comfort them, to help them to understand what has happened. This is the Holy Spirit. The second promise is from Jesus. It is peace, Jesus' own peace. Jesus says (v. 27):

> Peace I leave with you; my peace I give you. I do not give to you as the world gives. Do not let your hearts be troubled and do not be afraid.

What then is this peace of Jesus? It is not the peace of lack-of-conflict: Jesus was just about to be swept up by conflict. It is not the peace of serenity, of peace-and-quiet: Jesus' life was not serene; it was struggle and hard work. It is not the peace of security or safety: Jesus knew he was about to be killed. Yet, Jesus promises this 'peace', and tells his friends not to be worried or upset: 'do not be afraid'. This peace he promises, Jesus' peace, is a peace to overcome fears, and it will enable Jesus to overcome his own fears. It is the peace of knowing with certainty that what we are doing is right, and so God is with us. This peace does not come from what is happening around us, it is the peace that comes from within. And this is how Jesus could remain peace-full, at this tumultuous time in his life, and in the lives of those around him.

It is a peace Jesus wishes for us. After he has died and risen, Jesus comes to the disciples, who are behind locked doors in fear, and greets them with 'Peace be with you!' (v. 19). From these passages of those first days, John tells us that Jesus says this not once, or twice, but three times: 'Peace be with you'. The disciples were afraid of what might happen to them if they were arrested and put on trial. They could be whipped, beaten, even killed. Likely, they were talking about what had happened; perhaps they had been mistaken in following Jesus, had Mary really seen Jesus? Was Jesus really alive? They were not at peace, not in their situation, not with each other, not within themselves. It is hard to imagine what it would have been like for them, really, but there must have been confusion, doubt, disappointment, and maybe anger. But Jesus comes to them, and immediately offers them peace. And Jesus says that just as God had sent him, so he now sends the disciples, out into the world.

With Jesus' peace, we are not asked to sit around and enjoy it, in our comfort, we are sent out to be part of the world, taking that peace into the world, to live as people who bring peace. And we are given a clue as to how we can live 'full of peace', how we can live as peacemakers every day, wherever we are, and even when we are afraid, unsure of what is happening, and of what will happen. We can always seek the peace that comes from doing what is right, doing what God would have us do, and so being who God would have us be. It is the peace of the life that God would have us live. It is the peace of God with us. It is the peace that is not dependent on our surroundings, and that does not leave us.

> **HOW DO YOU LIVE PEACE?**

Jesus
we thank you for promising peace
your peace, that comes from knowing
that we are doing what is right

help us to have that peace
when we fear failure
when we fear danger
when we fear the unknown
when we fear what is beyond us
when we fear tomorrow

help us to live as peacemakers
taking your peace with us
into the world

Amen

Susan Joy Nevile and Maurice Nevile

Light

Isaiah 9:2-3 (NIV), John 1:1-14

GOD'S LIGHT SHINES IN THE DARKNESS, AND THE DARKNESS DOES NOT OVERCOME IT

In worship, we use candles to represent Jesus as the light of the world. Here, we will reflect on God as light, and the coming of the light into the world. Some people are afraid of the dark; they find it unsettling because they cannot see and know what is around them. Their immediate surroundings become worryingly mysterious. I find that if I am in the darkness, being still is okay, but problems begin if I try to move. If I get up in the night and think I can manage without putting a light on, I will usually trip over something, or walk into the corner of the bed. And I recall walking home from a night meeting at my children's school, along the unlit public path, and without my torch. I 'found' every dip and bump, and I was thoroughly barked at by a dog which sounded as if it wished to leap the fence and savage me. Had I brought my torch, I could have seen the unevenness in the path, and I could maybe have seen that the dog was not large and menacing, but just a feisty Jack Russell. But in the dark, I could not see, I was not certain, I could not think and react in the best way, with the awareness I needed. That is the power of the dark. It is the kind of experience that makes our reading from Isaiah so striking (vv. 2-3):

> The people walking in darkness have seen a great light; on those living in the land of deep darkness a light has dawned. You have enlarged the nation and increased their

joy; they rejoice before you as people rejoice at the harvest, as warriors rejoice when dividing the plunder.

To physically walk in darkness is daunting enough, but Isaiah talks of something even more difficult to negotiate than a dark path: 'The people walking in darkness have seen a great light'. Isaiah was using the image to describe people on their journey of life. So, I wonder about journeying through life without light. How would we know where to go, how would we know where the obstacles and dangers were, how would we see and meet others along the way, how would we know who was friend and who was foe? We would just ignore or become afraid of what was happening around us, simply because we could not see clearly.

The image of light and darkness bookend the two readings in focus here. Like Isaiah, John also refers to the coming of light: 'In him was life, and that life was the light of all humankind. The light shines in the darkness, and the darkness has not overcome it' (vv. 4-5), and 'The true light that gives light to everyone was coming into the world' (v. 9). It is a text familiar from Christmas services, when we celebrate the coming of the true light. But what does that mean? We understand the effect of turning on a light in a darkened room. We can see that everything is alright. The shadows that lurked in wardrobes, or behind half open doors, are seen to be nothing. The light reveals to us, comforts us, makes us feel safe, it shows us what is really there. But what does 'the light of the world' do? Jesus' birth as Immanuel, God with us, is a light to help us see clearly, and not to stumble in life. It is a light enabling us to take a good look at what is around us, helping us to begin to see, understand, and draw closer to God. We have many images of God. Some can seem troubling, like the God who watches over us, trying to catch us doing something wrong, to then condemn us. Or maybe we know images of God in the clouds, an old man ready to drift off to sleep, not caring for our pains and struggles. But at Christmas, light shows a God who acts, who is not distant but comes to be one of us, born as a fragile vulnerable baby, dependent on his mother's love, and his father's protection. We see God's amazing love, not a frightening shadow of our own imaginings.

In the light, we can see the people around us more clearly. In the Christmas story, it shines on the shepherds, at the social edge, but the ones chosen by God to hear first the good news. It shines on the wise men, the magi, strangers in the town but who saw the light and were drawn to it to come and worship. The light does not overlook the unimportant and the stranger. The light allows us to see all people as God sees them.

And, importantly, light gives us a chance to really see ourselves, perhaps at first in comparison to people of the Christmas story. We can wonder: do I have the faith of Mary and Joseph, who received amazing news, and did not reject it? They acted on the news, even at personal risk of social rejection. And the light shows us the choices God made, to give totally, not stand back, to be born in a stable, not a palace, and to respond with love, not with anger.

As we can open our eyes to the light of God, we can allow it to guide us in the dark around us, helping us to see and navigate life's circumstances, events, and dangers, and to see what is really there. But more, the light of God will also show us many unexpected gifts. We can see hope where we expected disappointment, peace where we expected conflict, joy where we expected sadness, and love where we expected hate. We can have a life of light.

> HOW DOES GOD'S LIGHT SHINE
> IN YOUR LIFE?
> WHAT CAN YOU SEE?

God
with your light we can better see
what is really there
where we are going
who is around us
who we are
and who you are

with your light we can better see
life's unexpected gifts
of hope
of peace
of joy
of love

so help us always to seek the light
to remain in light
to be light for others
to have a life of light
Amen

Susan Joy Nevile and Maurice Nevile

Belonging

Matthew 22:15-22

LIKE ALL THINGS, WE TOO ARE GIFTS FROM GOD

What is it that belongs to God? In the text here, the Pharisees plot a way to trap Jesus into saying something damaging. Is it right to pay tax to Caesar? It was a clever trap, and Jesus gives a clever answer. Using a coin showing Caesar's image and inscription, Jesus says give to Caesar what is Caesar's, and give to God what is God's. It is interesting that they used money to try and trap Jesus, because money is something we use constantly and that stirs our interest. Do you know whose faces are on your money? Certainly, a royal head is on the coins, but what of the notes? I did some homework for the Australian ten dollar note. At the time, it featured the poets A. B. ('Banjo') Paterson (1864-1941) and Dame Mary Gilmore (1865-1962), and it incorporated micro-printed excerpts of their work.

Who and what is represented on money is important to many people, and we saw this before the introduction of the Euro across many European countries. There was much disappointment at the loss of national currencies (the German Deutsche Mark, the French franc, etc.). So while Euros are of the same value, same size, and same colour, each country has its 'own' Euro in that the money also incorporates nationally distinctive imagery, someone or something that is familiar, important, a part of that country's sense of shared history, identity, accomplishment, or aspirations: something of their national story. The money shows what or who belongs, as Banjo Paterson belongs to Australians' sense of themselves. For the Romans, there was no one more significant than Caesar, so he was on the Roman money.

Let us just imagine for a second that Christians had their own currency, and we would want to show on it what is really important to *us*. So, what kinds of pictures or symbols might be on the 'Christian 10 dollar note'? Maybe something related to Jesus' command to love? We do not know what God looks like, but actually we could put anything on this fictitious 'Christian' money. We come back to the answer that Jesus gave, and it helps us to see just how clever that answer was – because in fact all things belong to God. All people, all relationships, all creatures, all of creation, are God's – God just lends them to us for a while.

How then do we recognise God's ownership? How do we give to God what is God's? One way is to better appreciate what we have been given by noticing and being thankful for who and what is around us. For example, we can try to find something beautiful, or surprising, in every day. It could be as simple as sitting still to watch a sunset, really tasting a meal, or appreciating a warm smile, or someone's simple presence with us. Another way is to treat everything and everyone that comes our way with care – as they are gifts from God. So, this is true for the physical world around us, as well as the social world, the people within our lives. And it is true for us, to treat ourselves with care. A last way is through prayer, by telling God about the things of our lives, the painful, our sadness, struggles, worries, and fears, but also the joyful, the exciting, and our triumphs! We can share all of these with God, who promises to listen, for we too belong to God who loves us.

> **YOU BELONG TO GOD: CARE FOR YOURSELF,
> SHARE YOURSELF**

God
to whom all things belong
we belong to you

we appreciate your gifts
of opportunities
of relationships
of creation
of ourselves

we will treat them all with care

Amen

Susan Joy Nevile and Maurice Nevile

Promises

Jeremiah 31:31-34 (MSG)

GOD PROMISES THE CHANCE TO BEGIN AGAIN

There are many stories of God's promises, or covenants, in his relationships with us as his people. For example, there's Noah, where God begins again. God does not forget Noah. We have the beautiful point in the story where Noah calls out to God, and God remembers him and sends the Spirit as he breathes over the waters. There is the sign of God's promise not to give up on people: the rainbow in the sky. There is the story of Abraham and Sarah, and God's promise to make a people, his people, with more descendants than stars in the sky. We can read of Abraham's great-great-great-grandchildren wandering in the desert, when God again puts his claim on the Hebrew people, 'I am God, your God, who brought you out of the land of Egypt, out of a life of slavery' (Exodus 20:2, MSG), and so establishes the rules to live by. But the people start complaining against Moses: why did we follow you, we hate the food, there's not enough water (Numbers 21). We get the idea. So, God sends poisonous snakes, but also gives a solution. God tells Moses to make a bronze snake, place it on a pole, and set it up in the centre of the camp – anyone who is bitten and who looks at the snake will be saved. Here God is promising healing. Many people see this as a shadow, or foretaste, of Jesus' hanging on the cross.

Here we look at the book of Jeremiah, who was a prophet. In his time the Hebrew people had been divided into two kingdoms, and Jeremiah was in Judah, the southern kingdom. It was his job to give the king bad news – the people had turned away from God and the Babylonians were going to conquer Judah (Jeremiah 25). Jeremiah was branded a traitor, but he was right – the Babylonians came, Jerusalem fell in 587 BCE, and many were forced into exile. But at this moment of national catastrophe Jeremiah again prophesies of a new covenant. If we look closely, we have two promises, two amazing promises: 'I will put my law within them – write it on their hearts!.. I'll wipe the slate clean for each of them' (Jeremiah 31:33-34).

When we say that we know something by heart, what do we mean? When I think about the things that I know by heart, it is as if the knowledge has sunk in so deeply that I know it without thinking at all. Probably the first was my address and phone number, which I learned as a small child. Knowledge by heart becomes part of who we are. But here it is not just knowledge as information that God is promising. It is not that we will be able to recite the commandments: in knowing the law in our hearts, we know what or who lies behind the law. God says, 'they will know me firsthand' (Jeremiah 31:33-34).

We all have at least one person whom we know by heart, someone, probably a family member, partner, or close friend, whose face we can see in our mind's eye without the slightest effort. We know them so well that we know immediately what they would say or do in a certain situation. This is the kind of knowing that God is promising. God is not removed from his people. In fact, God became one of us – it is in Jesus that we see the new covenant. Churches in every part of the globe celebrate this every Sunday in a simple story: during the meal, Jesus took and blessed the bread, broke it, and gave it to his disciples (Matthew 26:26-29, MSG): 'Take eat. This is my body'. Taking the cup and thanking God, he gave it to them: 'Drink this, all of you. This is my blood, God's new covenant poured out for many people for the forgiveness of sins'.

Forgiveness of sins was the second part of the promise the Jeremiah foretold: 'I'll wipe the slate clean'. Sin is a word that we tend to hear mostly in church. For me, it is clearest to understand sin as those things we do that cause separation. Sins separate us from God, separate us from one another, and separate us from the person God knows we can be. Forgiveness restores relationships, and that is what God is all about. The image of a clean slate is a powerful one. God offers us promises, that chance to begin again, fresh, anew, a clean slate, and white as snow.

> **WHAT DO YOU KNOW BY HEART?**
> **WHAT CAN YOU BEGIN AGAIN?**

God of promises
you write on our hearts
and we have knowledge
you forgive our separation
and we have another chance

we are restored
we are white as snow
we can begin again

thank you

Amen

Susan Joy Nevile and Maurice Nevile

Grace

Matthew 20:1-16 (NIV)

GRACE IS GOD'S UNDESERVED LOVE, GIVEN TO EVERYONE

We often like to think that the world is fair, or at least that it should or could be, but deep down we know that it is not. People start off in life across a wide variety of situations; they have different opportunities, different resources, and forms of support. And along the journey of life, bad things can happen; there are events and changes beyond our control, like illness and misfortune, and we can all make poor choices, mistakes, and have failures. If we reflect on God's kingdom, the text here – the parable of the vineyard workers – is crucial to understanding what the kingdom is all about. Yet it is a parable that people often do not want to talk about, perhaps because in one sense it runs against our expectations. We want to complain along with those who were hired first! They are right, it does not seem fair, and surely God should be fair! Fairness is a concept we grasp early, something no child needs to be taught. All children have an inbuilt radar about fairness: 'his piece of cake is bigger than mine, that's not fair!', 'when she was my age she had more time on the computer, that's not fair!', 'he got more presents than me, that's not fair!'.

I reflect elsewhere (see 'Forgiving', 'Father') on the idea of fairness in Peter's very human question – do I really need to forgive every time? We can almost hear Peter say 'that's so unfair' – he keeps doing the wrong thing. Part of his question involved wanting everything to balance out – it is a way of thinking that is based on rewards, punishment and just desserts. It comes from a way of looking at the world that assumes there is not enough to go around, not enough cake, not enough time, are not enough presents. It assumes that everything is limited in some way – even forgiveness (see 'Abundance'). So, we must measure and count what everybody else gets, to make sure that no one gets more than their share. This is why we can be jealous of someone's generosity.

Here is the story. A landowner goes out early to find and hire workers for his vineyard. He offers to pay a certain salary, and the workers agree and go off to work. The landowner goes out again in the morning, at lunch time, and at late afternoon, each time hiring workers and *each time offering the same salary*. In the evening, when the workers are paid, the workers who began early in the morning grumble at the landowner, expecting to be paid more for their longer hours worked. The landowner responds (vv. 13-15):

> I am not being unfair to you, friend. Didn't you agree to work for a denarius? Take your pay and go. I want to give the one who was hired last the same as I gave you. Don't I have the right to do what I want with my own money? Or are you envious because I am generous?

Jesus sums up the message of the parable like this (v. 16): 'So the last will be first, and the first will be last'. It is not just us – the first time this story was told the listeners would have had the same reaction: 'Huh? That does not make sense'.

To make sense of the parable we need to spend some time with a significant word – GRACE. It appears in that beautiful, moving, and widely known song 'Amazing Grace' (see 'Lost'). It is not about a girl with wondrous abilities, it is about

God's grace given to us. What then is grace? It has various meanings. When we say someone is 'graceful', we mean they have an elegance in their movements. When we say someone was 'gracious', we mean they were kind. Sometimes when we return library books a bit late and we do not get a fine it is because the library has a 'grace period'. Some families say a prayer before a meal and call that 'saying grace'. In their song, the band U2 claims that 'grace' is 'a thought that changed the world'.

Grace is God's gift of undeserved love. So how does this help us to understand the story of the vineyard workers? Well, let us say that God is the vineyard owner and the workers to be paid are people who respond to God's invitation to join him, to be his followers, to live his way as members of the kingdom. What is the payment? It is God's love, which he gives freely to all, and is not dependent on how hard or long we have 'worked'. In fact, there is nothing we can do to change God's love for us: nothing can make God love us more, and nothing can make God love us less. We find that hard to grasp, to understand, to believe. Often, we are used to the Santa Claus model: have we been naughty or nice? have we worked hard? are we deserving of reward? But God does not do 'I will love you if...?'. God just says, 'I will love you - no matter what'. God lavishes this love on everyone. That is grace. It is extraordinary.

With this idea of grace, the picture we have of God's kingdom makes more sense. It is not a kingdom where things are going to run out. It is not a place of competition, of 'fairness', where we have to worry about what everyone else is getting. It is not a realm where positions are earned. There is no hierarchy of clouds with some larger, or rounder, or floating higher than others, or where some people have halos that are more gold or shinier. God's kingdom is a place where the last will be first and the first will be last, and where all will be invited for there is more than enough for all. We can remember too that the kingdom is not just some far away time or place, it is about how we live right now (see 'Kingdom'). So, let us allow that thought to change the world, or at least our world, in how we see and treat ourselves and others.

HOW CAN YOU LIVE GOD'S UNDESERVED GRACE?

God
your gift of grace
is amazing
is undeserved
is outrageous
is extraordinary
and it changes our world

we accept it!
we love it!
we live it!

Amen

Susan Joy Nevile and Maurice Nevile

Father

Luke 15:11-32 (NIV)

IN GRIEF, WE OPEN OUR HEARTS TO OTHERS, AND WE CAN FORGIVE

One ancient saying is, 'Like father, like son', or from Ezekiel 16:44, 'like mother, like daughter', the idea being that some aspect of a person's appearance, or a characteristic, manner, interest, etc., is evident from one generation to the next. So, as God's children, how can we be like God the Father? At the beginning of the passage here, people were gathering to hear Jesus talk. Some official figures grumbled about the kinds of people Jesus associated with – 'sinners' – that they would consider unacceptable, as people outside the reach of the church. We can imagine them rolling their eyes in disgust. In response, Jesus tells some stories, from which we get a picture of God's unlimited love, and of how God feels about the people to whom Jesus was often drawn.

One of the stories we know as the parable of 'the lost son'. It tells of God's lament, his deep sadness, for his lost children. We have the image of God longing for the return of his children, for the day when, like the father of the story, he will look out and see a child making the way home. We can think about the two brothers, the one who left with his inheritance and wasted it foolishly, and the one who stayed home working dutifully. And we can think how we are like them. We can think about wanting to be welcomed home with compassion. We do not hear the end of the story, and so we do not know what happens next for the father and his two sons. But, as Henri Nouwen suggests in his extended discussion of the parable (see 'Child'), for us there is more to the story because we can wonder what it means to be home, rather than to be called home. How do we live and grow as God's children? Nouwen comments that children grow up, and can themselves become parents, and if we grow as God's children and heirs, then we grow to be like the father. It is excellent to be welcomed home as the errant returning son, to be forgiven, blessed and receive gifts, but much harder to be the one, like the father, who welcomes, blesses, gives and forgives.

For us, it can be easier just to hear the story tell of God's forgiving love, than it is to hear Jesus' message: 'be compassionate, as your father is compassionate'. We are called to love one another with the same selfless and generous outgoing love that we see from the father in this story. This father cannot wait to be with his lost son, and runs to greet him, so that the son does not make alone the last part of that difficult journey home. The father does not abandon the son but wants both his sons with him. This is a God whose love is all inclusive, caring for each child as unique and precious. This is a God who cannot compel us to stay, and who is devastated when any of us 'leave home', longing always for our return. The father of Jesus' story is filled with compassion and throws his arms around his returned son. The father does not make the son feel guilty, and his love is faithful and not conditional on the son's response. His love just is. It is the love of grace (see 'Grace').

If we are to be not only received by God, but also to receive others as God does, we must become like the father, and see the world through God's eyes (see 'God's eyes'). How are we to do so? Nouwen (pp. 128-133) argues that grief is a way to compassion, and forgiveness. Grief involves allowing our hearts to be pierced by the sin of the world: 'when I consider the immense waywardness of God's children, our lust, our greed, our violence, our anger, our resentment, and when I look at them through the eyes of God's heart, I cannot but weep and cry out in grief' (pp. 120-121). Nouwen believes that this grief is praying, and indeed that much prayer is grieving. He suggests that by allowing our hearts to be broken, by being moved to tears, our hearts are prepared to receive anyone, and to forgive them.

This forgiveness is not the forced 'okay, I forgive you', said through clenched teeth, which is still wanting apologies, or praise, or excuses. As Nouwen describes it (p. 130), it is God's unconditional forgiveness. It means that we must step over all the worldly views that forgiveness is unwise, unhealthy, or impractical, and step over all our needs for gratitude and compliments. And perhaps hardest of all, we must step over the part of us that feels wronged and hurt and wants to stay in control. It is as if we have built a small wall around ourselves, for protection, a wall of arguments and angry feelings, of fear of being damaged again, of pride and the desire to be in command. Grief enables us to see beyond these walls, to empathise with others' suffering. Forgiveness enables us to step over the walls, and when we do, we enter the house of our father where we can then welcome others into our hearts, without expectations in return. And like the father in Jesus' story, forgiveness allows us to celebrate someone's return with great generosity, and love.

> ## WHO CAN YOU WELCOME BACK?

God, Father
we long to stay home with you
but we know we often leave
and that saddens you
yet with compassion you forgive us
and welcome our return

help us to forgive others
and to welcome their return
just as you do for us

then we can all celebrate!

Amen

Susan Joy Nevile and Maurice Nevile

King

Luke 23:1-16 (NIV); Psalm 95:1-7

OTHERS CAN RECOGNISE CHRIST AS KING THROUGH HOW WE LIVE

How might we recognise a king? Do you know Hans Christian Andersen's fairytale *The Princess and the Pea*? A young lady turns up at a castle and claims to be a princess, and the prince, of course, falls in love. The queen, however, wonders who this lady is – she is not going to let her son marry just anybody. So she sets up a test. On the guest's bed, the queen places many, many, mattresses, and underneath them all she places a pea. Just the one. The following morning, when asked how well she had slept, the princess complains of a sleepless night, being kept awake by something hard in the bed. The queen, knowing that only a true princess would feel such a slight imperfection, then gives her permission for the wedding. The couple, we assume, live happily ever after. The queen's knowledge helped her to recognise a true princess, and she put this knowledge to good use.

The crime on record for Jesus' crucifixion was 'King of the Jews', so it is worthwhile reflecting on just what the King of the Jews should mean. Let us divert for a moment and go back into Jewish history. After the Exodus, when the Jews escaped from Egypt and returned to the promised land, the land was divided between the family groups. Originally the people were governed by judges, local people who would settle disputes and lead their people into battle. They did not have a king;

121

God was the king of his people. But the people wanted an earthly king, 'everybody else has one' and so on. Well, God gave them their wish and the Jewish people got a king, but it was a vastly different type of king.

Kingship at that time was all about power – a king could and did do exactly what he liked, his subjects were simply his possessions and their reason to exist was to serve him in whatever way they could. The Jewish model of kingship was different. Yes, the king had a more comfortable lifestyle than the people, better clothes, and houses and servants etc., but the king was responsible for his people. He was meant to care for them, to rule them with justice. The image in the Bible is that of a shepherd. Kings in the Bible did not always get it right, indeed there were some spectacular failures, but the model was one of service to the people, rather than dominance over them.

It seems to me that this model of kingship was a sign of things to come, for in Jesus this model of kingship is fully realised. Jesus fulfils what it means to be a king, and in doing so appears to be the opposite of what a king should be. No wonder people were saying, 'You claim you are the one, the king, the saviour – go on save yourself'. But there were those who could see it, who could recognise him. Crucified with Jesus, the thief says 'Jesus, remember me when you come into your kingdom' (Luke 23:42). Somehow that thief recognised and had faith in Jesus' kingship. We do not know if the thief had other contact with Christ or if he just looked over from his cross and saw a king.

I will pose a last question, and I will suggest a possible answer: how would you recognise Christ the King? We are called to recognise not just who Jesus is, but how Christ reigns. We are called to recognise him by living lives that reflect Christ's character – living with truth, justice, love, peace, and service to others. When we do this, we enable others to recognise Christ the King, in and among us, in what we do and who we are.

> **HOW IS JESUS THE KING RECOGNISABLE IN YOUR LIFE?**

God
we recognise Jesus as a King
who cares
who loves
who serves
who died for us
who reigns for us
who lives in us
for others to see
in our truth
in our justice
in our love
in our peace
in our service
Amen

Susan Joy Nevile and Maurice Nevile

Kingdom

Mark 4:26-34

THE KINGDOM IS HOW WE NOW LIVE

What is the kingdom of God like, and what is it to be part of that kingdom? I will begin with something that never ceases to amaze me. As I have grown older, I have discovered the truth of things my mother told me as a child, words of great and valuable wisdom, like 'the dishes won't wash themselves', or 'the laundry fairies won't pick your clothes up'. Her favourite in the car on the way home from church was, 'we spend our time talking about Jesus, Jesus spent his time talking about the kingdom'. And she was right. Jesus' first recorded sermon was to 'repent for the kingdom of heaven is near'. When he sent his friends, he told them, 'as you go, preach this message – the kingdom of heaven is near'. For Jesus, the kingdom was so close he could taste it – I imagine like when driving down to the sea, we can taste the salt in the air as we get closer.

So, Jesus wanted everyone to understand what he meant by the kingdom. For his Jewish listeners, the idea of 'a kingdom' would have suggested a return to the great days of David and Solomon, a leader for the nation backed by God. Jesus is at pains to show them that this was not what he was talking about. On the other hand, as modern listeners, we tend to pick up the heaven part of the phrase. When I asked one of my young sons what he thought of when he heard 'the kingdom' he said, 'an amazing castle, paradise, you know, everyone is happy, and it is all beautiful'. Well, Jesus was not talking about a political state, he was not talking about life after death. Jesus was talking about being one of God's people now. So, it is worth spending some time with the images of kingdom that Jesus draws for us, as outlined in the book of Mark.

The first image is of seed scattered in a field. We are reminded that the seeds take time to *grow*, first the stalk, then the ear, then the grain grows to its fullness. The farmer must wait for the harvest time. In a similar way, David did not step immediately into his kingship. He was anointed and continued as a shepherd boy, spending his days out on the hills with some of the silliest creatures of God's creation. Like the wheat, he needed time to grow, to mature, to reach the potential that God saw in him. The timing of the kingdom can seem slow, different to the way we might think it needs to happen. In our time, in our culture, we want it now: why wait? Everyone seems to be in a rush. We do not have the patience to wait for growth to occur. Not only do we rush, we also like to be in control. Yet in the picture that Jesus draws, we are told that the seed grows, no matter what the farmer does, if he is asleep or awake. Sometimes it is hard to remember that it is God's work we do, not our own. *We* do not control the growth of the kingdom, *God* does. *We* do not bring about the kingdom, *God* does. But we are asked to be active, not passive, in doing God's work.

Again, the second image contains elements of growth – the tiny seed, once it is planted, will become the largest plant in the garden. In this second image, the small, the insignificant, becomes the greatest. As a youngest child myself, I like to point out that David, the youngest of Jesse's eight boys, becomes the King. The one that probably spent his childhood being left out and forgotten is the one who is chosen by

God. In the kingdom, small things, small people, can make a big difference. When the tiny seed has grown it becomes something that is not big and grand for its own sake, but we are told that the birds of the air can find shelter on its branches.

If the kingdom is about how we live now, what are the kingdom principles that we can draw from the stories? One principle is not to be fooled by what is on the outside – God looked at David and saw the potential within. A second principle is that God's work often seems to take time to develop. There is a time of waiting, of nurturing, of trusting in God for things to come to their potential. Even small things we do can make a big difference for other people. When we look at the world around us, we can take the time to look at it in God's way.

How much more care would we take, of others, and of ourselves, if we saw the world with the creator's eyes? How differently would we treat people and situations that we take for granted, or may dismiss as unimportant? Very often we overlook how even the little things we do, and give, can be points of substantial transformation for others, like an act of kindness, an encouraging word, a warm smile, a quiet hug, an ear ready to listen, or a shoulder to lean on. It can mean just being there, present for someone. These small acts are part of the larger picture of our lives, of how each of us slowly becomes the person God knows we can be – and it takes our lifetime. And not only do we need to be careful and patient with others, but we also need to be careful and patient with ourselves.

> **WHAT CAN YOU GROW WITH CARE AND PATIENCE?**

God
yours is a kingdom of people
taking time to grow
so even the least
can become the greatest

help us to live the kingdom now
in who we are
in what we do
in how we are to others
in how we are to ourselves

with patience
with care
to bring transformation

Amen

Susan Joy Nevile and Maurice Nevile

Authority

Matthew 21:1-46

IF WE ACCEPT JESUS' AUTHORITY, HOW WILL WE RESPOND?

When a child is baptised in the church community, it is a demonstration of God's undeserved and outrageous love for all. If the child is a baby, or too young to speak for her/himself, others will speak on the child's behalf, accepting God's call to be recognised as part of the family. At my church, people close to the child will stand in front of the priest and congregation and answer for themselves the questions put to them:

> Do you turn to Christ?
> Do you repent of your sins?
> Do you reject selfish living, and all that is false and unjust?
> Do you renounce Satan and all that is evil?
> Will you by God's grace strive to live as a disciple of Christ, loving God with your whole heart, and your neighbour as yourself, until life's end?

The people stand up to be counted on God's side. It is a time of excitement and celebration for all involved, but sometimes another question lurks in my mind. It is a question once asked of me by a confirmee – what will it be like afterwards, after the questions are answered, after the promises are made, to live as a disciple of Christ? Would it be easier than before? We discussed the question in the wider confirmee group, and there were mixed responses.

Authority

The question effectively prompts us to ask ourselves: 'having talked the talk, how will I walk the walk?'

The gospel story here is one of three told after Jesus' dramatic arrival to Jerusalem and his subsequent shocking behaviour in the temple, described earlier in Matthew 21. And those who felt that they had the right to control the temple, those who believed they had the authority to teach, needed to reassert their position. The chief priests and the elders moved in to attack Jesus. 'By what authority are you doing these things?' (v. 23). The stage is set by Matthew for a discussion of Jesus' authority and the appropriate response. The stories are part of Jesus' reply. They come directly after Jesus, in rabbinic fashion, asks his questioners a question, about the authority of John's baptism: did it come from heaven or was it of human origin?

Jesus stumps them and then tells three stories. The first is about two sons, and the choices they make when asked to work in their father's vineyard (see 'Failing to act'). Jesus was suggesting to the elders that were like the second son: they could talk the talk but could not walk the walk. They knew all the rules but lacked the heart to bring them to life. Jesus even rubs it in at the end, with his comment about tax collectors entering the kingdom of God before chief priests. Then comes 'The parable of the wicked tenants'. The common title immediately suggests issues of responsibility and resulting judgment. Jesus was not letting his questioners off the hook. He follows up with the third story, that of the banquet and those who accept the invitation and those who do not (Matthew 22) (see 'Invited').

In the case of the wicked tenants, who brutally and greedily mistreat the landowner's servants and son, there seems to be a direct correlation between elements of the story and the world of its hearers. The image of *the vineyard* was familiar, not only practically but also theologically. There was a pre-existing image of Israel as a vineyard (Isaiah 5:1-7), so it would have been familiar to most in Jesus' day. Similarly, the Old Testament prophets were described as servants sent by God, for example in Jeremiah, Amos and Zechariah. And everyone knew what had happened to the prophets. Little wonder that the chief priests, scribes and elders were able to identify themselves as the wicked tenants to be judged. In this light, the story can be seen to position Jesus with the authority of the son. The term 'son' has been heard twice already in Matthew, and in both cases, it came as a voice from heaven. At Jesus' baptism, it is not clear who heard the voice, other than Christ, and at the transfiguration it was only Peter, James and John, whom Jesus ordered not to speak of what they had seen (see 'Seeing Jesus'). But in this story from Christ, 'son' is heard and understood by all.

When *we* hear it, or read it, it is easy for us to identify the bad guys, to pick up that judgmental vibe. We can say, 'Yeah, Jesus, put it to them, you really got them, they can't argue their way out of it', and we can position ourselves comfortably on Jesus' side. We are there with him, taking on the narrator's position. Or perhaps if we place ourselves in the story, we are the good guys, the ones who get given the vineyard at the end.

While we hold this understanding, let us consider its implications for a minute. The Christian church today is in the position of being the tenants, and so now the parable begins all over again. For is it not also true that if *we* are now the tenants, the owner will be asking *us* for the fruits of *our* labours? We are responsible for the harvest. For some, this can be a much needed wake up call, a reminder that perhaps we have become too comfortable, it has all become too easy. It acts as a prompt to ask ourselves, 'how am I living? am I like the tenants, wanting to keep the fruit of the vineyard for myself?' For others, this understanding can be carried as a burden: 'what fruits are there in my life?', 'what harvest have I brought in?', 'I'm not and never will be good enough'. We can experience the understanding as judgment, as a sense of permanently disappointing God, of not being able to live up to expectations: 'It wasn't easy, it was too hard, I failed.'

Fortunately, we can turn to Paul's answer to such questions in Philippians chapter 3. There, Paul considers all those things that might be thought of as profit, the things that may give him credit in the world's eyes as his accomplishments (by birth and effort), are wiped aside, as garbage (Philippians 3:7-9). This is another jolt for the complacent. All that we think we have done, as significant, does not count. Yet there is hope too for the uncertain, for the downhearted, for Paul, and for any Christian, because there is only one item on the credit side: it is Christ, the cornerstone on which all will be built and which utterly transformed Paul's life. This removes the burden of disappointing God, of not living up to expectations, for these are met in Christ. As we have reflected before (see 'Grace'), there is nothing we can do to make God love us more, and nothing we can do to make God love us less. This gives us freedom to respond to God's love, just as the supporters at a baptism do, to commit ourselves to the work of the vineyard, to bringing the kingdom to fruition.

What help do we have in doing this? What guidance is there for us as labourers in the vineyard? Well, for a start, we can remember the people of Israel in the desert, how they were brought out of Egypt, through the Red Sea, and how God gave them water from the rock. And we can remember the covenant between God and his people in the commandments, not as a burdensome list of negatives, but as helping us to understand more of God, and to see the world as God sees it, and as one day it will be (see 'Rules?').

We are challenged to be people who produce the fruits of that world, God's kingdom. The gospel story is about authority, the authority of the son, the authority of the vineyard owner. If we accept the authority of Jesus' guidance, of his way of living, then it is all about our response. Jesus expressed the goal of the kingdom of heaven as a tiny seed growing into a large bush. It is not so much a place as a state of growing to maturity, the capacity to bear fruit which nurtures and nourishes others. Will it be easy? We must try it and see.

Authority

> **WHERE IS JESUS' AUTHORITY IN YOUR LIFE?**

God
we turn to you
we accept your authority
but we get things wrong
and we disappoint you

thank you for always loving us
to set us free
to hope
to respond
to do your work
to grow your kingdom
Amen

Susan Joy Nevile and Maurice Nevile

Power

John 1:1-5, 10-12, 14

GOD'S POWER IS LOVE, AND IT IS GIVEN TO US

'Dusting off your savior' is how the band Red Hot Chili Peppers begin their song 'Savior', and I have always loved that opening line. It creates an image for me of that time of the year when we unpack the family Christmas decorations, uncovering the nativity scene and blowing the dust off the figures and placing them one by one, until finally we get to the baby Jesus, the saviour, and placing him right in the centre, in pride of place, ready for the celebration. From the Gospels of Matthew and Luke, we can get the familiar Christmas scene, with the shepherds and angels and wise men, but here I want to focus on John's Gospel. The early verses of John are not the most straightforward passages to understand, but they give a different and beautiful way to hear the Christmas story, and they tell us something about God's kind of power. In verse 14 we hear:

> The Word became flesh and made his dwelling among us.
> We have seen his glory, the glory of the one and only Son,
> who came from the Father, full of grace and truth.

The Word became flesh. God was not content with being a distant God, somewhere out there, but chose to become one of us, fully human, a tiny, frail, vulnerable human life, to grow and walk beside us. If we stop to think about it, it is astounding, breathtaking, stunning, staggering. From being one with God, from whom all things were created, to come to a dirty stable, from limitless power and freedom to be born into poverty, to a teenage mother, and into an occupied country with unstable rulers.

The paradox of the Incarnation, where God relinquishes power and becomes a baby, defies even our imagination. We cannot get our heads around it. To us, power, all kinds of power, is so very attractive: we seek it, we value it, we hold on to it, we don't want to lose it, and very often we are not keen even to share it. It could be the power of popularity, the power of wealth, the power of authority, the power of influence, the power of competence, the power of success, the power of might, the power of security, the power of certainty, or power of whatever other form. And we do not have to look far to see people abusing their power. So, the notion of relinquishing power seems to us bizarre, and goes against all the norms we see around us. God seems to be intentionally choosing the wrong option.

How are we to explain it, to understand God becoming human, becoming one of us? It can help to think of love, of God's love for us. For in that love is power, the power to overcome death, the power to remove our separation and bring us back to God, the power to give eternal life. It is power that we cannot imagine, but we do not need to. By turning to God, we can feel God's power, and it changes our lives.

HOW DO YOU USE LOVE'S POWER?

God
sometimes we are attracted to power
for what we think it gives us
but your power is in love
and it is astounding
breathtaking
stunning
staggering
beyond even our imagination

your love brings us back to you
it overcomes death
it gives eternal life

we hold it
we feel it
we cannot lose it
and it changes our lives
Amen

Susan Joy Nevile and Maurice Nevile

Rules?

Exodus 20 (NIV)

GODS' RULES ARE REALLY A PROMISE
FOR HOW THE WORLD WILL BE

For all of us, and maybe especially for children, sometimes it seems that our lives are full of rules of different kinds – do this, don't do that, do it like this, don't do it like that, be like this, don't be like that. We have rules in wider society, at work, at school, or home, for ordering and conducting our lives. There are rules about what we can do, say, how we can dress, and how we should spend our time (exercise more, have less screen time...). From a child's point of view, adults seem to have it made – no one is telling them what food to eat, when to do their homework, or when to go to bed! But really, we know it does not get any easier as we age.

Are you someone to always keep the rules? Or if you are told not to walk on the grass, do you just have to do it? For some of us, rules are a heavy burden, cramping our style – 'why can't I do what I want, when I want?' But I wonder how it would be if we were all like that? What would the world be like if there were no rules? As a school chaplain and teacher, when I asked that to children, they would often say, 'Oh yes, please!' They imagined staying up late, being free to be use electronic devices and be immersed in social media, having music blaring, eating junk food. But I encouraged them to really think – what if nobody kept any rules, and only did what suited themselves? I would prompt the children to think just about the morning, from getting up, getting dressed, having breakfast, and getting to school – what would those be like in the 'no rules world'? What if they got up whenever they wanted, wore whatever they felt like, ate whatever they chose (sugary cereal every day?!), and turned up to school any old time in the day? The children realised quickly that it might not be so easy, or even much fun. Instead of chains that only restrict us, rules can actually protect us, from other people as well as from ourselves.

The story we focus on here is one of the significant ones. It is right up there with creation, with the flood, and it is perhaps one of the most influential legal texts in human history. It is the story of the giving of the commandments. It begins (vv. 1-4):

> And God spoke all these words: 'I am the Lord your God, who brought you out of Egypt, out of the land of slavery. You shall have no other gods before me. You shall not make for yourself an image in the form of anything in heaven above or on the earth beneath or in the waters below.

And likely you know the others as it continues, including 'You shall not murder. You shall not commit adultery. You shall not steal. You shall not give false testimony against your neighbour' (vv. 13-16).

It is astonishing to think how far these rules have spread, from the community guidelines of a small tribe at the foot of Mount Sinai to become the basis of the legal system across western cultures. The Hebrews had, just months earlier, been rescued from slavery in Egypt. There had been miracles of protection, provision, and guidance in the desert. They had arrived at Sinai, the holy mountain, and Moses tells them to prepare themselves as he goes up to speak to God. The

Rules?

mountain is covered with smoke, the mountain trembles, and there is thunder and lightning. And Moses hears the voice of God.

Often people think about the commandments as only a list of negatives, 'You shall not...', to take the enjoyment out of life, well exemplified in the judgmental Reverend Lovejoy of the TV show *The Simpsons*. But this is unfair and limited. The commandments give ten quite clear and surprisingly simple 'rules' to live by. Actually, it is better to see how they help us to understand more of God, and to see the world as God sees it. In the first three commandments, the Israelites are shown how to live, and with the reality of the God they serve as 'El Shaddai' – God the almighty and all-knowing one. In the fourth commandment, the people are called to live as God lives, to match the rhythm of their lives with God's rhythm. Then Commandments five to ten give ways of living as God does.

I asked children to imagine what it would be like with *no* rules, but then I also asked them to imagine what it would be like if everyone followed the rules, if we kept the commandments. There would be no fear of violence, or of stealing, or of betrayal. We would be content with who we are, and with how we treat others and how others treat us. We would be satisfied with what we have, and we would be happy to share that with others. We would respect the range of people's responses to God, and the diversity and the varieties of religious experience. We would take time to rest properly, and no one would be overworked and overstressed. We would celebrate God. So, we can see the ten commandments in a new light: as ten possibilities, as ten hopes, as ten dreams, as ten ways to live. The commandments offer a glimpse of the world that God promises will one day come about. One day 'you shall not' will no longer be a command, an instruction for how to live in the world, a rule. Instead, one day 'you shall not' will be a description of how we are, and how the world is. This is the promise we can celebrate.

> **HOW DO RULES HELP YOU TO UNDERSTAND?**

God
in your rules, your commandments
we can understand you
and what you promise for us

ten possibilities
ten hopes
ten dreams
ten ways to live

we look forward to the day
when your promises are fulfilled
and we can celebrate
because we are finally who you know we can be
and the world is finally what you know it can be

Amen

Susan Joy Nevile and Maurice Nevile

Riches

Mark 10:17-27 (GNT), Matthew 19:16-30, Luke 18:18-30

IN GIVING OF OURSELVES TO OTHERS
WE CAN RECEIVE SO MUCH MORE

What really matters in life? Where are we to find life's true 'riches'? After a major tragedy, like a transport accident, natural disaster, or mass criminal event, people commonly say that they are prompted, even compelled, to identify and reflect on what is important in their life – on what really matters to them. This is what Jesus is doing in the story here, forcing the rich young man to see what is important to him. It is not as though the man was on the wrong track – he asks a great question, perhaps *the* great question: 'What must I do to receive eternal life?' (Mark 10:17). In one sense, he knew what was important, certainly he knew enough to ask Jesus, but he seemed to have the intuition that he needed more. He had kept the commandments, he had played by the rules, done the right things, yet he knew that something was missing, something was not quite right. And so, he asks, 'What must I do...?' The Bible says that Jesus looked at him with love, as he answered: 'You need only one thing. Go and sell all you have and give the money to the poor, and you will have riches in heaven; then come and follow me' (Mark 10:21). The Bible tells us that the man's face fell with gloom – he was very wealthy.

Was Jesus saying it was wrong to be rich? No, at least not really. Jesus was trying to encourage his followers to live differently, to prepare themselves for the upside-down kingdom of God. Thinking about this story encourages us to ask ourselves, 'well, what are my priorities, what is important to me?' Is it being accomplished and successful, with an impressive career, a new car, a nice house, and having grand holidays? If not that, is it living well? Is it family? Is it friendships? These might be reasonable answers, yet I wonder if Jesus would look at us with love and ask, 'are any of these more important than following me?'

Sometimes it is good to hear stories of others who have asked themselves similar questions of life's priority and importance, and so here I give some snapshots of people who reflected on what matters to them, resulting in turning points in their lives. For example, one friend was planning to do a weekend course in mosaics. In passing she told me of the course presenter who had been a tax accountant for a large multinational company, earning $340 per hour, until she realised that she really wanted to be an artist. By developing her creative side, and sharing that with others, she estimated her new income at less than $5 per hour, doing what she loved. Or, after struggling for most of his own life for secure employment and financial security, the original Colonel Sanders became very wealthy as an innovator in the fast food business. He was later determined to change others' lives for the better and so became a substantial donor for charities caring for women and children.

I think too of St Francis of Assisi. He was born as Giovanni in the late 12th century to a rich family and enjoyed a life of wealth and comfort. He then had some experience away in the army and returned home a quite different man, before an illness and some visions led him to begin to re-assess his life. He gave up everything he had, took vows of poverty, and began to attract followers, later starting an order of monks. Among other things, St Francis is known for his compassion and deep concern for the poor, and for animals and the natural environment. As a deacon and preacher to ordinary people, he was dedicated to live and work in Christ's way, caring for the vulnerable. Here are verses from the hymn known as *The Servant Song*, which is often ascribed to St Francis and captures a sense of his faith life.

> Brother, sister, let me serve you
> let me be as Christ to you
> pray that I may have the grace to
> let you be my servant too.
>
> We are pilgrims on a journey
> and companions on the road
> we are here to help each other
> walk the mile and bear the load
>
> When we sing to God in heaven
> we shall find such harmony
> born of all we've known together
> of Christ's love and agony.

Servant Song. Words by Richard Gillard

In each of these cases, the individuals found joy and peace in discovering what really mattered for how they lived and lived with others in the wider world. So, it is important to remember that Jesus' call is not only about giving up, but also about receiving. It is a little like the upside-down logic of the first will be last and the last will be first, the rich shall be poor, and the leaders shall serve. In giving we can receive so much more, and these are the riches that matter.

WHAT ARE YOUR RICHES?

God of riches
you call us to give up
but also to receive
your riches
the true riches
the riches that really matter
the riches of your kingdom
joy
peace
grace
love
and eternal life

we hear your call

Amen

Susan Joy Nevile and Maurice Nevile

Abundance

Matthew 14:13-21, Mark 6:31-44, Luke 9:12-17, John 6:1-14

AN ATTITUDE OF ABUNDANCE CAN LEAD TO TRANSFORMATION

Here I reflect on an attitude that seems particularly widespread and taken for granted: it is the attitude of scarcity. We often treat good things as scarce, as if there is simply not enough to go around. Imagine if there was a last ever piece of chocolate fudge banana cake, made to a unique recipe. Word has got out that it is the most delicious cake ever, but the recipe has been lost and the cake can never be made again quite like this. There is one last piece of cake, and many people want to buy it, and eat it. So, what happens? The seller can charge a premium price, automatically cutting out many potential buyers, but still there are some who can pay. Then someone buys it. Others feel annoyed that they could not get it, and are maybe angry at the seller, and envious of the person who enjoys that last piece of chocolate fudge banana cake. These people become unhappy with the ordinary chocolate cake that they have. And maybe the buyer does not really enjoy it but must gobble it down fast in case other people have ideas to take it, or before it gets dropped to the ground or goes bad. Keeping to the chocolate theme (sorry!), I think too of Roald Dahl's book *Charlie and the Chocolate Factory* and the clamour worldwide for the five Golden Tickets. Scarcity can bring out the worst in us.

This is the attitude of scarcity, and we begin to see the problems it creates. We see it operating around us. What happens when we live with an attitude of scarcity? We become always worried about what we have, and the possibility of losing it, and we become worried about what others have and the possibility of missing out. When I just think on this, I can find myself almost hunching over, my arm curving around my imagined treasures. The attitude builds a sense of competition between people, where we must beat others, to be smarter, faster, better, stronger, to have more, to get the prize and to stop others getting it. It is an attitude where walls between people become higher.

I want to tell a further story, and it is one that likely you have heard before. It is a story that is told by John, Matthew, Mark, and Luke – in all four Gospels! – which means that it is one of the most familiar of Jesus' miracles. Jesus feeds 5000 people with five loaves and two fish. In this story we can see two hugely different attitudes running throughout. The attitude of scarcity is there when the disciples say, 'we don't have enough', 'we can't feed them', 'send them away'. The implication is that the people are to look after themselves. Except for one young boy who brings forward his lunch, and so shows us the way that God looks at things (John 6:1-14): *his* is an attitude of *abundance*. What a contrast to the others.

We are prompted to wonder: if an attitude of scarcity creates problems between people, then what comes from an attitude of abundance? First, there is the spirit of generosity: the boy brings forth all that he has. He does not quickly cram a fish and three buns into his mouth and then give his leftovers! He happily gives it all. Where scarcity builds mistrust, abundance brings trust. The boy did not worry about getting his fair share but trusted Jesus to do the right thing. And second, from trust comes transformation, the miracle that thousands of people were fed from the two fish and five loaves. Everyone had more than enough, and there were leftovers – not a few crumbs, but twelve baskets full.

Some people have no problem with the idea of miracle; after all, if God made the world then why cannot the physical rules, as we understand them, be bent every now and again? But other people really struggle with the idea that Jesus fed all those people with that boy's lunch: it is impossible, one just cannot make more than there is. But I wonder what is harder, making that lunch go around or changing people's hearts so that they were moved from an attitude of scarcity, of holding on to their own, to a spirit of abundance, where people come together, all sharing whatever they have? Either way, it is a miracle to me. As we think about how to respond to the story, we need to ask ourselves what attitude do we live with, scarcity or abundance? And how do we want to be living? An attitude of abundance represents trust, hope, and generosity, and can lead to transformation.

DO YOU HAVE ENOUGH?

God of abundance and miracle
in you there is more than enough

help us to be generous with what we have
to share with those who need

help us to trust and hope
to bring transformation

Amen

Susan Joy Nevile and Maurice Nevile

Miracles

John 2:1-12 (NIV)

**MIRACLES MAY NOT BE SPECTACULAR,
THEY CAN BE SMALL, SLOW, GENTLE ...**

It is a common enough expression, 'It's a miracle!', but do you believe in miracles? And can we experience them in our own lives? This story is found in the book of John, and does not appear in the other Gospels, so John must have felt that it was somehow remarkable. In fact, it comes right at the beginning as John tells us about Jesus. It is the first time Jesus does something miraculous, something that cannot be explained other than by saying that it is God's awesome power. At a wedding in Cana, Jesus turns water into wine, indeed six stone jars full, each holding at least 75 litres, of high-quality wine. After telling the story, John writes 'What Jesus did here in Cana of Galilee was the first of the signs through which he revealed his glory; and his disciples believed in him' (v. 11). It is a particularly significant event!

John described this act, this miracle, as a sign. Let us think about that. What is it that signs do? They tell us something, give us information, they alert us, like what is up ahead, or to look out for something, or where something can be found, or if we have to do something, or should not do something. What then does this sign - the miracle of turning water into wine - tell us? What information and alert is there for us, about Jesus, and about God? Well, at the very least, it tells us that Jesus can do things that are just simply amazing. It shows us that Jesus is special, different to the rest of us, and this is probably what immediately impacted his friends, the disciples. We must remember that this occurred just after Jesus began teaching, and the disciples did not yet know much about him. They probably went away thinking 'wow, who is this guy?! What else can he do?' And if we learn nothing else from this story then that is one great thing to hold on to – that Jesus did astonishing acts which show and remind us how he was truly special.

But there is more to this story because it tells us about God as well. We see how God can change things, how God can turn around situations of trouble. The family holding the wedding was no doubt feeling dreadful – how embarrassing to run out of wine! They would never live it down; it would be remembered as the wedding when there was not enough wine. We cannot know if Jesus had concerns about that, but what could have been a social disaster became a triumph. God has a knack of turning things upside down, and we can remember that too. When we are in difficult situations, when we cannot find an answer to a problem, when we cannot see how to move forwards or find a way out, if we take time to talk to God, God will be there, God will listen, and God will help us to find a solution.

Yet there is a more important message in this story – it tells us something about Gods' character, about what God is like. The story gives us a picture of God's love for us, a picture of wild, generous, extravagant love. Thinking practically, what is also utterly amazing in this story is the amount of wine that Jesus offers the wedding party. Jesus transforms at least 450 litres of water into wine. And it is not just any wine, but the best the steward had ever drunk! This is so typical of God. Therefore, the wine becomes a symbol of God's love for us, a symbol that Jesus picks up on three years later. God gives us much more than is needed, and he gives us the very best.

The story helps us to know something about Jesus; it reminds us that God is there when we are in trouble, and it shows the generous extravagance of God's love. The story tells us that God loves to celebrate. Jesus changes ordinary water into wine, the symbol of celebration. The Bible tells us that when people change, to try to live in God's ways, to be as God wants and knows they can be, God throws a party in heaven. God is really a party God. God knows how important it is to feel joy, and to share life's joyous moments.

And still one last thing, it is a story of miracle, and reminds us to be open to miracles in our lives. They may not be spectacular, and they may not be physical – miracles may be small, slow, gentle, quiet, and social. Maybe it is a change in yourself, or in someone you know, like a new way of responding or being. Or maybe it is a change in some situation that allows for new opportunities for insight and action, or new possibilities for goodness and joy. In miracles, we can see God's work, love, and power to transform.

> **WHAT ARE THE MIRACLES OF YOUR LIFE?**

Miraculous God
we want to know you better

help us to see
your small miracles
your slow miracles
your quiet miracles
your gentle miracles
your social miracles
your joyous miracles

help us to recognise
your generosity
your change
your solution
your triumph
your extravagant love
your power to transform

Amen

Susan Joy Nevile and Maurice Nevile

Not alone

Matthew 4:17-25, Mark 1:14-20

WE ARE NOT ALONE ON LIFE'S JOURNEY

What will 'the new' be like and how are we to face it? Often it is easier when we are not alone. The beginning of anything new can be a scary just because it *is* new, we have not experienced it, we do not know it. Starting something brings a mixture of excitement and challenge, even uncertainty and fear (see 'Beginning', 'Trusting'), and so the thought of facing it alone can seem daunting. The story here happened right as Jesus is starting something new, his work as a preacher, as someone who travels around explaining God's message. Jesus' message was quite simple – he kept going where John had left off. We can remember that John was a 'wildman': 'he went into all the country around the Jordan, preaching a baptism of repentance for the forgiveness of sins' (Luke 3:3, NIV). John was saying 'the Lord is coming, the one we have been waiting for is nearly here! Things are going to be different, and you need to get ready for it!' Jesus continues this: 'Repent, for the kingdom of heaven is near.' (see 'Kingdom'). Like John, Jesus was announcing the beginning of a new time, and that a new start is possible, as Peter, Andrew, James and John found out when they literally dropped what they were doing, in order to follow Jesus.

I think on what this story has to say for our lives as we start something new, like a new situation, a new relationship, even just a new year. God is all about new beginnings; it is his specialty. The opportunity to start anew lies at the very heart of God's message to us, so when we face the new, we can always ask God for help, and look for people we can turn to. Jesus shows us that we do not have to do it alone. He does this in two ways: he builds on what John had done – he extends on what was already there; and he asks others to join him. New circumstances, new demands, new tasks, new struggles, are much easier when we have others with us to share them. We can have guidance, we can have support, and we can have care.

I think too that the disciples give us a great example. Often when we hear about the disciples, we think, 'how could they have thought that?', 'how could they have done that?!' Like us, the disciples often miss the point and seem to muddle along until they get it. But this time they are spot on, in their complete trust of Jesus. They did not say, 'oh that's too hard, you don't really want me, I haven't done that before'. When Jesus called them, they went with him. They gave up what was familiar, and comfortable, to do something new and risky. We do that when we give up something old and known for something new and unknown.

Jesus invites us to follow him to start living a new way, the way that God wants us to. But as we feel both the excitement and the uncertainty, we can know that God is always there alongside for the journey, and we can look for others to be with us and to help us along the way.

Not alone

> **WHO IS WITH YOU?**

God
when facing the new
the challenging
the unknown
and the risky
we are excited
we are uncertain
we are scared
and we are often alone

thank you for being alongside
and sending others to help us

Amen

Susan Joy Nevile and Maurice Nevile

Sacrifice

John 3:1-20 (NIV)

Mary Batchelor (1985) *Mary Batchelor's Everyday Book*. Lion Hudson, Oxford.

IN CHRIST'S SACRIFICE, OUR SEPARATION FROM GOD IS OVERCOME

When I was a school chaplain and teacher, sometimes the little ones would ask me, 'Mrs Nevile, which is more important, Christmas or Easter?' I know that from a child's perspective, Christmas is so important: the buildup is more exciting, for example, with decorations and lights; the Easter bunny (or bilby) cannot compare to Santa; families will get together; and there are more presents. I can understand why, to children, Christmas would feel like the most important Christian festival. And it is indeed amazing that in Jesus we have God on earth. God showed us how much love he has for us by becoming Immanuel, God with us. But that was just the start of God's plan, because God knew there was a problem...

What typically happens when someone really wrongs us, or hurts us? We can be less inclined to be near them, and if we could, we would close a door, shut them out, stay away from them, even have them out of our life. And when people hurt each other, God feels that hurt also. God is love, and so when love and hate meet, when generosity and selfishness come face-to-face, they repel each other. I would demonstrate this in class with the like poles of two magnets: they push each other away. Even though God loved people, the results of our actions often lead us to be separate from God. God needed a way to bridge the gap, to reduce this separation, and that is why Easter is so important. Jesus, who had done nothing wrong, took the consequences, by dying on the cross. Jesus, as fully human, chose that fate of sacrifice, for us (John 3:16-17): 'For God so loved the world that he gave his one and only Son, that whoever believes in him shall not perish but have eternal life. For God did not send his Son into the world to condemn the world, but to save the world through him.'

In talking about love, Jesus said that the greatest love a person can have for his friends is to give up his or her own life for them. We seem to have a natural, intuitive, understanding of this. Acts of sacrifice crop up in much loved books like *I am David* (by Anne Holm), and *The Lion, the Witch, and the Wardrobe* (by C. S. Lewis). War heroes are formally recognised for such actions, and not all war heroes are soldiers or other fighters. For example, Mary Batchelor (p. 78) tells the story of a nun, Mother Maria, of Ravensbrück concentration camp, from 30 March 1945, the last year of the Second World War. The appalling conditions of the camp eventually overcame one young girl who could not wait quietly outside the bath house, knowing that a horrible death would come. She began to scream with terror. As the guards approached, Mother Maria got to her side first, put her arm around her shoulder, and whispered assurance. Some say they entered the gas chamber together; others say that Mother Maria took her place. At Easter, we have Jesus putting his arms around the whole human race, and saying 'Don't be frightened, I'll come with you', and undergoing, for us, sacrifice, and terrible separation from God.

But Easter does not end there! On the Sunday, the women discover that the stone has been rolled away, and the angel announces that Christ is risen. Death itself has been overcome. God's power for creation and re-creation is such that life bursts out of the tomb. Hope is born out of despair; God, in his son, has paid the price, and triumphed. In my services, I would use signs and symbols of Easter to remind us of that, to remind us of new life. The *rainbow* is a sign of God's promise of enduring love. Some *flowers* point to Easter at Spring in the northern hemisphere, to reinforce the message of life, that the ground recently dull and snow covered is now full of colour and beauty. A *butterfly*, which seems dead and lost in the cocoon, emerges transformed. A *sun* signifies a new start, with each new day, and the darkness broken by light. *Water* sustains life. And from *eggs*, new life breaks out, just as the stone of Jesus' tomb was pushed aside to reveal the new life within.

So, is it Christmas, or Easter? Both tell of life. Easter tells also of sacrifice, so that the separation between people and God is overcome, and love emerges victorious.

> **HOW DO YOU FEEL JESUS' ARMS AROUND YOU?**

God
as a baby you came to us
as a man you walked with us
on the cross you left us
in sacrifice
only to rise and return
so that together again
we can share your victory
in light
in life
in love

victorious loving God, we praise you

Amen

Susan Joy Nevile and Maurice Nevile

New ways

John 21:1-19

IN CHRIST WE CAN FIND NEW WAYS OF BEING

This story gets to the heart of Jesus' message, to teach new ways. The story comes right at the end of the book of John, as he finishes his account of Jesus' life with the disciples by the lake. It is a neat finish, for Jesus' ministry starts by the lake as he calls the disciples to follow him, to change what they did, from being fishermen to 'fish for people'. Now, the disciples have gone back to fishing, to what they had done before they were followers of Jesus. It is almost as if they have written off that part of their life, as if it were good while it lasted but now it is back to reality. Now it is back to a real job, back to the smell of fish that you can never rinse out; back to the hard labour of the sail and the nets; back to the long nights out on the lake. But it is just not working, there are no fish! And then Jesus asks them to do things in a *new way*. Jesus calls out, prompting them to try fishing from the *other side* of the boat. And when they do, it is a huge success! The net is full of fish. They are re-called by Jesus: he wants them to do things differently.

Jesus taught a *new way of living*. When people said that God only accepted certain kinds of people, Jesus accepted everyone, and welcomed the people that were considered the bottom of the heap. Children, Jesus said, are precious to God, and all adults needed to learn from children how to accept and love God. Jesus went out and invited himself to dinner with someone who was considered beneath contempt – a tax collector. Jesus did not avoid lepers, as everyone else did, and not only spoke to them but reached out and touched them.

Jesus taught a *new way of looking at things*. He watched people giving money at the temple and said that the gift of two cents was worth more than the hundreds of dollars that were lying on top of it. He said that if you want to be a leader – one who is followed, looked up to – then you must be a servant. You must do those things that no one else wants to do, like wash people's dirty feet.

Jesus taught a *new way of treating people*. He said that if someone slaps you on the right cheek, then let them smack your left cheek too; if someone takes your shirt, then give them your coat as well; if one of the despised Romans asks you to carry his pack for one kilometre, then take it for two. And perhaps the hardest of all, for us even today, when people said that you should only love your friends, Jesus said, love your enemies.

And that is what is most significant: Jesus taught a *new way of love*. He asks Peter that question three times – 'Do you love me?' You can hear Peter's frustration by the third time – 'Lord, you know all things; you know that I love you' (v. 17). What is it that Jesus tells Peter to do?... to care for his sheep. We remember that God is like a shepherd, and people are his sheep. Peter is to show his love for Jesus by caring for God's people, through actions. Which is fair enough when we think about it. After all, how do we show someone that we love them? We can tell them, we can spend time with them, doing things together, we can give to them or make them something, and we can do things for them in just the way they like.

All this is true for God. When we talk to God, when we come together to be with God as well as with each other, and when we make choices for how we are going to live, for how we are going to treat people around us, we share a new way to be, as revealed in Jesus.

> HOW CAN YOU SHARE JESUS' NEW WAYS?

God, teach us
a new way to live
a new way to look
a new way to treat others

we want to learn
Jesus' new way of love
Jesus' new way to know you
Jesus' new way to be

Amen

Susan Joy Nevile and Maurice Nevile

God's eyes

Mark 12:41-44

WE CAN TRY TO SEE WITH GOD'S EYES

How could we see the world and its people with God's eyes? Our story here is set in Jerusalem in the days before Jesus' crucifixion. In Mark chapter 11, we hear of Jesus' triumphant entry into the town, and his cleansing of the temple. He overturns the tables in the outer court and says the merchants have made a house of prayer into a den of thieves. The crowds were spellbound by Jesus' teaching, but the chief priests and scribes were looking for a way to kill him. At the end of Mark chapter 11 and throughout chapter 12, they try to test Jesus with a series of questions. They try to show him up, and find a weakness: 'by what authority do you teach?'; 'should we pay tax to Caesar?'; 'if a widow remarries, to whom is she married in heaven?'; 'what is the greatest commandment?' Jesus answers, and delights the crowd. Much of his teaching carries warnings about the scribes and Pharisees, of their hypocrisy, and to whom one should place trust. In the midst of this teaching and engaged debate is our focus story. Jesus sits and watches as people place their offerings for the temple treasury. Many rich people give large amounts, but Jesus draws his friends' attention to a widow who gives two small copper coins, worth much less in comparison.

Often when we hear this story, we focus on her giving. We are encouraged to be like her, to give all that we have. And that itself is a huge challenge! It asks us to give with an attitude of generous abundance, rather than scarcity (see 'Abundance'), to give much because we have ourselves have received so much. But here I would rather focus on Jesus, and the fact that, of all the people in the temple at that time, he saw and drew attention to her. Jesus noticed and valued a woman who was usually invisible. Widows in Jewish society had no man, and so had no social standing. Yet Jesus saw her, and he understood her. Again, and again, Jesus is drawn to the vulnerable, the outsiders. He mixes with tax collectors, prostitutes, lepers, foreigners and children.

We see once more God's way of looking, inside out, upside down, reversing how we see the world. We see with blinkers, focused on ourselves and what suits us, on what we need, on what we want. We miss the bigger picture, and we miss the people at the edges. Jesus never did, he would bring them into the centre, like using a child to demonstrate who is important (see 'Great', 'New ways'), and like using the widow to show who gives more, and what it really means to give. How different might the world be if we could look with God's eyes? We would see each other with gentleness, understanding, generosity, and care, and we would see others for their potential. We would love, and not judge, and we would know that we too were loved, and not judged. And I think this would give us the freedom to live truly as children of God, and to be part of his kingdom, and of his work.

> **CAN YOU LOOK, AND SEE SOMEONE AT THE EDGES?**

God, creator, maker of heaven and earth
we long to see the world through your eyes
inside out... upside down

help us to see the bigger picture
with gentleness
with understanding
with generosity
with care

help us to see beyond ourselves
to give to others because you give to us
to include others because you include us
to love others because you love us

help us to see
and to change the world

Amen

Susan Joy Nevile and Maurice Nevile

God's vision (all about Mary)

Luke 2:1-21 (NIV)

Ana Maria Bidegain (2004), in Christopher H. K. Persaud, *Famous People Speak About Jesus: A Compendium of Expressions of Praise and Reverence*. Xlibris

Joyce Johnson Rouse, song lyrics, 'Standing on the shoulders', via https://earthmama.org/lyrics/ (accessed 11 September 2020).

MARY IS AN EXAMPLE TO US
OF CATCHING AND KEEPING GOD'S VISION

It is one thing to see or hear God's vision, for ourselves, for our lives, or for people and the wider world around us. It is another thing to truly catch and keep that vision, no matter its cost to us to carry it through. In this extended reflection we will consider Mary, Jesus' mother, as someone who did just this. I was once struck by the words of a song by Joyce Johnson Rouse:

> I am standing on the shoulders of the ones who came before me.
> I am stronger for their courage, I am wiser for their words.
> I am lifted by their longing for a fair and brighter future.
> I am grateful for their vision, for their toiling on this earth.
> I am standing on the shoulders of the ones who came before me.
> I am honoured by their passion for our liberty.
> I will stand a little taller, I will work a little longer.
> And my shoulders will be there to hold the ones who follow me.

It prompted me over the next few weeks to ask my friends and family a simple question, and it is where I would like to start. Where does your mind go when I say 'Mary'? What is the first image that comes to you when I say that name, the name of Jesus' mother? For many, it will spark some kind of picture. It may be, as it was for my older son, a nativity picture, a young mother bending over a crib. Or perhaps like my friend, working at a major art gallery, your mind goes to a beautiful work of art. For her, it was Michelangelo's *Pietà*, with Mary holding her crucified son. Or maybe, like a friend in pastoral education training, you respond in terms of words. She said, 'calm, peaceful, comforting'. It could be that your mind goes to scriptural words, to the *Magnificat* – amazing words of praise, a vision of God's reign and purpose (see 'Trusting'). Or maybe your mind wanders to images of burnt toast, which some have claimed to reveal the face of Mary! Perhaps just seeing the name 'Mary' conjures up memories of statues, processions with candles and flowers.

Most of us carry around some form of image of this woman – picked up from all kinds of places, like childrens books, Christmas cards, the media, Bible readings, and church teaching. Mary has worked hard for the church! From the earliest of times, Mary took on any and every female deity. Like Athena she protected cities; like Isis, she watched over seafarers; like Juno, she cared for pregnant women. Within the church, she has carried potent Biblical symbols. As the New Eve of Genesis chapter 3, she is often depicted crushing the serpent's head. She is seen as the bride of Yahweh, and some theologians tell us that in John her placement at the cross represents the church tenderly caring for us.

Over the years, the church has promoted many different images for Mary. In the Constantine era, she was depicted as the Egyptian desert nun – she only ate and slept when her body demanded it, she modulated her voice, and was so modest she shut her own eyes when dressing and undressing! In the middle-ages, Mary became a fair lady, for the knights a symbol of chaste love. In the renaissance, she was the tender mother caring for her spiritual children. Early in the twentieth century she was exalted as part of the holy family. Little wonder then that late in the twentieth century, feminist theologians saw Mary as domesticated and needing to be liberated. As the idealised, submissive woman, for the male higher powers, she had become a tool to oppress women. While liberation theologians seemed to discover what the people had always known, there was always running alongside the church's official theology another Mary; she was that aspect of divine love that was interested in the daily needs of ordinary people. Mary was merciful, close and responsive.

As on Saints' Days, when the church specifically celebrates Mary, Mother of our Lord, here now we can take the opportunity to connect with her story. It is a chance to draw closer to the ones who have gone before us, and to allow ourselves to be encouraged in our faith by their actions, standing on their shoulders. Within the Gospels, we hear of Mary as she grows from what we would see as a young teenager to a mature woman. While Mary appears in all the Gospels, it is from John and Luke that we are given the clearest pictures. Two pictures from Luke are in our focus text here. John's depiction of Mary focuses on the end of Jesus' earthly life, but Luke focuses on the beginning, the birth story.

In his description of the birth of Christ, Luke paints Mary as the central figure. The angel visits her, and Mary gives consent, after asking for clarification. For those of us who have lived with teenage girls, here is a great miracle. Mary says 'yes', not a flat 'no', not 'ahh it doesn't fit in with my plans', not 'whatever', but 'yes'. Mary empties herself and gives herself to God's purposes. So often this has been presented as Mary passively, submissively saying 'yes' – a form of self-denial which was presented as the essential if not the only attribute of a good woman. But as Ana Maria Bidegain (p. 185) emphasises, Mary is not taken by God, she is not passive but gives her 'free and responsible' 'yes', and hers 'is not the yes of self denial, almost of irresponsibility... Mary knows to whom she is committing herself'. Mary commits, knowing the risks she takes. She risks losing Joseph as a partner, she risks rejection, she risks ridicule, she risks injury: and still she says 'yes'.

And we have a picture of Mary as a determined ally of God's plans. In the book of Luke, Mary goes to visit Elizabeth, her cousin. It is an ordinary, commonplace occurrence, the meeting of two pregnant women, and as always with God, the ordinary is transformed, and we are given a picture of Mary as a prophetess. The words of the *Magnificat* are given to Mary, words that capture the heart of God's mission (see 'Trusting'). Mary joins that group of wise women and prophets of the Jewish scriptures. They are women who acted and articulated God's vision, women whose lives reflected God's purposes, such as Huldah (2 Kings 22), Deborah (Judges 4), Miriam (Exodus 15), Tamar (Genesis 38), the unnamed woman of Isaiah 8, Ruth, Esther, the mother of the Maccabees, Judith and Hannah.

In the songs of both Judith and Hannah, we see many of the images of Mary's song. There are elements of the threefold revolution of God's reign – cultural, political, and economic – divine power being exercised in caring for those in need. Here we have Mary as a disturber of the comfortable rather than a comforter of the disturbed. Furthermore, in Luke's birth story, it is Mary whom the other actors address: the shepherds speak to her; and when Jesus is brought to the temple for dedication, the prophesies are made to her. And Mary's response is to store the prophesies, to ponder on them.

She does not passively let things pass, but actively tries to understand the meaning of these events, and so in many ways Mary is a contemplative.

We do not hear much of either Jesus or Mary for the next thirty years. We can guess at some of her life experiences, as a woman who had carried her head high through a questionable pregnancy, and as a refugee in exile from her homeland, who in all likelihood was a migrant worker with no rights or protection. Reflecting on these experiences of being on the outer, of very real marginalisation, coupled with Mary's earlier proclamation of Holiness revealed through mercy, perhaps it is not unrealistic to say that Mary was a pivotal influence over her son Jesus in his formative years. We know of Jesus' radical inclusiveness, his teaching of God's love for all, his call to move from selfishness to other-centredness, towards love, sharing and communion. Certainly, in the one story we have of Jesus' childhood, in Luke 2, when he stays in the temple and his parents head home without him, it is *Mary* who addresses Jesus. As I have been the mother of two 12-year-old boys, I am with her in her worry: 'Son, why have you treated us like this? Your father and I have been anxiously searching for you' (Luke 2:48). And so, it is Mary who receives the rebuke: 'Didn't you know I had to be in my Father's house?' (Luke 2:49).

In this we see Mary's next task – having accepted her part in God's plan, having caught the vision, having carried, and cared for this child, she must now let Jesus go. She must relinquish her role in his life. In each of the Gospels, we catch a glimpse of this, as Jesus' family seek him out, to control what is happening, to protect him from the obvious consequences of his behaviour. In each Gospel, we hear Jesus' reply that 'whoever does the will of God is my brother, my sister, my mother'. In John, we have the wedding conversation at Cana, where Jesus addresses his mother as 'woman', effectively telling her that she does not understand what is happening. In Luke, a voice from the crowd calls out, 'Blessed is the mother who gave you birth and nursed you' (Luke 11:27) – but Jesus corrects them with 'Blessed rather are those who hear the word of God and obey it' (Luke 11:28). Great news for us. Jesus reframes that comment about his mother from a blessing for one individual to a blessing for all who want it! But what if you were that one individual, the one who *had* carried and suckled? Mary seems to be pushed out of Jesus' ministry. She is forced to re-examine, to keep on contemplating, pondering her understanding of who she is and her relationship with Jesus. It is not a popular or common image of this remarkable woman.

Yet, through this, Mary remains faithful, and she is there at the most difficult moment in Jesus' life. Most of his male companions have fled, but Mary is there with the women, watching as he undergoes the immense pain of crucifixion, bearing the shame of a punishment imposed on common criminals, experiencing its rejection and isolation. Mary is there in a position of powerlessness, doing all she can, just being, offering her presence as the one she loves, her son, our Lord, dies. Mary is there too in Acts, part of the birth of the church as the Spirit is poured out, and perhaps it is this, just as much as those early stories of her life, that enable us to see Mary as someone who caught God's vision – not in one peak experience but in the totality of her life.

We can see through the layers of meaning and symbols placed on her over the centuries. We can see past the statues, past the face on toast (!), and past the trite Christmas card images. We can see Mary very clearly as someone who heard the word of God, as ally, as prophetess, as teacher and disturber, as contemplative, as influencer, as companion, and above all as joyful. She is an example to us of someone who truly captured God's vision, and who kept it.

WHAT IS YOUR IMAGE OF MARY?

God
we are lifted on Mary's shoulders
we thank you
for her faith
for her caring
for her mercy
for her wisdom
for her presence
for her commitment
for her extraordinary courage

give us strength
so that we too can lift and hold
the ones who follow us

Amen

Susan Joy Nevile and Maurice Nevile

3 Along the way

Committing: saying 'yes'

Luke 1:26-38, 46-55

WE CAN SAY 'YES' TO GOD, AND TRANSFORM OUR WORLD

It is a massive challenge to believe, decide, commit, and act; and so allow your faith in the future to transform the now. As we read Luke 1:26-38, we see surely one of the most amazing moments in history, the moment when God's plan is announced to Mary, and Mary accepts: Mary says 'yes' (see 'God's vision'). In art, literature and other representations, people have imagined for hundreds of years what this moment looked like. Perhaps my favourite is a picture which captures the feel of the moment. We see a young girl, Mary was probably about 14 or 15 at the time – and she is facing not a friendly looking messenger but a being which is beyond imagination. She is listening intently and is about to give her answer: she is about to respond to God's plan of salvation.

Sometimes, I think about what Mary *could* have said... She could have said: 'No, I'm not ready'; 'No, it doesn't fit with my plans'; 'No, I don't want to, that's too hard'; 'No, what would people say?'; 'No, that's impossible'. These are the kind of responses that go through my head sometimes when I think about what God wants me to do. And I do not think I am so unusual. I suspect that we all have similar thoughts: 'You want me to forgive them? I'm not ready!'; 'You want me to help? That doesn't fit with my plans'; 'You want me to share? I don't want to, that's too hard'; 'You want me to spend time with them? What would people say!?'; 'You want me to love them? No, that's impossible!'.

How often do we offer excuses to God? How often do we say we cannot, we do not want to, that it is impossible? Not Mary though. Mary was troubled, shaken, but she said 'yes', even though she was not ready. Mary said 'yes' even though it was not what she had planned. Mary said 'yes' even though it was going to be hard. Mary said 'yes', even though people would judge her, laugh at her, talk behind her back. She said 'yes' even though it seemed impossible. We know Mary's response as the *Magnificat* (see 'Trusting').

As we read further of Luke 1:46-55, we can see just how Mary's 'yes' is utterly remarkable. Mary said 'yes' even when she did not know how it would turn out. When *we* hear this passage, we *do* know: we know what comes from her acceptance of God's will. Christ is born, and Christ changes everything. Mary does not know the future for her son, yet she responds with joy. She is willing to make a claim on the future that transforms her experience of the present, and that transforms our experience today. Mary's simple 'yes' changed the world. It is the 'yes' of love, which offers itself to others. Mary's love for God enabled God's love for the world to be born. Our challenge is to be ready to be part of that love, to offer our own 'yes' to God's call to us.

Committing: saying 'yes'

> SAY 'YES': WHAT WILL YOU DO?

God
thank you for asking
thank you for the challenge

yes, we are ready
yes, we want to
yes, it is possible for us
to help
to share
to care
to forgive
to love
to transform our experience
to transform ourselves
to transform our world

Amen

Susan Joy Nevile and Maurice Nevile

Doubting, believing, following

C. S. Lewis (1971) *Prince Caspian*.
Penguin Books (first published 1951).

> BELIEVE, AND FOLLOW GOD'S LEAD,
> FOR THE STRENGTH TO CARRY ON

What is it that we believe in, and what can stop us from believing, and from following our beliefs? In C. S. Lewis' book in the Narnia series, *Prince Caspian*, the Pevensie children are walking together when the youngest, Lucy, sees the great lion, Aslan. Lucy cries for others to look but they do not see him. Lucy's face changes completely, and we are told 'her eyes shone'.

Oldest brother Peter and sister Susan are doubtful, and question Lucy who replies that she saw Aslan up among the ash trees, in the *opposite* direction to the way they are wanting to go. She tells her siblings that Aslan wanted them to go where he was, up, not down. Lucy's other brother, Edmund, asks her how she knows what Aslan wanted, and Lucy says that she just knows, by Aslan's face. After discussion in the group, they head down, not up, on Peter's decision, and Lucy walks last, crying bitterly.

What stopped Lucy this first time Aslan calls her to follow? It seems that she did not have the courage to do what she knew (deep down) was right. Why not? She did not have enough trust. She did not have enough trust in herself, in her own convictions, to stick up for what she believed was right when others said that it was not logical, or sensible, or that they could not believe in Aslan. And Lucy did not have enough trust in Aslan. She did not believe that if she obeyed him it would be alright, that Aslan would take care of things, even if she could not yet see how. What Aslan had asked her to do, to follow him up the gorge, seemed too hard, so she followed the others.

But Aslan calls Lucy a second time. She reveals how she had seen him earlier but that the others would not believe her. She begins to criticise her siblings but stops at the suggestion of a lion's growl. As Aslan looks straight into her eyes, she begins to wonder aloud if she could indeed have gone up to him that first time. She realises that she would not have been alone because she would have been with him. As Aslan says nothing in reply, Lucy wonders further if things would have turned out alright but asks him how she could know. Aslan tells her that nobody is told what *would have* happened, but anyone can learn what *will* happen. They must act. He instructs her to wake the others and tell them a second time that she has seen him, and that they must all get up and follow.

What then was different the second time Aslan calls Lucy to follow? One difference is that by this time she had found out that *not* following Aslan had been unsuccessful; they had walked straight into their enemies. So, she had learnt from her mistake. But the big difference was that for the second call she had a real and physical encounter. She could hug Aslan; she could talk to him face-to-face. Meeting with Aslan gave Lucy a much clearer and better understanding of what she had to do, of what he expected of her. However, as the story continues, we see that even that was not enough. It was still too hard to follow – until Lucy buried her head in Aslan's mane and she felt his lion strength going into her. It is that strength that enables her to go back to the others, to wake them up, to explain what happened, and this time to stand up to her older siblings, Peter and Susan, and to Trumpkin. With Aslan's lion strength supporting her, what was previously too difficult becomes achievable. And if you know the C. S. Lewis books, or if you have seen the movies, you will know that in the end, all Narnia is renewed.

Now it is always a joy to read the Narnia books, but especially so at times in life when we pause to reflect and ask questions of ourselves. We explore elsewhere about how we make decisions (see 'Choosing', 'Deciding'). From another Narnia character, Digory, we are reminded that we can imagine what someone we trusted would do, not relying on ourselves, and so we could better understand how our choices would affect others. That can help us to resolve dilemmas. So, I come to ask a simple question. What would it be like if we believed and followed like Lucy eventually did? What would it be like if we *knew* that God was there, and we relied on him to lead us, just as Aslan led Lucy? But we may wonder, 'how can God lead me? He is not going to appear and tell me where to go'. Well, maybe not literally! But God sometimes *does* guide us to do things that are the opposite of what people around us may say, things that maybe seem to make no sense. For example, whereas society might say that if someone hurts you then get your own back, God says no, do the opposite. God tells us to love our enemies, to forgive them, and to pray for them. That is very much like going up a difficult rocky path when others want to go down the easy way.

God does give us directions about where to go in life, and how to get there, and gives us people for the journey. If we remember that no matter what, even if it looks too hard, if we listen, trust and believe, if we stay close and follow God's lead, he will give us the wisdom and strength to carry on.

> **HOW IS GOD APPEARING BEFORE YOU,
> CALLING YOU TO FOLLOW?**

Guiding God
when walking your way
sometimes we doubt
we hesitate
we do not believe
we do not follow
we are led by others
and we go the wrong way

help us to trust you always
to show us the way forward
to show us how to follow you

Amen

Susan Joy Nevile and Maurice Nevile

Seeing Jesus, listening to Jesus

Matthew 17:1-13 (NIV), Mark 9:2-13

NO MATTER HOW WE SEE JESUS, WE CAN ALWAYS LISTEN TO HIM

We all have different ways to see Jesus. Maybe how we see Jesus is influenced by our experience of him, or of how we came to our belief and faith, or of the traditions we are used to. Maybe it is influenced by how we see and experience people. The passages here tell of Jesus' transfiguration. When upon a mountain, and before some disciples, Jesus becomes radiant in glory, shining in bright rays of light like the sun (Matthew 17:2-5).

> There he was transfigured before them. His face shone like the sun, and his clothes became as white as the light. Just then there appeared before them Moses and Elijah, talking with Jesus. Peter said to Jesus, 'Lord, it is good for us to be here. If you wish, I will put up three shelters – one for you, one for Moses and one for Elijah'. While he was still speaking, a bright cloud covered them, and a voice from the cloud said, 'This is my Son, whom I love; with him I am well pleased. Listen to him!'

And then Jesus tells them not to tell anyone what they have seen! It must have been immensely hard for them not to talk about it. What a story, what an awesome story! Jesus' face starts to glow, like light itself had somehow become human, then the clothes, so white they hurt your eyes, then two people who have been dead for hundreds of years appear. And not just any old people but two of the most important people in Jewish history. A cloud descends, also radiating light, and then it finishes with the voice, 'This is my Son, whom I love... Listen to him'.

They could have dined out on that event for years. But they did not. Perhaps it was because this experience really shook them up. The story comes late in Jesus' life. The disciples had been around him for three years. They felt, especially the three here, Peter, James, and John, like they really knew him. They had been there when it had been tough, when Jesus had been thrown out, rejected by the people in his hometown. They had been there on the dusty roads as Jesus travelled from town to town, got cold, tired, hungry, just like the rest of them. They had been there on the good days as well, when Jesus had fed the multitude – they had passed around the baskets themselves. They had seen him calm the storm, and they had been amazed at his power over wind and water. But Jesus had still seemed human – after all they knew his mother, his brothers, and sisters.

But now, this, this was different. This forced them to see Jesus in a different way, as God's beloved son. They could no longer hold on to their familiar, comfortable ideas about who Jesus was, and what he might do. I think they were pushed out of their comfort zone when confronted by the mystery of the mountain. Okay, we may be thinking, but so what, what does their experience on a mountain top have to do with us, for how we see Jesus, and other people? Well, most of us are like Peter, James, and John. We like to keep people within the categories that we have formed for them. We like to know who they are, where they fit, what they do, and what they can do. We are a bit uncomfortable with people who do not fit easily into our boxes, who are a bit of a mystery. This is true for the people we see every day, and it is also true for how we see Jesus.

Whether we are conscious of it or not, we all 'see Jesus'; not in a physical, perceptual way, like we see each other now, but in our minds and imaginings. All of us walk around with a familiar sense or image of Jesus in our heads. Probably the pictures will be slightly different among us, but I think many will cluster together and we can establish some common categories of how we see him. We can see him as a *baby*, swaddled in a manger, cute, cuddly, maybe surrounded by the familiar parts of the story, shepherds, angels, wise men. It is a safe image, wrapped up in cotton wool. Then we have the *nice guy*, do-gooder image of Jesus, the one who comes to fix things up, helping and healing those he comes across. There is also the image of Jesus as the *preacher*, teacher, a charismatic speaker, who could hold a crowd in the palm of his hand and inspire people with great ideas. Perhaps we see him *on the cross*, a man who miscalculated, who took on the authorities and lost, and ended up dying. Or maybe we see him as the *risen Lord*, who from that cross turned defeat into victory, sadness into joy, and darkness into light, by overcoming death itself.

So, we can see Jesus wherever goodness, light, life, and love, shine through. We can always see Jesus as *God's beloved son*, with whom God is well pleased, and to whom we can listen.

> **JESUS IS SPEAKING TO YOU,
> WHAT DO YOU HEAR?**

God
Jesus is your son
your beloved son
whom you love

we can see him
as newborn baby
as helper
as healer
as inspiring teacher
as walking in the dust with us
as fully human in life
and in death

glorified in light
and shining like the sun
he speaks to us
if only we will listen

Amen

Susan Joy Nevile and Maurice Nevile

Welcoming Jesus

Matthew 25:31-46 (NIV)

Bernadette Watts (1997) *Shoemaker Martin*. Adapted and illustrated from original story by Leo Tolstoy. North-South Books.

WE CAN RESPOND, AND WELCOME JESUS, IN THE PEOPLE AROUND US

Sometimes it is hard to know how we should respond when we see situations of need, and especially people in need. What are we to do? Should we help, and if so, how? The book of Matthew tells of Jesus' pronouncement for how nations will be judged and divided, as a shepherd separates the sheep from the goats. The righteous, who give food to the hungry, drink to the thirsty, shelter to the stranger, clothing to the naked, and who visit the sick and imprisoned, will inherit the kingdom and eternal life: they are the sheep, and gain entry to heaven. Those who do not give food to the hungry, etc., are the goats, and are cursed and sent to the eternal fire. On one hand, this passage seems straightforward to understand, but on the other hand, it seems challenging to think on, let alone to reflect on. That is because of the image of judgment, or more particularly because of the idea of eternal punishment. These ideas can be frightening, and if we get caught up in them, we miss the heart of what is said.

I think about the story of Martin, a shoemaker who simply wanted to welcome Jesus into his house (story originally by Leo Tolstoy, adapted by Bernadette Watts). As he mended shoes in his basement, Martin could look through his window and see the legs of people passing by. Each evening, he would read the Bible, and one evening he read the story of the rich man who invited Jesus into his home. As he fell asleep, Martin imagined what it would be like to have entertained Jesus: 'If Jesus came to visit me, what would I say? What would I do? How would I welcome him?'

Martin is woken by a voice telling him to watch the street tomorrow, 'because I shall be coming!', the voice said. The next day, Martin sees and welcomes inside Stefan the street sweeper, who is struggling in the winter cold. He also welcomes a young woman in a shabby dress with a baby, offering her his coat, and food for them both. And then Martin stands up for a poor boy being dragged along by a woman for apparently stealing an apple. Martin says to the woman, 'Let him go... He won't do it again. If we punish someone so harshly for taking an apple, what punishments should we expect for our sins that are far, far worse?' The boy asks the woman for forgiveness, and they walk away together. Martin comes to understand that Jesus really had visited him, and he is overcome with joy.

What happens when we welcome someone into our home, and we spend time together? We can define and strengthen our friendship, build connections, understand, and appreciate each other better, and become closer. This is what Martin is longing for, and this is what he succeeds in doing: he gets closer to God as he cares for the people around him. He does not invite Stefan the street sweeper in because he knows he is going to be judged; he does not help the young mother and baby because he wants to avoid eternal punishment; he does not settle the dispute between the shopkeeper and the boy because he wants to earn brownie points in heaven. No, Martin simply sees the need, and he responds. He wants only to welcome and be with Jesus, and he takes the opportunity when it arises, by giving welcome to others. As Matthew 25:37-40 records:

> Then the righteous will answer him, 'Lord, when did we see you hungry and feed you, or thirsty and give you something to drink? When did we see you a stranger and invite you in, or needing clothes and clothe you? When did we see you sick or in prison and go to visit you?' The King will reply, 'Truly I tell you, whatever you did for one of the least of these brothers and sisters of mine, you did for me'.

And that is how we tell the difference between the sheep and the goats.

HOW CAN YOU WELCOME JESUS?

God
Jesus comes to us
as people in need
the cold
the poor
the wronged

forgive us
when we do not respond
when we watch him walk past
when we leave him outside

remind us to welcome him, inside
into our hearts
into our lives
to be closer to you
to know your great joy!

Amen

Susan Joy Nevile and Maurice Nevile

Growing

John 15:1-2, 12-17

GOD LONGS FOR US TO GROW AND TO BEAR GOOD FRUIT

We reflect elsewhere (see 'Accepting gifts', 'Forgiving') on perhaps the best-known image of God, as shepherd, and I think it is so familiar because it is comforting, giving us the idea of the care and protection that God offers. Unfortunately, the image of God in this passage from John is not so comforting. It is the image of God the gardener. Certainly, a gardener does take care of plants, and makes sure that they have what they need to thrive and grow, but here there is also mention of trimming, and even worse of cutting off branches if they do not bear fruit. We may be concerned at the thought of being trimmed, pruned, or even cut off! The text is a warning.

Picture in your mind a plant – maybe a rose, or a fruit tree – being pruned. Pruning involves cutting small parts off the plant so that the whole plant is healthier, or will have more flowers, or bear more fruit. So then, how would God prune a person? We might imagine a giant pair of secateurs, but I doubt it is like that, at least I hope it is not (!), and the idea of bearing fruit is not so simple. Jesus is not talking literally, he does not expect people to suddenly sprout grapes or dates or figs, the common fruits of the area. And I do not think Jesus is talking about our children, or offspring – what we produce.

Jesus is not saying that if we produce fine children then we will be okay.

So, what is it that Jesus is trying to warn us about? What is it that will enable God the gardener to judge how we are going and growing, and what fruits we bear? Do we deserve to stay on the vine, in the garden, or to be cut off, and thrown on the fire?

My suggestion is that it is our actions, how we live, how we treat people, that is important to God. The criterion being used is apparently quite simple: it is spelled out for us at the end of the passage. Do we love? Do we love one another just as Christ has loved us? This criterion may be simple, but living it, actually seeing it in our own lives, is much much much harder.

Just one way we can see how we love others is in the language we use, the basic truth of how we talk to each other. Do we, as is so easy and common, criticise others and use words to hurt? Are we humble in how we talk of ourselves and gracious in our victories, and our defeats? Do we recognise others' strengths with praise, without feeling threatened ourselves? We know that we often fall short in our language, in how we talk to and about others, and this is the kind of thing that I am sure God would love to prune from us – some dead wood that needs to go! On the other hand, in our language we can describe the good in someone, offer to help, speak up for them, and forgive them if they hurt us, even when that seems very hard to do. These are some good fruits that we can bear. This is what God longs for in us, to grow and bear such fruit (see 'Bearing fruit'). So, while the image of God the gardener is maybe not as comforting as God the shepherd, it gives us not only a richer sense of God, and God's care, but helps us to answer the great and crucial question: so how shall we live? (Ezekiel 33:11-20).

> **HOW CAN YOU GROW
> AS GOD WOULD HOPE?**

Gardener God
thank you for tending to us
you prune away what we do not need
and can harm us
you give us what we do need
and can make us grow

we will try to grow and bear good fruits
for ourselves, for others, and for you
by living with love

Amen

Susan Joy Nevile and Maurice Nevile

Bearing fruit

Acts 2:1-41

WE CAN KNOW GOD'S PRESENCE BY THE FRUITS OF THE SPIRIT

Birthdays are an occasion for gifts. The church's birthday is Pentecost, and not any particular church, but the whole Christian church: and we receive the gift. In terms of Christian festivals, I wonder if Pentecost is underrated. Everybody knows Christmas – there is a huge build up, decorations, marketing campaigns, and the familiar symbols. We look forward to time with family, the food, and children especially look forward to the presents. Most people could even say something of what Christmas is about – the baby in the manger is recognised and understood. Easter is nearly as well known, with lots of chocolate and familiar symbols of eggs, which are maybe not quite as well understood (and there is also the bunny, and now the bilby). Like Christmas, at Easter we get some holiday time. In the wider community, however, Pentecost passes without a blink. It marks the day when Jesus' followers changed from being a fairly disorganised and fearful group of people that hung out together, to having the sense of purpose of being God's body on earth, and of telling others of God's love for them. It marks a huge change. How did it happen? The story is found in the book of Acts (2:1-41).

They were all together, when suddenly there was a sound like a massive wind, filling the whole building, and they saw tongues of fire that came to rest on each of them. The Spirit filled them, and they spoke in many other languages. Jewish pilgrims staying nearby came running to see, and they were stunned. Well, Jesus had promised his followers a gift before he ascended into heaven, but he had not really spelled out what would happen. And I think it is fair to say that the gift of the Spirit really blew them away. It is as if they had no choice but to accept it. Peter spoke up. I don't think when he stood that he was reading the room and debating in his mind, 'Hmm, should I say something, is it the right time and place, what if I get into trouble, or arrested?' No, it is as if the Spirit came bursting out of him, full of excitement, full of energy, full of life. This is, after all, the Spirit's job.

Right back in the beginning of all things we are told that the Spirit was hovering, brooding, waiting to breathe life, form and beauty into existence. Throughout the Bible, we hear of the Spirit's work, as when the prophet Ezekiel has a vision of the Spirit bringing to life a valley of dry bones. Jesus, in his first sermon, recorded in Luke 4:18 (GNT), quotes Isaiah (another prophet) saying 'The Spirit of the Lord is upon me, because he has chosen me to bring good news to the poor. He has sent me to proclaim liberty to the captives and recovery of sight to the blind, to set free the oppressed'. The Spirit does not come for no reason, the Spirit comes to inspire and empower action – creating laughter, peace, imagination, change, life, love – the Spirit is the opposite of inaction, the reverse of not caring, the enemy of apathy, and is constantly working to bring about God's kingdom.

What I find amazing is that the Spirit works both on a grand scale, like the global outpouring of concern for victims of natural disasters, and very much on the small scale, in our ordinary everyday actions, in how we treat the people around us, and as a result what kind of community we make. In fact, in Galatians 5:22-23, Paul describes the effects of the Spirit, the enduring marks that it leaves on a community, a bit like scars, or tattoos, or even dental records. The image Paul uses is 'the fruit'. Even someone who knows nothing about botany can tell an apple tree from an orange tree by looking at the fruit it bears.

So, what are the fruits born of the Spirit? Paul describes a community marked by love, joy, peace, patience, kindness, generosity, faithfulness, gentleness, and self-control. When we see those qualities, either in a community or an individual, we can see the power of the Spirit working. These are the marks of God's presence – we may not feel the might of the wind, or be touched by tongues of flame, and we may not hear many languages, but we will see and understand those qualities, the fruits born of the Spirit. We will be warmed by love and kindness, comforted by peace, patience, and gentleness, inspired by joy, overwhelmed by generosity, encouraged by faithfulness, and strengthened by self-control. In these ways, we as individuals, and our communities, will be changed, moved, brought to life by the Spirit, by God's gift to us. So, it is worth regularly reflecting on the fruit that we bear, to see if there is a need in our own lives for love, for joy, for peace, for patience, for kindness, for generosity, for faithfulness, for gentleness, or for self-control.

> **WHAT FRUITS OF THE SPIRIT CAN YOU SEE,
> AROUND YOU ... OR IN YOU?**

Giving God
you made your Spirit present
in the sound of massive wind
in the tongues of fire
in the multitude of languages

help us now to make your Spirit present
in love, in joy
in peace, in patience
in kindness, in generosity
in faithfulness, in gentleness
in self-control within us
and within our community

Amen

Susan Joy Nevile and Maurice Nevile

Understanding

Matthew 21:1-11

WITH COURAGE, WE CAN UNDERSTAND AND ACCEPT GOD'S WAY

Often it is easy to understand things in retrospect, with hindsight, especially when we are faced with problems, or something surprising or unusual. And we do not always ask for help when we cannot understand. The Palm Sunday story gives a good example. Jesus comes to Jerusalem after three years in the countryside, wandering, telling stories about shepherds, farmers, housewives, beaten travellers, and lost sons of fishermen. After bringing hope to those who had given up, healing and wholeness to the broken, Jesus takes on the big city. Jerusalem was not a quiet, peaceful place; it was a city with a history of invasion, a seat of the mighty Roman empire. It was a city full of rumours, threat and discontent, where the poorest suffered most and cried out for change, buoyed by hope in the promise of a Messiah. They wanted an end to occupation, and they wanted bread in their stomachs and a better life. They wanted to be saved. The city was going wild!

Think of your own experience of being in an exceptionally large crowd, perhaps at a New Year's celebration, a major music concert, or a sporting event. Can you remember what that is like, the sense of expectation, the roar of excitement, the feeling of power from being part of something big? Well, the people of Jerusalem had an idea that they were onto something big. 'Hosanna! Hosanna!' they cry. A rough translation of Hosanna is 'SAVE US!' They called Jesus 'Son of David'. David was the great King, so in their cries the crowd identifies Jesus as a political leader, as one who would come, overturn the government, and sweep the rotten Romans out of their lives forever. Surely this was what the prophets of old had foretold: the Messiah, the saviour, would come, entering the city on a colt.

Jesus was being provocative. He could have slipped into town quietly. He could have stayed with his friends in Bethany. Jesus wanted to make a clear statement, to the temple priests, to the Roman troops, and to the people of Jerusalem. He made his choice years ago, back in the desert, when he faced the temptations of power (see 'Tempted'). Whoever heard of a great political leader arriving on a donkey?! You need more than a donkey and a few fishermen from up north to throw out the Romans. By choosing to enter the city this way, Jesus said that he was the one, but he came as the prince of peace, not as a warrior king.

But they all misunderstood. The *priests* did not want to understand, they did not want anything to upset the Romans and threaten their religious freedom. They were made to feel uncomfortable by this carpenter who would not be part of their debates, but whose actions made all their intellectual arguments look foolish. The *military* did not understand how to deal with someone who did not offer violence to anyone, who in fact discouraged his followers from violence, yet still posed a threat to public order. And the *people of Jerusalem*? Well, they heard only that royalty was on its way. That is a lot of misunderstanding, and we know what can follow when people do not understand each other: disappointment, hurt, anger, and worse. These are the seeds of the crowd's reaction later that week, in Pilate's courtyard, when the cry turns from 'Hosanna!' to 'Crucify him!'

Understanding

It is easy for us now, looking back, to shake our heads and scoff, 'how could they do that, how could they have misunderstood? It is so clear, so easy to understand what Jesus meant.' But when we are immersed in a situation, understanding is not always so straightforward. There are times when we feel like those in the crowd, that we are under threat, that we need to be saved. Maybe there are tensions with friends or family, a pile of bills to pay, a chaotic house to clean, work deadlines to meet, a crisis of health, a substantial life change or challenge. We feel under pressure, but we do not necessarily see and understand what can save us, what could be a way forward. We may not admit that we need help. Often, we can want an easy way out, a quick solution, or to avoid the problem entirely. But that's not God's way, as Palm Sunday reminds us. It marks the start of Holy Week, and we know the cross is there, waiting, showing us God's way, if only we can see it. The hope is there as well, the promise of salvation – we need the courage to *understand* it, and to *accept* it as God's way.

> **WHEN HAVE YOU NEEDED COURAGE
> TO UNDERSTAND AND ACCEPT?**

Provoking God
too often in life we are unsure
we are surprised
we are pressured
we are uncomfortable
and we just do not understand

we need help
to know the cross
to see what can save us
to wait for the right solution
to have courage to understand
and accept your way
Amen

Susan Joy Nevile and Maurice Nevile

Risking faith

Mark 5:21-43 (NIV)

HAVING FAITH MEANS SOMETIMES TAKING THE RISK TO ACT

Here we think about how faith figures in our actions and lives, and specifically on *risking faith*. Elsewhere, I reflect on David, the shepherd boy whose actions became legendary (see 'Facing giants'), and later we think too about Indiana Jones' step into the abyss (see 'Living with faith'). David was able, with nothing more than a stone, a slingshot, and faith in God, to defeat the giant Goliath. Now we *might* think that David was different, because after all God had chosen him to be the next king, and David had been anointed with oil by Samuel. The oil had represented God's Spirit falling upon him, so it is not that surprising that David was able to defeat a giant. We might think too that David's success was to be expected, really, because he was a special case, someone to be looked up to and admired. And Indiana Jones is a fictional action hero! We might think that, surely, *we* are not meant to believe that with *our* faith *we* can do anything remarkable, like David, and Indiana Jones, because we are just ordinary, everyday people. Well, the story in the passage here focuses on some very ordinary everyday people. They are people just like us.

The first is the story of Jairus. A friend once described this story to me as 'the miracle on the way to a miracle'. It starts with Jairus, who, as a synagogue leader, had a lot to lose by coming to Jesus. Remember it was synagogue leaders, the scribes, and Pharisees, who were in positions of authority in the Jewish faith, and who therefore were most threatened by what Jesus was saying and doing. Jesus had already had run-ins with them over issues like eating with tax collectors and working on the Sabbath. Jairus risked his job, and what his friends thought of him, by humbly and publicly asking for Jesus' help. When Jairus saw Jesus, he fell at his feet and pleaded with him: 'My little daughter is dying. Please come and put your hands on her so that she will be healed and live' (v. 23). Jesus went with him to find the household grieving for the daughter who had since died. But Jesus says 'Why all this commotion and wailing? The child is not dead but asleep' (v. 39), and he brings her to life.

Then we have the story of the woman who had been bleeding for twelve years. Technically, being sick meant that she should not have been out in public. Sick people were unclean and so not able to come before God. If she touched anyone, technically she made them unclean also. So, she risked being humiliated and turned upon if anyone recognised her and knew of her condition. In the large crowd following and pressing around Jesus, she comes behind him and touches his cloak, thinking and believing that by doing so she will be healed. Her bleeding stops immediately, and she felt freed from her suffering.

What is it that made the difference for these two ordinary people? Jesus identifies it when he says to Jairus 'Don't be afraid; just believe' (v. 36), and when he says to the woman, 'Daughter, your faith has healed you. Go in peace and be freed from your suffering' (v. 34). What made the difference is having faith. How can we understand faith? Well, having faith does not mean that we always get it right (see 'Failing to act'), and faith does not make sense until it is used (see 'Living with faith'). The promises that faith holds are not reached by merely agreeing to them, and then putting them aside: they are reached by acting on them.

And in the stories here, we are reminded that acting on faith can be risky. The risk is not always one of danger, as when David believed that God was on his side but still had to put his body on the line against Goliath's sword and spear. The risk might be more subtle. Jairus and the woman may have believed that Jesus offered healing, but Jairus risked continuing believing even when his friends told him that hope was gone, and his daughter was dead. The woman, after reaching for help, could have walked away, but she risked staying, 'trembling with fear' (v. 33), to fall to Jesus' feet and 'admit' what she had done. She is a woman of courage.

Having faith means taking the risk to put our thoughts and beliefs into action. Faith is lived, it is not a remote idea or part of a distant philosophy, but something practised daily for all to see, even when there is risk of loss, of rejection, of defeat, of failure, of disappointment, or of hurt. When times get terribly hard, we can have confidence to take the risk of faith and hold on to what we know to be true. We have a God who is with us, who loves us, who wants us to be whole.

HOW CAN YOU RISK FAITH, AND ACT?

Faithful God
you show us that ordinary people
can do extraordinary things
with courage
with action
with truth
with faith

help us to see faith miracles
help us to live our faith
because by risking faith
we become whole

Amen

Susan Joy Nevile and Maurice Nevile

Loving

1 Corinthians 13:1-13 (NIV)

LOVE IS AN ACTION
LOVE IS HOW WE LIVE

Think of the wording 'Love is...'. What words come to your mind to finish the sentence? Do those words help you to understand what love is? What thoughts, feelings and images does the word 'love' create for you? Does 'love' prompt any specific experiences and memories? And the big question: how do we know when someone loves us? In music, it sometimes seems that more than half of all songs are about love (!), and love comes up one way or another in most movies. In art, love has always been a common subject. As a word, I think that 'love' is overused. In everyday talk, we mention love all the time: 'I love my new shoes', 'I love walking', 'I love a morning coffee', 'I love starting a new book', 'I just love what you've done with your hair'. Around Valentine's Day we hear about love even more than usual. The word 'love' appears in advertisements, on cards, and with chocolates and flowers.

But 'love' is not just a word, love is an action, it is what we do and how we live. And perhaps, as a *way of life*, love is very much *underused*. That is because we do not always think through what we are talking about, about what our words are doing.

Now, the Bible has a rather good explanation of what love is like. It was written by Paul to the church in a town called Corinth. It is an exquisite and enduring piece of writing.

> Love is patient, love is kind. It does not envy, it does not boast, it is not proud. It does not dishonour others, it is not self-seeking, it is not easily angered, it keeps no record of wrongs. Love does not delight in evil but rejoices with the truth. It always protects, always trusts, always hopes, always perseveres. Love never fails. (1 Corinthians 13:4-8, NIV)

Sometimes, when we read a part of the Bible, we need an explanation of what it all means. But other times, we can read and know it immediately because it resonates so deeply. That is how many people feel about this passage, and why people choose it to be read aloud at their weddings. It guides us on how to act if we love someone, and I think it is a pretty high standard! We need only pause for a minute to think of the people we love, and how we treat them, to know just how high a standard it is, and how often we fall short. But this passage really gets scary when we recall Jesus saying, 'love your neighbour as you love yourself' and 'love your enemies'. It is easy to feel like saying 'Come on, God... It is hard enough treating the people I really care about this way, but how can I do this for people I don't even like?!'

How can we live the challenge of this way of love, to show our love to others? Maybe we can start by focusing our effort on just one or two areas: can I be more patient?; can I be kinder, and more caring?; can I be slower to anger?; what can I hope for?; can I better see and rejoice in the truth of someone's love for me?; where can I persevere? The passage is indeed challenging, but it is also inspiring and empowering for how we can live. It can comfort us because we know of God's love for us, and that God *does* get it right. With us, God

Loving

is patient, God *is* kind, God *rejoices* in truth, God *protects*, and God *perseveres*. God's love *never* fails. We can know that when we love others, we are being like God.

> **LOVE IS...?**

Loving God
help us to love
with peace, with patience
with honour, with kindness
with goodness, with forgiveness

help us to love
without envy
without pride
without boasting

and in your love
challenge us
inspire us
empower us
to hope
to protect
to persevere
and always to rejoice!

Amen

Susan Joy Nevile and Maurice Nevile

Taking a journey

Genesis 6 to 9

A NEW LIFE JOURNEY CAN ALLOW FOR PRAYER AND REFLECTION

In our lives, we take many journeys. Some are short and some are long. Some we take alone and some we share with others. Some are physical and some are emotional, mental, or spiritual. Some are easy and over quickly; others are difficult and demanding, and can extend for years. The story of Noah and the great flood is one of the Bible's best known, at least for its basic elements. It has been the subject of major movies, even in recent years. For Noah, the journey was not only physical but was also a journey of faith. He had to put his trust in God. Despite what his neighbours said, he built the ark, which was a huge endeavour, he collected the animals, organised the food, and loaded everything on board, all the time relying on the truth of what God had said: that it would flood, and that God would preserve him. As he boarded the ark, it was time for the test. Now we have heard this story, and so we know how it turns out, but for Noah, his family, and the animals, there are forty days of rain, of waiting, of hoping, of not knowing, of praying. I would think that in a situation like that, what is important to you would become very clear. You would have time to think about the kind of person you wanted to be, the kind of world you wanted to build, and exactly how you could go about doing it.

We can think of this as we begin a journey, especially a spiritual journey like those built into the church calendar. For example, the journey of Lent takes us on a path that heads towards the cross and tomb of Easter, and, because of this, Lent is sometimes seen as a bleak time, a time of suffering, a time to give things up. Some churches choose not to have any flowers as decorations, others choose not to sing songs with the word 'alleluia', as ways of marking this season. For many people, Lent equals sacrifice, giving up the nice things in life, like sugar in your coffee, that glass of wine with dinner, or chocolate and cake, after all, that is why we have Pancake Tuesday – to use up all the delicious food before Lent starts. Yet to think of Lent only as a time of sacrifice short-changes it, particularly with the Bible stories like Noah that focus on God's promises.

Spiritual journeys are also times of prayer and reflection. As for Noah, they provide times when we can take stock, both of ourselves and of our community and wider society. Each church season gives a unique opportunity to slow down and look inside ourselves to see who we are and where we are heading. Life often does not allow us time to do this. We live in a world where 'busyness' is often valued and equated with 'importance', for surely if you have a lot to do then you are greatly needed. But busyness without direction leads to ever-decreasing circles, going nowhere. So it is good to take the chance to think about the journey we are on.

Symbols can visually mark the journey path for us. For example, in Lent I use an altar cloth in the colour purple, not because I like the colour (though I do!) but because purple is the colour of Lent, the colour of repentance. As we look at the altar, the purple cloth is a reminder: have I said or done something that does not sit right?; do I need to fix something with someone, have I treated someone unfairly?; am I holding a grudge?; do I need to say sorry?; do I need to tell God?; do I need to ask for help? Or a crown of thorns can remind us directly of Christ. The season of Lent comes from Christ's time in the wilderness, when he struggled with what kind of Messiah he would be, with how he would use his power. The crown of thorns reminds us of the answer Jesus reached, that he would not use his power for selfish ends, but to serve. The crown is a sign of Jesus' love and sacrifice for us. And there is a rainbow, the sign of God's promise never again to destroy the earth in flood. Throughout Lent and other journeys, we can focus on the promise of God. The rainbow reminds us that we do not make our journeys alone, we make them always with the promise and presence of God.

Thinking back to Noah, whenever I plan a service, in school, church, or hospital, I have a vision of what I would like to happen. Sometimes this vision is practical and realistic... and sometimes it is not. When using a text such as the story of Noah and the ark, I would dearly love to create a ramp for people to walk up, and have some sprinklers going out the front – to give a sense of rainfall. I would love to create the feeling that we, along with Noah and the animals, are entering the ark, and going on a journey. Imagine now that you are boarding. You will take that journey. And on that journey, you will have time to reflect, to feel sorry, to know God's love and sacrifice, to know God's promise to be there alongside you. And you will have time to ask yourself, 'who do I want to be?'

> ON YOUR JOURNEY,
> WHO DO YOU WANT TO BE?

God
as we journey, we will try to slow down
to look inside, to see who we are
to look outside, to see where we are heading
to look upwards, to see your rainbow
and in this way to remember your promise
to be with us, in love, always

Amen

Susan Joy Nevile and Maurice Nevile

Searching

Charles M. Schulz (1964) *Christmas is Together-time*. Paul Hamlyn, London.

Susan Summers and Jackie Morris (1998) *The Fourth Wise Man. Based on the Story by Henry Van Dyke*. Dial Books for Young Readers, New York.

IF WE SEARCH, WE WILL FIND CHRIST IN UNEXPECTED WAYS

There are many ways to search for Christ, and the new life he offers. Here, I will focus on a Christmas story, of one man's long search for the newborn king. It gives a different perspective to the story of the wise men that we are familiar with. One of the advantages of my work as a school chaplain was that I got to think and talk about Christmas with many different children, for example about what Christmas means to them, or what their favourite Christmas memories are.

One of my strongest Christmas memories is of reading a book called *Christmas is Together-time* by Charles M. Schulz, creator of the 'Peanuts' cartoons. Each of the characters comments on what Christmas is to them. For Charlie Brown and his little sister Sally, Christmas is a box of tree decorations that have become part of the family. For Sally it is also 'a time of waiting... and waiting... and waiting... and waiting...'. For Lucy, Christmas is wishing that an awkwardly shaped present were finally wrapped! Linus looks wistfully out the window

Searching

and wishes he could have seen the star of Bethlehem. That too is a familiar sense of longing, to have seen the star, marvelled at its beauty, to have felt both terror and amazement at the angels, and to have travelled far to find the baby.

Now *that* would be something to treasure as a Christmas memory, to see Christ, and even hold him! It is not hard to drift off into that daydream when we hear the Christmas story retold, when we listen to heavenly music, and it is not too hard to wonder what it would mean to see the Christ child. We are told of the impact Jesus had, even at that age, as a newborn. The shepherds returned, rejoicing, and telling others of what they had seen. The poet T. S. Eliot reflects on the experiences and difficult journey of the three magi, the wise men, and their radically changed perspective after seeing the Christ child.

How would we look at the world, at others, at ourselves, if we had looked on Jesus? What a pity that we are over 2000 years too late! With my school classes I shared a story of someone else who was too late, *The Fourth Wise Man*, a picture book originally written by Henry Van Dyke and retold by Susan Summers and Jackie Morris. Artaban was an astronomer who planned to join his friends and colleagues, the wise men Caspar, Melchior, and Balthazar, to bring gifts to Jesus, the newborn King of the Jews. He sets out to meet them, so they can journey together, taking with him a sapphire, a ruby, and a pearl, to be his gifts for the child. Yet Artaban never meets up with his friends, and so fails in his quest. He never sees the Christ child: like us, he is too late. Why does he not meet them? Along the way Artaban comes across a man who is sick and dying. By stopping to care for the stranger he misses his friends, who could wait for him no longer. So, he continues, travelling alone, and by the time he arrives the wise men have left, and Jesus' family has fled. Artaban misses the chance to see the newborn Jesus.

However, he does not give up. He spends years searching for the King. Following the advice of a wise rabbi, Artaban searches not among the rich and powerful but among those who are most vulnerable. And he finds many to help, feeding the hungry, clothing the naked, healing the sick, and comforting the captive. But he does not find and see the King he is searching for, and in the process, he gives away in kindness the jewels which were to be his gifts.

Artaban's search ends thirty-three years later, in Jerusalem, during Passover, when he hears of a crucifixion taking place that day – the crucifixion of Jesus, of Nazareth, who calls himself the Son of God. Artaban knows this must be the King of Kings, but before he can, at last, see the one he has been searching for, the sky darkens, the ground shakes, and Artaban is struck on the head by a heavy tile. As he lies there dying, he hears a voice saying 'Peace be with you, Artaban. When I was hungry, you gave me food...', continuing and ending with 'As often as you did these things for the least of my children, you did them for me'. A calm radiance lights up Artaban's face as he makes a last sigh, realising that his journey was ended, and that he has finally found his King. There is no doubt that just as the other wise men had found the King, so too had Artaban, in his own way, in his determination, and his compassion, care and love for others.

Like Artaban, we are too late to see the Christ child at his birth, but also like Artaban we can still search for and find Christ. In fact, we do not have to search all that hard. Christ is not confined to the manger far away: he is with us, in the person of the homeless, the elderly, the sick, those seeking refuge, those who are pushed to the side, and those we find easy to overlook, and forget. Christ is there if only we open our eyes to see him. Or, perhaps it is more that we need to change where we are looking. Our eyes can easily become fixed on the goals we have set ourselves. They may be life goals, like Artaban's to find the Christ, or shorter-term goals, like making sure we and our family are happy. Or maybe the goal is just to get through our list of tasks for the day ahead. In the end, Artaban found that by stopping and taking the time to see and respond to those in need around him, who could have been classed and treated as distractions, side issues, unimportant, he actually achieved his goal in a totally unexpected way! For all of us, at Christmas, or whatever the time of year, amidst all the joys and frustrations of life, we can still find and see Christ in unexpected ways, if we search for him.

> **WHERE DO YOU FIND AND SEE CHRIST?**

God
we are too late to see Jesus
as a poor and vulnerable baby
help us to search for him
help us to find him
help us to see him
in the poor and the vulnerable
around us today
and to share with them
our many gifts

Amen

Susan Joy Nevile and Maurice Nevile

Trusting

Luke 1:39-55 (GNT)

WE CAN ALWAYS TRUST IN GOD'S LOVE

Trust is at the heart of living. 'Who can you trust to take care of the economy?' So began one political party's pitch in yet another Australian national election. To trust that party would be to choose its representatives, allowing them make decisions on our behalf, believing that they have our best interests at heart. We must often put our trust in institutions, in technologies and objects, in social structures, and in the people around us, especially those closest to us. The Bible is rich with stories of trust, of nations and communities, and of individuals. Here we focus on Jesus' mother, Mary, and her wonderful act of trust (see 'God's vision'). We are reminded that we can always trust in God's love.

But first, let us put this passage from the book of Luke into context. Mary has just been told that she – an unmarried teenager – is going to have a baby. Now in that place and at that time, for a girl or woman to have a baby when not married meant big trouble. It was punishable by death. Is Mary worried? No, she is excited after her visit from the angel. So, she goes to see her cousin Elizabeth, who lives up in the hill country, to share her good news. And as it turns out, Elizabeth is also pregnant, very unexpectedly considering her older age and how long she had waited for a child. Now this is something I really love about Bible stories, how we can look at them and see two different things happening. Like in this scene, we could hardly imagine anything more ordinary than two pregnant women talking in a small town. Yet in this very ordinary moment we see the start of a revolution – the world is about to be turned upside down. We can hear it in Mary's Song, the *Magnificat*, a song of radical justice (Luke 1:46-55).

> Mary said,
> 'My heart praises the Lord;
> my soul is glad because of God my Savior,
> for he has remembered me, his lowly servant!
> From now on all people will call me happy,
> because of the great things the Mighty God has done for me.
> His name is holy;
> from one generation to another
> he shows mercy to those who honour him.
> He has stretched out his mighty arm
> and scattered the proud with all their plans.
> He has brought down mighty kings from their thrones,
> and lifted up the lowly.
> He has filled the hungry with good things,
> and sent the rich away with empty hands.
> He has kept the promise he made to our ancestors,
> and has come to the help of his servant Israel.
> He has remembered to show mercy to Abraham
> and to all his descendants forever!'

The song reminds me of Jesus' comment about the first and the last (Matthew 20:16). It is a song which celebrates God's action in the world. And it is easy for *us* to understand and appreciate, for in one sense we have seen the end of the story – *we* know what they are celebrating. But these two women talking, Mary and Elizabeth, do not. Both women have unusual pregnancies – to say the least! But they both respond with joy, not knowing the future for their sons, but trusting in God's love. We know that Elizabeth's baby is born safely, that he grows into a fine young man called John, John the Baptiser, the one who, from before he was born, was excited about Jesus' coming. And we know how Mary's child, Jesus, turned out as well. But these women did not know, they simply trusted in God, and in the promise that he gave to them. This is something we can learn from them, that no matter what happens in our lives, what surprise, what change, what challenge, what disappointment, what sadness, what loss, we can trust in God's love.

> YOU ARE BEGINNING, LOOKING FORWARDS,
> AND YOU DO NOT KNOW WHAT IS AHEAD:
> HOW CAN YOU TRUST IN GOD'S LOVE?

God
it is easy to trust when we know
when we look back
when we are at the end

help us to trust in the confidence
of your promises
of your presence
of your love
for the times when we do not know
when we look forwards
when we are only beginning

then we can respond with joy

Amen

Susan Joy Nevile and Maurice Nevile

Praying

Luke 11:1-13 (NIV)

FROM JESUS, WE CAN KNOW HOW TO PRAY, AND THE GOD TO WHOM WE PRAY

Jesus' friends, the disciples, had been watching him, and they could see that, for Jesus, prayer was much more than saying the words. Prayer refreshed him, and it sustained him. So they asked Jesus to teach them his way of praying. In response, Jesus does two things: he tells them about *talking to God*; and he tells them *about God*, with some images.

Let us start with the second, telling 'about God', to set the scene. The first image of God refers to a neighbour who refuses to provide hospitality. This would have seemed absurd to these first hearers of the story, because at that time, in first century middle eastern cultures, customs of hospitality were a social requirement. In such an inhospitable natural environment, one never refused a request for hospitality because everyone shared the same circumstance, and you never knew when you yourself would need help. Jesus concludes (vv. 9-10): 'Ask and it will be given to you; seek and you will find; knock and the door will be opened to you. For everyone who asks receives; the one who seeks finds; and to the one who knocks, the door will be opened'. A second image is perhaps easier to appreciate. It is the bizarre picture of a parent who gives their child a snake or scorpion, when their child asks for a fish or egg. Jesus clarifies it for them (v. 13): 'If you then, though you are evil, know how to give good gifts to your children, how much more will your Father in heaven give the Holy Spirit to those who ask him!'

The message to the disciples, and to us now, is that God is good, and wants to give to us what we need, when we ask. It is God's nature to care for his children. This is the context, the background, to praying as Jesus does. And it sets us free, because it tells us that God does not listen only because we are good, because of who we are, but that God listens to all, because of who God is. We do not have to promise anything to God, we do not have to pay anything to God. Prayer is not about what God can receive, but about what God can give. We need only to talk, and God will listen. And prayer is not about posture and procedure, the right words, kneeling, hand position, open or closed eyes. God's response is not about how we pray, because it is not about what we do. Again, it is about who God is. God always listens to us, and God always answers us, though sometimes we may not hear, or understand, or it may not be the answer that we expected, or thought we wanted.

So now to the first thing that Jesus responded about, when the disciples asked him how to pray. He tells the disciples about 'talking to God'. He tells them to pray this (vv. 2-4):

Father
hallowed be your name
your kingdom come
Give us each day our daily bread
Forgive us our sins, for we also forgive everyone
who sins against us
And lead us not into temptation

Jesus gives his followers a pattern, or model, for prayer, and it is quite simple. It starts with 'Father', though the word Jesus actually used is 'Abba', an Aramaic word equivalent to 'dad'. It is the word that children use, and it shows affection and closeness. Jesus chooses to start the prayer by emphasising the familiar, loving relationship with God. But then, as if for balance, he continues with 'hallowed be your name', that is, may your holy name be honoured. 'Holy' means set apart, different from the world, and from all the things that drag us down. This opening pair captures a profound truth, that we can think of God as both 'dad' – perhaps with an image in mind of a father reaching down to pick up a small child – but at the same time knowing that those reaching hands also set the stars in their places, and the planets on their paths. Jesus' prayer opening conveys both intimacy and greatness.

Jesus continues the prayer with four requests of God, of different forms. The first is that 'your kingdom come'. This is an affirmation, a statement of hope, as a request for God to be active in the world, that is, for God's way of being, thinking, and of treating others to become the world's way. It is an extremely far-reaching prayer, for imagine what the world would be like if God's way really became *our* way. The second request 'Give us each day our daily bread' is a simple prayer for the essentials of our physical life, food, shelter and rest. Jesus' prayer then asks for forgiveness, touching on our social and emotional needs, both the need to be forgiven and the ability to forgive others. Forgiveness allows us to be free to move forwards. Jesus' final prayer request, 'lead us not into temptation', recognises that we will be faced by choices, that we will be tested. Some tests will be hard to withstand, so this is a request for wisdom and discernment, and protection when times get tough.

Praying

The disciples had asked Jesus (v. 1), 'Lord, teach us to pray', and this is what Jesus taught them. He taught them a pattern for prayer, and he taught them about God, so that they would understand. From this, we can know that God is good, wants us to talk to him, will always listen, and wants to give to us, because that is who God is, a father who cares for his children. We can also know that in how we pray we are talking to a God who is both close and great, and to whom we can make requests, to help us to live his kingdom.

> PRAY: GOD IS CLOSE BY, AND LISTENING
> PRAY: GOD IS GREAT, AND LISTENING

Jesus
you teach us how to pray

to God who is holy
to God who is close
to God who is good
to God who is great
to God who cares
to God who gives
to God who loves
to God who forgives

we pray with eyes eagerly open, or calmly closed
we pray with hands together, or arms outstretched
we pray with a gentle whisper, or a painful cry
we pray standing tall, or kneeling low
we pray looking to the ground, or up to the stars
we pray in a cool shadow, or under a bright sun

but always we will pray
because always God is there
and always God will listen

Amen

Susan Joy Nevile and Maurice Nevile

Accepting gifts

Luke 2:1-20, Matthew 2:1-12

IN ACCEPTING GOD'S UNEXPECTED GIFTS, LOVE IS BORN AGAIN

Sometimes I wonder what everyone made of it at the time, that star that shone so brightly and seemed to hang over Bethlehem for so long. What did people make of shepherds – considered at the bottom of the social hierarchy – who claimed to have been visited by angels? What would they think of the so-called wise men searching for a king among cattle? And how would they react to the news that the long-awaited Messiah had been born? Here are three different responses, and they help us to reflect on the challenge to accept the unexpected, and on the choices we make.

Of course, as one response, many people may simply not have noticed. They just got on with what they had to do. After all, they were busy – there was the registration for Caesar, all the administration with a new tax, and then much work to catch up on, important work, crops to grow, houses to build, cloth to weave. And there were always meals to cook, clothes to clean, children to care for. It is no surprise at all that many would have missed the event in a small country town.

Or, some people might have thought... 'why do we need another king? Kings are a waste of time and money! All they do is raise taxes, send their soldiers to push us around, or even worse, call our sons into the army and then send them away to fight'. And some people could have thought: 'what's the point of a baby? What we really need is someone who can save us from the Romans. Here, we are an occupied country – what we need is another David – someone who could knock out our enemies just like David defeated Goliath. What on earth is God doing sending a baby? It will never work!'

For sure, as a third possible response, there were some people who did see the signs, who listened to the messengers and opened themselves to what God was doing. I wonder what it was like for the shepherds after they went back to their sheep. Maybe they found it easier to look others in the eye, having once looked not only at angels, but also at the Christ child. What about the wise men who returned home along a different route; were they, as T. S. Eliot suggests in his poem 'Journey of the Magi', no longer at ease with the way things were? And maybe there were others – those who saw the newborn king, small and vulnerable, surrounded not by courtiers and the usual trappings of royalty, but by oxen and bales of hay. They could see what he would grow up to be – a new kind a king: a king who knows what it is like to feel tired, cold and lonely; a king who is quicker to give than to make demands; and a king who came willing to serve and die for his people, not to rule over them. They accepted that Jesus was God's kind of king.

So, those are three vastly different responses to the arrival of the long-awaited Messiah and, it seems, some things just do not change. There were different ways of responding to God's action 2000 years ago, and we seem to have remarkably similar choices today. First, it is easy to miss what is happening, especially at Christmas. After all, we know how busy Christmas is, with presents to buy and wrap, cards and messages to send, a tree and decorations to put up, food to cook, on top of the everyday things to be done. With all the rush it is not surprising that we often do not notice God's work in the world. Secondly, there are times when we still look around us and say, 'God, I think you have lost the plot, what are you doing? We need you to overthrow the evil in the world – people are starving, whole countries are in the grip of hatred and war, children go to sleep scared and crying. Whatever you are doing, God, it is the wrong plan'.

The challenge for us is to be able to see and accept that third response, the unexpected one, to look at the world from another perspective. We can recognise that God has acted, he has come to be with us, alongside us in the world, and in so doing he has transformed the world forever. We have the choice of allowing ourselves to be open to that transformation: to be like the shepherds who heard amazing news, and then responded to it; to do as the wise men did, who accepted the unlikely and found their king in a stable.

Who knows what we will find when we listen and look, when we accept God's unexpected solutions, and when we all join in. It may be as simple as picking up the phone and calling someone we have not spoken to in a long while. It may mean including someone we may usually not think of. It could be taking time away from the hustle and hassle of life to seek some calm. And perhaps, when we allow ourselves to be part of what God is doing, like others before us, we will receive unexpected gifts. May we accept them. May we find hope where we expected disappointment, peace where there was normally conflict, and joy where there was mostly sadness. For not just at Christmas, but always, love is born again.

> WHAT UNEXPECTED GIFT
> HAVE YOU RECEIVED?
> WHAT CAN YOU GIVE UNEXPECTEDLY?

God
you gave a star, for all people to follow

forgive us when we are busy
and do not notice it
forgive us when we doubt
and think we do not need it

help us to see the signs
of your unexpected gift
... your son among us

help us to find him
help us to accept him
help us to share him
as a gift of love to others

Amen

Susan Joy Nevile and Maurice Nevile

Waiting

Isaiah 2:1-5 (NIRV)

WE CAN WAIT, IN GOD'S WAY, WITH HOPE AND TRANSFORMATION

Whether we like it or not, waiting is a common scenario of life! For example, we wait for our turn to be served, and then for the coffee we ordered. We wait to find and buy that perfect item, and then for it to be delivered. We wait for our bus to appear, and then to arrive at our destination. And we wait to meet a friend, for a partner or parent to come home, and for a baby's birth. We wait for a medical appointment, for test results, and for recovery from illness. We wait for a birthday, an anniversary, and for holidays. Waiting can involve expectation and excitement, but also doubt, worry, and even fear.

I do not think waiting is something we do well. Indeed, my husband insists he will not queue for anything. Maybe it is because when we wait, we are often waiting for something we want, something we are longing for, and so waiting forces us to put ourselves and our desires aside, and that is difficult. Waiting also usually involves something that is beyond our control. We are restricted to the timing of someone or something else, whether that is the person ahead of us in the line, the busy barista, the bus, or just for time to pass. Waiting seems to remind us that we are not in control of everything in our lives. But we can have hope. Hope seems to go hand-in-hand with waiting. As we wait, hope sits with us, spurring us on, keeping us going. Hope convinces us that what we want is there, that it is just beyond our grasp, and if we keep going, we will reach it.

Waiting is also marked for key parts of the church calendar, for example for Lent or Advent, as we look forward together to what will come, and its significance for us. With Lent, we wait for the death and resurrection of Christ, for the promise of forgiveness and new life. With Christmas, we wait for the family get-togethers, the tree and decorations, the food, the presents, and that seems hard enough. But more importantly, Christians are also waiting for something else, for all of God's hopes for the world to come to pass in the birth of Jesus. We wait for the joy of life.

This is what the Isaiah (2:1-5) passage is describing. When we look at the world sometimes it seems like that is an impossible wait – how on earth will we get there? Well I think we get a hint when Isaiah says 'People of Jacob, come. Let us live the way the Lord has taught us to.' (v. 5). How do we wait in God's way? What does that 'waiting' look like? Maybe it is like an Afghani man, in Qandahar, working hard and patiently in the darkness to fashion Russian-made bomb shells into flower plots. He transforms weapons of death into what will become instruments of beauty, peace and life. Transformation lies at the heart of God's way – 'they will hammer their swords into ploughs' (Isaiah v. 4) – the despised tax collector becomes a child of Abraham, a carpenter becomes a king, a cruel death on a cross becomes new life. As we wait, we can also hope, we can transform, and we can know there will be God's joy.

> ## WHAT ARE YOU WAITING FOR?

Patient God
we do not like to wait
and we do not do it well

show us your way to wait
with hope and transformation
assured of your great joy

Amen

Susan Joy Nevile and Maurice Nevile

Choosing

Mark 1:40-45 (MSG), 2 Kings 5:1-14 (MSG)

OUR CHOICES CAN BRING HEALING, WHOLENESS, AND JOY

'If you choose...' The two focus texts here have something clearly in common. They both deal with healings. Yet for me both these passages are also about choices: 'If you want to... if you will... if you choose... you can make me clean'. These are the words that jump out at me when I read the two passages. In the Mark text, a man comes to Jesus seeking healing, and for us it seems hardly surprising that Jesus chooses to heal him; he is Jesus, it's what he does: a sick man comes to Jesus, Jesus feels pity, the man gets better.

So, what does it tell us about choosing? What is there of special value for us here? We need to look at the bigger picture. Let us start with the man. People with skin diseases were totally cut off from the normal activities of their community. Such diseases prevented people from working and supporting their family, from being with friends, from being part of the religious community. It was a big risk for the man to approach Jesus because he could easily have been rejected. It was considered dangerous and contaminating to touch these sufferers. People who cared for them had themselves to go through cleansing rituals before they were again able to participate in society. Yet Jesus deliberately breaks these taboos and constraints. He reaches out and touches the man, someone who has been avoided, looked upon with contempt, and mistrusted. Jesus reaches out to him and brings healing, and in so doing reconciles the man to his community. This act sheds light on making choices, with Jesus showing us that sometimes we need to do what is risky, even against socially conventional thought, practice and acceptability, if we are going to do God's way, and to bring about care and healing, both for others and ourselves.

The story of Naaman (in 2 Kings) is even more interesting and revealing, and not only because it is full of choices – and unusual ones at that. First, we remember that this is an Israeli story, yet it clearly shows God acting to heal the enemy. God was not confined to one side or other in this story. It starts with the choice of a slave girl, a child who was captured in war, to tell her master Naaman, an army general, of a prophet who can heal his disease. She does not rejoice in her master's vulnerability, she does not long for revenge. Instead, she is moved to compassion and does what she can in what appears to be an extremely powerless position, acting to bring about healing. Secondly, we have the choice of a senior military man to listen to the story of a slave. In this society, for a man to take advice from a female is unusual, from a child is unheard of, and from a slave is near unbelievable. It is extraordinary! We cannot know whether this is a measure of his desperation or his enlightenment, but either way, because Naaman was open to listening to others, he was open to healing.

Then we have the choice of the prophet Elisha to offer that healing, even though the one with leprosy is an enemy and commands the occupying army. Elisha chooses to extend God's mercy to an enemy. The message then comes, go and wash in the river, and when Naaman is about to go off angry and dismissive his servants remonstrate with their master, urging him to try. Presumably, to disagree with and push your master was rather dangerous, yet the servants take a risk to achieve his healing. Finally, we see the choice of Naaman to follow the servants' advice and prompting and so be healed. He does something for which he is reluctant, and which is likely demeaning for someone in his position, yet it is this that brings about his wholeness. As I suggested, this is a story rich with choices, and in fact most stories are! This is true of stories that we read, or watch in movies or media, and it is true of the stories that we live ourselves, that we create in our own lives. Each of our lives, just as each moment in history, can be examined according to the choices that we and others make, and their impacts.

So, it is worthwhile reflecting on our choices, and those made around us and for us. It is especially through our choices for how to live, for our actions, that good news and joy can come to us and to those around us. With compassion we can bring healing and wholeness to ourselves and to others, but sometimes pride, arrogance, anger, or fear can prevent us. To whose voices do we listen, and how can we participate in God's healing power? We can confidently choose to follow in God's way, even if it might mean risking to break with convention and expectation.

Choosing

> **AS YOU CHOOSE, TO WHOSE VOICES ARE YOU LISTENING?**

God
through our choices
we create our lives
and we impact others' lives

help us ...
to listen
to risk
to be open
to be compassionate
so that our choices can bring good news
healing, wholeness, and joy

Amen

Susan Joy Nevile and Maurice Nevile

Deciding

Genesis 2:4 - 3:24

C. S. Lewis (1980) *The Magician's Nephew*. Fontana Lions, Chapters 13-14. (first published 1955).

WITH GOD, WE CAN DECIDE WITH RESPONSIBILITY AND LOVE

How do we decide, and on what basis? Here I connect two stories, the foundational biblical story of Adam and Eve, and the story of Digory and his ailing mother, from C.S. Lewis' book *The Magician's Nephew*, part of the Narnia series. Digory is sent by Aslan to fetch an apple from a sacred tree to protect Narnia. These two stories have a great deal in common. They have two beautiful gardens. There are two wonderful fruit trees, with fruit that offer amazing possibilities: the knowledge of Good and Evil; the apple of life. Both trees have restrictions placed on them. In both stories, the people are tempted to eat the fruit to take the wonders that they offer.

But then we can see some differences between the stories. For while the Adam and Eve story is a tale of selfishness, Digory's is not. Adam and Eve are not satisfied with the gifts that God had given them. The serpent tells the woman that they can have more... if they eat the fruit they will become like God. Adam and Eve wanted to be God-like, but what they found out was that to have that knowledge they also had to accept consequences, and to take responsibility for their own actions. It is not as easy as just eating a piece of fruit. The fruit is almost a symbol for seeking the easy way out – they can get the accomplishment without the effort, gain privilege without responsibility. It is like driving a car without paying for the petrol, or getting selected for a sports team but never doing the training. Life is never that easy. We can see their attitude. They hide from God, then they try blaming someone else for their greed. The woman blames the serpent, and the man blames the woman. Neither one of them was willing to take responsibility for their own decisions.

What about Digory in the Narnia story? He is also tempted, not by what the apple could bring him – he does not want to stay eternally young or to rule as king alongside the witch – but he does want a cure for his mother. Digory is tempted by something good for someone else. The witch plays one loyalty against another; his mother against Aslan the great lion. This is when decision-making becomes difficult: when we can see the good that will come. Two things get Digory out of the hole. First, he refers to a higher authority, his mother, and realises that she would say 'no'. When unsure what to do, he thinks of someone he can trust and considers what they would do. Secondly, what really clears Digory's head is seeing the impact his choice could have on his relationship with Polly – the witch suggests leaving her behind. Digory knows that this is not an option, but if he took an apple, his friendship with Polly would be different – *she* would know what he had done. Digory can take a step back from deciding and see what might happen, the wider implications, the responses of others, and this enables him to make the better decision.

How do the stories end? Well, Adam and Eve were turned out of the beautiful garden, forced into accepting the consequences of their actions. Digory? He is given another apple, which not only cures his mother but, if you know your Narnia books, also sets off a whole series of other adventures. So, although the stories have much in common, one is about selfishness, but the other is about selflessness, about responsibility, about care, about trust, about love. They prompt us to reflect: how do I make decisions?; are my decisions based on greed, on what I think is good for me?; do I see how my decision can affect those close to me, and others?; do I think of those I trust and value, and wonder what they would do, or have me do?; do I wonder what God would have me do? In life we must face and make decisions great and small, so it is a comfort to know that we do not have to decide on our own.

HOW CAN YOU DECIDE WITH LOVE?

God
what would you do?

when we decide, help us to act
with selflessness
with responsibility
with care
with trust
and with love for others

Amen

Susan Joy Nevile and Maurice Nevile

Forgiving

Matthew 18:10-14, 21-35 (NIV)

FORGIVING CAN BE HARD, SO WE NEED THE PRACTICE

How many times must I forgive? Peter's question to Jesus about forgiveness (v. 21) is a very human one, isn't it? Any of us could have asked it – Peter wants to know what he can get away with, what is okay. What are the rules about forgiveness? Peter probably thought he was being quite generous in suggesting seven times. It reminds me of a child learning a musical instrument, who asks, 'how long do I have to practise?' Practice is the hard work that must be done to enjoy the later rewards of performing and creating music for yourself. But how much practice is *really* necessary?...

Forgiveness is like that, in that it is hard work, but it is necessary if we are to enjoy a good relationship with someone. In some ways, it is strange that we often find it so hard to forgive – we all know what it is like to be in the wrong, we know the consequences and guilt of having made a bad choice, or having done the wrong thing, of having not done the right thing. And it can be a physical feeling. I feel it in my gut, and the knot in the pit of my stomach gets tighter and tighter. For others, it is an iron bar of tension that forms across the shoulders, or a headache that lurks just behind the eyes. We know from experience that it feels terrible to stay in that state, yet somehow we can cling to the idea that the offender deserves to be punished, that we are owed something for what they have done, that they need to feel some pain to balance out ours. This is another very human aspect to Peter's question. It assumes that everything is counted, that everything has a number next to it, can be measured and quantified and evened out. Jesus' response, however, transforms the question: it becomes a question of attitude, not magnitude.

In the story Jesus tells here (Matthew 21-35), we have images of forgiveness. A king takes pity on a servant who begs for more time to pay a debt. The king cancels the servant's debt and lets him go. However, that same servant then shows no such mercy to a fellow servant indebted to him. He has the fellow servant thrown into prison until he can pay the debt. The story inevitably leads us to ask ourselves, 'what am I like at forgiving?' Am I ready to forgive, but then ready to take it back when it suits me? Do I have somewhere in the back of my mind, half hidden, a list of all the wrongs done to me, ready to be pulled out when needed? We can think, 'last time you kept me waiting twenty minutes', 'last time you lost the book I lent you', 'last time you didn't thank me', 'last time you let me down', 'last time you hurt my feelings'. This is yo-yo forgiveness – now it is there, now it isn't; now you see it, now you don't. It sits next to conditional forgiveness – I will only forgive you if you do this and that, if you jump through this hoop.

What then about the servant in Jesus' story? We can ask ourselves, 'am I maybe more like the servant?' Are we happy to be forgiven, and experience the relief that goes with it, but not willing to forgive others? Do we expect others to grovel before we will accept them, watching them squirm? Do we look for opportunities for point scoring, for payback, or for revenge? What is the effect of our responses like these? They can make forgiveness, or lack of it, into a weapon – something that can be used to manipulate or control other people. These responses can create barriers between us and others. And to be clear, it is not only to other people that we can do this – we can also be unforgiving to ourselves, holding ourselves back. We can think... 'last time I did this I failed, I didn't try hard enough, I did the wrong thing, I let myself down, I let others down. I won't try again'. Withholding forgiveness creates barriers for and around ourselves, it limits what we can do, and the person we can be. It is just like being limited by holding on to all the hurts that we have suffered, and defining ourselves as victim, rather than moving on and beyond them.

Having dismissed these two examples as unsatisfactory, where is the alternative? We need to look at the story that comes *before* Peter's question (Matthew 18:10-14). It is one that you might know well – the lost sheep. The shepherd has 100 sheep, and he leaves 99 of them to go in search for the one who has wandered off. In this case, forgiveness is not just *un*conditional: the shepherd does not stand there, hands-on-hips, demanding that the sheep re-enters the fold. No, forgiveness is *active*. The shepherd goes out looking for the sheep, he re-gathers it, he brings it back into relationship with himself and the other sheep. In the book of Luke, the message is strengthened with the image of the forgiving father who runs down the path to embrace the lost son he had given up for dead (see 'Child', 'Father'). In these stories, we see God's position on forgiveness – God longs to forgive and be reconciled with those who have turned away, who are lost but can be found.

In answering Peter's question with 'not seven times, but seventy times seven' (v. 22), Jesus does not give a numerical answer. He is saying that the bottom line is, always forgive. That is what God does for us, and that is what God expects we will do for others. Yes, it can be hard work, so we need the practice.

> **WHO CAN YOU CAN FORGIVE, TODAY?**

Forgiving God
you ask us also to forgive

we know it is necessary
we know it brings healing
we know it brings reconciliation
but still we find it hard work

please give us practice

Amen

Susan Joy Nevile and Maurice Nevile

Standing, kneeling

Acts 6 and 7

WITH GOD AS OUR ROCK, WE CAN STAND FOR WHAT WE BELIEVE IN, AND KNEEL FOR FORGIVENESS

At times, we must think on what is worth standing for, and at times we must kneel before God. Here we reflect on the story of Stephen's stoning. Stephen was a follower of Jesus, 'a man full of faith and of the Holy Spirit' (Acts 6:5). He had been performing signs and wonders among the people, and this drew opposition from some who then told lies about him to stir up trouble with the authorities. And so, Stephen is brought before the tribunal and high priest to have charges laid at him. They see that Stephen's face 'was like the face of an angel' (Acts 6:15). Stephen speaks up to challenge them, standing up for his beliefs, and they become furious with him. But Stephen, full of the Holy Spirit, looked up to heaven and saw the glory of God, saying to them, 'Look', he said, 'I see heaven open and the Son of Man standing at the right hand of God' (Acts 7:55-56). This is too much for them, and they rush and grab Stephen, and stone him to death. While they are stoning him, Stephen prays, 'Lord Jesus, receive my spirit', then falls on his knees and cries out, 'Lord, do not hold this sin against them' (Acts 7:59-60). And then he dies.

First, before we rush to judge those who condemned and stoned Stephen, let us think about when we are on the side, condemning and throwing stones. We are often easily angered with others, without always thinking through, from their point of view, what they have said, or done, and why they might have done so. They could be family, friends, colleagues, even strangers. It might be a situation of the moment or extend over time. We too have thrown stones, not real ones, but stones of words, actions, attitudes, or feelings, when we have responded in ways that hurt, diminish, or reject others.

What are we to make of the story? Here is Stephen, someone who, by all accounts, was close to God, a good man, doing what God had wanted in reaching out to people, and yet he ends up dead, stoned as the punishment for blaspheming. It is a cruel end to his life. We can have different reactions. We could be saddened at Stephen's painful death, seeing it as a waste. We could be angry at the mob that destroyed him. We could marvel at his bravery. We could wonder how he could have the confidence to stand up at the tribunal, and say what was for him the truth, what he believed they needed to hear. How was Stephen able to face his death so calmly? How was he able to kneel, and ask God to forgive the people who were killing him?

It all seems totally beyond us; beyond anything we could do. Yet Stephen was an ordinary man, doing extraordinary things. How? Well, from Stephen's point of view, God's love was the most important thing in the world, and that meant living how God wanted him to live. It meant saying what God wanted him to say, and not being afraid of what might happen. God's love strengthened and enabled him to do that. God's love was not something that kept Stephen 'safe' and isolated from the world and its dangers. It was something that inspired him to go out into the world to take risks, to stand up for what he believed in. It might help to think that, with God's love as his rock, Stephen could suffer the stones of people.

What, for us, is worth believing in, and standing up for? We might believe that all people are valuable, precious, created as gifts of God. We might actively support those who are in some way 'condemned' by society, because they are poor, vulnerable, persecuted, or somehow different and treated as unacceptable. And for whom, like Stephen, should we kneel, and ask God to forgive? Or, if we have 'thrown the stones', what should we ask God to forgive, in us? With God as our rock, we can always be confident to ask.

> STANDING ON THE ROCK OF GOD,
> FOR WHAT CAN YOU SPEAK?
> KNEELING BEFORE GOD,
> FOR WHOM CAN YOU ASK?

God
we are ordinary people
but with your strength
and on your rock
we can stand
to say what we believe
and we can kneel
to ask for your forgiveness
Amen

Susan Joy Nevile and Maurice Nevile

Resting

Matthew 11:28-30 (NIV)

WITH JESUS WE CAN FIND REST, FOR OUR SOULS

There are times in life, even just in the progress of the year, when we truly crave the chance to rest. With the demands of work, education, family, or whatever life throws at us, sometimes we just need the opportunity to lie in bed a little longer in the morning, read the pile of books stacking up, go for long walks, do something creative, tend to the garden, spend the day watching cricket. We all have our own ways of resting. But this is not actually the kind of rest that Jesus is talking about here (vv. 28-30).

> Come to me, all you who are weary and burdened, and I will give you rest. Take my yoke upon you and learn from me, for I am gentle and humble in heart, and you will find rest for your souls. For my yoke is easy and my burden is light.

Jesus is referring to a different kind of rest, 'rest for your souls'. He refers to the weariness from the burden of what weighs us down, the worries, struggles, and conflicts that we hold within us. Sometimes these are for us, like health and personal circumstances, or what we are thinking, feeling, doing, deciding, where we are heading, and how we are relating to others. Sometimes we are weary from our concern for others because they are sick, sad, and troubled, or away and distant. Sometimes we are wearied by the situations we find ourselves in, of which we are just a part, where we might have little control.

But what does Jesus mean by 'my yoke' and what does he mean by saying it is 'easy'? A 'yoke' is the wooden crosspiece fastened over the necks of two animals so that together they can pull a plough or cart. It is a metaphor familiar to Jesus' listeners; they knew it from daily experience, but it is much less familiar to us now. Of the things that weigh us down, Jesus says that we do not have to manage on our own. We are not alone, we are together, and he will be there with us to carry the load. He says, in words that are beautiful and deeply encouraging, 'learn from me, for I am gentle and humble in heart'. We can learn from Jesus. From Jesus, we can know to pray (see 'Praying'). We can take our concerns to God, express them, share them, have them heard, and have them responded to. In prayer, we can lay our concerns before God, and ask for help, strength, peace, and forgiveness. Prayer has the power to initiate change, especially in ourselves. And from Jesus we can get perspective. Sometimes I find that when I pause and take the time to reflect on Jesus' ways, it helps me to understand what is worth worrying about, and what is not.

Maybe a good way to understand Jesus' comment about the yoke being 'easy' is to think about a sense of 'comfortable', like when soldiers are told to stand 'at ease', or when we sit in an 'easy chair'. I recall one writer using the metaphor of wearing shoes, and the problems we have if they do not fit. If they are too small, they rub, and you get blisters; but if they are too big, they slip around, and you can step out of them and trip. In shoes of the right fit, right for you, you feel comfortable. So, Jesus does not mean that walking with him will be no effort at all, but that it will be doable, that it will be right, right for us.

Jesus says that if we can take his yoke, and learn from him, we will find the rest we need. It is not the rest we seek at the end of a busy week, or year. It is the rich and lasting rest we can receive by being together with God, by being right with God. It is the rest for our souls.

> **HOW DO YOU GET THE REST YOU NEED?**

God of gentle and humble heart
we get weary, so very weary
weighed down by the burdens of life
and sometimes it seems too much to bear
and we fear we cannot go on

we come to you
we bring our burdens to you
and we ask for rest
the lasting rest for our souls
that comes from being with you
Amen

Susan Joy Nevile and Maurice Nevile

Rejoicing!

Isaiah 61:1-4, 8-11 (NIV)

IN GOD WE CAN DARE TO REJOICE

Sometimes, it can be immensely difficult to feel like rejoicing, especially at times of trouble, despair, or worse, when our life can even seem to be crumbling around us. Here I reflect on 'joy'. Sometimes what I must write comes easily, with flowing strokes of the pen, or keys, and sometimes it seems like getting blood from a stone. It is like the words are there, lurking somewhere in the back of my mind, but they are just not coming. So who would think it would be hard to write about joy, after all 'Joy' is my name, I should know all about it! Maybe a prompt would come from the name for the third week of Advent, 'Gaudete Sunday', which comes from a Latin word meaning 'dare to rejoice'. It is actually not about being happy. Let us look at just some of what the writer of Isaiah says (vv. 10-11).

> I delight greatly in the Lord;
>   my soul rejoices in my God.
> For he has clothed me with garments of salvation
>   and arrayed me in a robe of his righteousness,
> as a bridegroom adorns his head like a priest,
>   and as a bride adorns herself with her jewels.
> For as the soil makes the sprout come up
>   and a garden causes seeds to grow,
> so the Sovereign Lord will make righteousness
>   and praise spring up before all nations.

Sounds good. I am not sure how you imagine the context for these words, whether you see the writer standing in the midst of a glorious temple, or on top of a green hill, addressing a crowd of happy and excited people. Actually, these words are uttered from the middle of a ruined city, to a group of ex-slaves. The people of Israel had been enslaved by Babylon, and at last, after years of hoping and longing, they were back in Jerusalem. But it was not the city their parents had been taken from – it was in ruins. Isaiah stands up and gives a promise of justice and new beginnings. The people rejoice, even though what they celebrate has not fully come to be. They are rejoicing in the ruins. Their rejoicing, therefore, is a daring act. They are willing to make a claim on the future that transforms their experience of the present.

If we stop and think about it, it is a big demand. They are celebrating because of what is to come, and their faith in that future changes how they live now. That takes real courage. Often, that is what is demanded of us, especially when we are faced with problems that seem huge, even impossible. How on earth are we to manage it? When we think about ending world hunger, war and terrorism, pollution, and climate damage, or seeking cures for illnesses, we hope that people would be thoughtful, merciful, and compassionate to each other – but we do not see these. In fact, we very often see the opposite.

So, how can we rejoice? To answer that, I would like to take a side-track, but I hope that it will make sense by the time we get to the end. I want to talk about books, especially big fat ones. Some people love them the bigger the better, and if it comes in three parts it is even more enjoyable. Perhaps there are two types of readers, those who open a novel at the beginning and read through to the end, and those who find themselves becoming involved and turn to the last pages, just to have a look. They want to know how it ends. I confess that

I am one of the latter – I do not want to know all the details, but I am keen at least to see if it all ends happily. As a Bishop in South Africa, Desmond Tutu worked tirelessly to bring about change for his country in the face of insurmountable odds. He was once asked, probably by a western journalist, how he did it. How did he have the strength to continue? He picked up the Bible and said he had strength because he had read to the end of the book – he knew how it finished, and God won!

At times we are encouraged to think about the hopes that we have for our community and the world around us. We can reflect on the need to change ourselves – from the inside out – and the peace, which flows from that change. Here we are offered a dare – we are asked to rejoice even when the things we have hoped for have not yet appeared. As Bishop Tutu says:

> Good is stronger than evil
> Love is stronger than hate
> Light is stronger than darkness
> Life is stronger than death
> Victory is ours through Him who loves us

To me those words give an answer to the question 'how can we rejoice?' We rejoice because we know that God has acted to change the world – he sent his son in love, not to judge it but to save it. So, we need to act on that truth. It does not mean that we can say it will all be OK in the end, and so we do not have to do anything about it now. No, it is just the opposite. If Isaiah's people had said that, then Jerusalem would have stayed a pile of rubble. No, they rebuilt, on the ruins. We need to be like that.

If we hope for a world without hunger, we rejoice that it will come, and then we think about what we spend our money on, and what we give away. If we hope for peace, we rejoice that it will come, and then we set about living as peacemakers. If we hope for a world without pollution, we rejoice that it will come, and then we live as people who value and care for our natural world. If we worry for the sick, we can be there for them offering support. Yes, we *can* 'dare to rejoice', both by looking for the things around us that show us God's love, and by living so that God's love can be seen in our actions.

> ARE THERE RUINS IN WHICH YOU CAN REJOICE, AND THEN REBUILD?

God, world changer
we dare to rejoice
because good is stronger than evil
because love is stronger than hate
because light is stronger than darkness
because life is stronger than death

we will hope and act
we will value and care
and we will rebuild from ruins
so that your love can be seen
Amen

Susan Joy Nevile and Maurice Nevile
(in part adapted from the words of Bishop Desmond Tutu)

4 Encountering troubles

Starting over

Luke 3:1-6 (NIV)

WITH GOD, WE CAN ALWAYS START OVER

Try as we might, we all make mistakes, we get something wrong, or we are not who we would like to be. For example, it could be something we said, or did, or felt, or thought, and it could be a decision, or how we treated someone. Maybe it is something we did not do, when maybe we could and should have. Sometimes, our mistakes impact only ourselves, and maybe nobody else knows. Other times our mistakes affect other people, and others' mistakes affect us. As we see the consequences of mistakes, sometimes even only small ones, we often yearn for the chance to do it again and get it right. This is exactly what John was about – starting over, or what we can call *repentance*. As Luke 3:4-6 tells us,

> As it is written in the book of the words of Isaiah the prophet: 'A voice of one calling in the wilderness, prepare the way for the Lord, make straight paths for him. Every valley shall be filled in, every mountain and hill made low. The crooked roads shall become straight, the rough ways smooth. And all people will see God's salvation'
> (see Isaiah 40:3-5).

The word of God came to John in the wilderness, and John went into all the country around the Jordan, preaching a baptism of repentance for the forgiveness of sins. John was saying that the Lord is coming, the one we have been waiting for is nearly here! Things are going to be different; we need to be prepared for it. We need to change how we live, to see how things are, and what can be different, what we can do differently, and better. We need to take the chance to start over again. We need to be confident to know that those things that we wish we had never done, all those things that we know in our hearts have saddened God, were not what God would hope for us, they can be gone. The slate can be wiped clean. We can be saved.

This was John's message. How would they have felt, hearing that news for the first time? Would they have been excited, encouraged, relieved? I think they would have felt a sense of peace. And the good news for us is that nothing has changed, the message is the same – we can still take advantage of the offer. We can start over. God can help us to change. We can be prepared by saying sorry, and by seeking ways to be closer to the person who God knows we can be.

Starting over

> **THE LORD IS HERE, YOU HAVE THE CHANCE,
> WHAT WILL YOU CHANGE?**

God
we make mistakes

we wish we had...
spoken differently
acted differently
felt differently
thought differently
decided differently
treated someone differently

we know that we have impacted ourselves
we know that we have impacted others
we know that we have saddened you

we feel low
we feel empty
and we yearn for the chance to start over
to get it right

please fill us with your loving spirit
please remind us...
that we can change
that we can start over
that we can feel your peace
and become the people you know we can be

Amen

Susan Joy Nevile and Maurice Nevile

Bound

Luke 13:10-17 (NIV)

GOD CAN SET US FREE FROM WHAT BINDS US

In this story, Luke tells us of a woman bent over for eighteen years, not able to look people in the eye, not able to look up to see the sky, and being judged by all who saw her as someone God had punished. She was living with both physical and emotional pain. It was indeed as if she was bound. How could we imagine what it would have been like for her? Sometimes we can get a glimpse of that, being bound, those times we feel trapped, desperate, in despair, when life seems unfair, when we feel that no one knows or cares, and no one helps. We can feel ourselves being pulled down, and into darkness. We can be convinced that even God has abandoned us. Or, there are times when we feel overwhelmed by what is happening in our lives, like worries about our health, our family, our work, our friends, our school, or something we have done, or something occurring in the world that is far beyond our control. To me, these worries can feel like a backpack full of bricks, a heaviness we carry with us, that weighs us down, that slows and restricts us (see 'Burdened').

We can also feel bound by things that other people have said to us, even if it was a long time ago. Maybe those people were friends, siblings, parents, teachers, colleagues – their words could have told us that we are not good enough, not acceptable, not welcome. I know of one man called John Bell who, when he was a boy, was told not to sing at school assemblies but to only mouth the words of the songs. The teacher said that John was such a bad singer he would put the other boys off. John carried that with him as he grew into adulthood, feeling inadequate, and every time people sang around him, he was too embarrassed to join in. He was bound by what that teacher had said to him years before.

But it is also possible that we bind ourselves. There is a good example of this in Luke's story. The synagogue leader was just as bound as the woman, only he did not know it. He was angry with Jesus for healing the woman on the Sabbath, being bound by his narrow understanding of what was right and what was wrong. He knew that no work should be done on the Sabbath, and that was that. He made no attempt to understand what it was like for the woman – he only judged her. And the danger is there are times when we can do exactly the same thing, when we make little or no attempt to understand other people's situations and what they are going through, when we look at someone and do not see the whole person. We do not see who they fully are or could be. Perhaps we see only a part of who they are, maybe even with a label, like 'disabled', 'old', 'child', 'teen', 'man', 'woman', 'retired', 'unemployed', 'immigrant', 'refugee'. We become restricted, bound, by the labels we give to other people.

Now the good news is that we can be set free, just as the woman was. God can break through whatever is bending us over, whatever is holding us down, holding us back. Earlier in the book of Luke, chapter 4 (vv. 18-19), we hear for the first time about Jesus preaching. Jesus quotes from Isaiah:

> The Spirit of the Lord is on me, because he has anointed me
>   to proclaim good news to the poor.
> He has sent me to proclaim freedom for the prisoners

and recovery of sight for the blind, to set the oppressed free, to proclaim the year of the Lord's favour.

This is Jesus' statement about what he is going to do – to set people free – and that includes us. He did not ignore the woman, playing it safe to focus on praying and discussing the scriptures. Jesus risks, he reaches out to her, and he humbles himself to bring her freedom. I imagine Jesus kneeling in the dirt to look into her eyes. Being free is about how we can live if God releases us from what binds us. We can live as free people, bringing freedom to others.

I will finish the story about John Bell. I am happy to say that he too was set free! He is now a songwriter and in my chapel classes we would often sing his songs. I met him when he gave a workshop on how to use music in worship. He was teaching us how to sing.

> **WHAT BINDS YOU?**
> **ASK JESUS TO SET YOU FREE**

God
when we feel bound
pulled down
in darkness
overwhelmed
abandoned
remind us that Jesus risks to reach out
and release us
so that we are set free
and can bring freedom to others
Amen

Susan Joy Nevile and Maurice Nevile

Tempted

Matthew 4:1-11 (NIV)

AS WE ARE TEMPTED, GOD GIVES US WISDOM AND STRENGTH

Sometimes we might ask ourselves, 'who am I?' and 'where am I going?' In a way, these were the questions that Jesus asked of himself during his time in the wilderness, when he was tempted by the devil. This part of Jesus' life story comes at the beginning of his time as a teacher, right after his baptism, right after the heavens opened and God sent his Holy Spirit, and right after God declared 'This is my Son, whom I love' (Matthew 3:17). Jesus was trying to get his head around what it all meant! What did it mean to be God's son, and what was he to do about it? In this wilderness story, from Matthew chapter 4, we are shown some of the battles Jesus was going through, and we are told of three temptations he faced. We also see the three choices he made, because temptations are all about responding, about choosing what to do. Here is the first temptation (vv. 2-3).

> After fasting forty days and forty nights, he was hungry. The tempter came to him and said, 'If you are the Son of God, tell these stones to become bread'.

Was Jesus to become the kind of leader who used his power to meet his own physical needs? He was very hungry, it was an easy point of weakness, he had fasted for many days and needed to keep his strength up. But Jesus decided, no, not that way, he chose not to be the kind of leader who thought only of his own needs. What about the second temptation? (vv. 5-6)

> Then the devil took him to the holy city and had him stand on the highest point of the temple. 'If you are the Son of God', he said, 'throw yourself down. For it is written:
>
> "He will command his angels concerning you, and they will lift you up in their hands, so that you will not strike your foot against a stone"'.

Jesus knew that as God's son he deserved to have all the world at his feet, and how quick and easy it would be to have it all with just a small compromise. He would only have to bow down to the devil, then all that he deserved would be his. Jesus was faced with the lure of the easy, but he chose to be the kind of leader who cared about how things were done, to be the kind of leader who did not believe that 'the end justifies the means'. Here is the third temptation (vv. 8-9).

> Again, the devil took him to a very high mountain and showed him all the kingdoms of the world and their splendor. 'All this I will give you', he said, 'if you will bow down and worship me'.

This temptation is particularly interesting. It did not come from Jesus' weakness like the first one, but rather his *strength*, his knowledge of God's love for him. After all, he went into the wilderness with the voice of God ringing in his ears, 'you are my son... whom I love'. Yet Jesus chose to say no, he would not be a grand leader who sought to control and impress. Of course, it was right for God then to send angels to attend to Jesus and protect him.

These three temptations are important because we see Jesus specifically deciding how he was going to live as God's son. Now I do not think that this was the only time that Jesus was faced with temptations, because he was fully human, just like us, so he was tempted as he went about ordinary life.

We are not out in the wilderness, but *we* do face similar choices. We get to choose how we live. We get to choose what kind of person we are going to be. We get to choose what path we will walk along, and how we will walk it, and what we will do along the way. And we make these choices every day. Sometimes we do not even know we are making them.

Often, we are tempted at our points of *weakness*, where we are vulnerable, the areas of our life where we know that we struggle. If you have a short temper then it does not take much to be tempted to lose it, and to say or do things that hurt people. If we really like what money can buy, then it can be easy to overvalue material things and how they can impress others. Then there is the lure of the easy way. If we want to feel better about ourselves, and maybe appear in a good light to others, we may put others down.

Sometimes when we are tempted at our points of *strength*, we do not even see it. If we are particularly good at something, we may not think it is boasting to talk about how well we have done. If we are socially successful then we may not notice those less successful, the people on the edge, the outcast, the lonely. We may not hear their voice or recognise their needs. If we are driven and diligent, we may work too hard, and not see its costs to others, or to ourselves. And we may not understand others' lack of motivation and empowerment.

When we are faced with temptations and choices, we can remember Jesus as an example. This does not mean that we must go off into the wilderness for weeks on end, but we can stop and think about what we are doing. And then we can know, as Jesus did, that God is with us. Jesus went into the wilderness full of the Holy Spirit, meaning that God was with him every step of the way. God is with us too and that means we are not alone in our responses to temptation; we are not alone when we make our choices. From God we can gain wisdom and strength. We are a child of God, so we can be confident as we answer the questions of who we are, and where we are going. We can decide what kind of person we want to be.

> HOW ARE YOU TEMPTED
> IN YOUR WEAKNESS?
> HOW ARE YOU TEMPTED
> IN YOUR STRENGTH?

God
Jesus was tempted, as we are
Jesus had to choose, as we do
Jesus decided how to live, as we must
but sometimes we are weak
and we choose poorly

forgive us when we fail temptation
and give us wisdom and strength
for choosing better next time

we long to be like Jesus
so that we can know, we can be sure
just who we are
and where we are going

Amen

Susan Joy Nevile and Maurice Nevile

Lost, found

Luke 15:1-10

WE ARE NEVER SO LOST THAT GOD CANNOT FIND US

One way or another, we have all lost something, or been lost ourselves. So, let us reflect on some 'lost and found' stories. Some people, the saying goes, would lose their head if it were not attached. I am not quite that bad – but I will confess that I have a problem with my keys. I try always to put them in the same spot – but my problem is that they do not always stay there! Once I was in my office at work, and I had been at my desk for a while. I got up and went to pick up my keys. They were not there. I searched my desk, no; in my carry basket, no; I looked on the floor, no; in my pockets, no; in my handbag, no; I checked next to the photocopier, but again no. Now my office was not excessively large. I started to get desperate – in the bin? under the desk? in the filing cabinet? The frustration at losing the keys was mounting. It had been over an hour! I just could not understand where they could be. I pushed my chair under the desk, maybe somewhat over vigorously... and there was a tinkle tinkle sound as the keys fell to the floor. They had been caught on the lever under the seat of the chair! My relief was enormous, and I can remember running out of my office to tell everyone that I had found them. I certainly felt like throwing a party to celebrate.

In Luke chapter 15, Jesus tells stories of things lost, and here I have most in mind the lost sheep, one of a hundred, and the lost coin, one of ten. Though in each case the item lost is just one of many, the owner searches with great effort and care until it is found, and then rejoices. I guess most people can relate to that feeling of relief and celebration at finding something lost, and I love the picture we get in our focus passage of the angels celebrating in heaven as one lost 'sinner' is found.

But what about from the point of view of the lost, of the sheep that wandered off, of the coin that had been misplaced – how would they 'feel'? Well, I do not know if you have ever been lost, really lost, and when I ask younger children that question usually more than half of them say 'yes' – often it was at the shops. I must have been good child because I never got lost at the shops, but one afternoon I did have problems getting home from school. I was aged just five, living in a new city, in a new house, going to a new school, and having to catch the bus home by myself for the first time (this was the 1960s!). My problem was that I was not quite sure which bus to catch. Mum and dad had told me to check with the teacher, but I did not quite understand the answer, and I was too shy or embarrassed to admit it. So, I solved it in my 5-year-old way. I got on the bus with my friends. But it was not the right bus. I can remember sitting on the back seat as stop after stop all the other kids got off. And I got more and more worried. The bus driver called me up to the front of the bus and asked me if I recognised anything, and sadly I did not, so he said he would drive me back to the school where we could find a teacher to help me. I can remember feeling scared, and worried that I had done the wrong thing. But my main memory of that afternoon is of the bus pulling up at the curb of the school and seeing my dad standing there, and I knew that now I was OK. All the fear had gone in that instant. For a child, it was the best feeling, and I remember that even the bus driver was happy. I think that the sense of relief at being found is also a feeling to which people can easily relate. It goes beyond the sense of just being safe to that feeling you get when you know that everything is going to be alright.

Jesus gives us images of God and of his work, helping us to understand God himself, and we can feel confident that we get it. Now Jesus is using the picture of something that is physically lost to help us understand about being spiritually lost. What does that mean? It means being apart from God. I chose to get on the wrong bus, and some people choose to live in a way that distances them, sets them apart, from God.

Think of the hymn 'Amazing Grace', written by John Newton, an 18th century sea captain. What kind of captain was he? He captained a slave ship, a ship that captured and took Africans to the slave markets of London. By reports, he was a cruel drunkard, greatly disliked by his crew. In 1748, his ship was caught in a violent storm which lasted twelve days. It was so rough that the crew tied themselves to the ship to stop from being washed overboard, and Newton himself was tied to the ship's wheel for twenty-four hours straight. Sometime at this point was 'the hour he first believed', as the hymn words it. He later left the sea and became a minister, writing many hymns and becoming a well-known preacher. At 82, shortly before he died, he said, 'Although my memory's fading, I remember two things very clearly: I am a great sinner and Christ is a great Saviour'. Here is some of that beautiful hymn and its telling of being found.

Amazing grace, how sweet the sound
That saved a wretch like me
I once was lost, but now am found
was blind but now I see

'Twas grace that taught my heart to fear
And grace my fears relieved
How precious did that grace appear
The hour I first believed

Through many dangers, toils and snares
We have already come.
'Tis grace that brought us safe thus far
And grace will lead us home

I once was lost, but now am found
was blind but now I see.

Selected from *Amazing Grace*, by John Newton (1725–1807)

John Newton is the classic lost sheep that was found, that came good, and this is why he could write a song that all around the world people still sing and love, more than two hundred years later. The song captures the relief of the lost and the wonder of knowing that now it will always be alright – not because of anything that we have done, but because of the amazing love of God, of what God has done for us. It is a love that can be understood in such simple stories of searching for a lost sheep or coin. It is a love that does not give up, that keeps on looking – even when all seems hopeless. It is a love that can change us, from being lost to being found.

Lost, found

> **HOW ARE YOU LOST?**
> **KNOW THAT GOD IS LOOKING FOR YOU**

God
along the way we become lost
we make wrong choices
we take wrong paths
we are not the people we wish to be
and we become apart from you

but in your amazing love
with your amazing grace
you look for us
you do not give up
you find us
you keep us safe
you change us
and you lead us home

with you we are always found
thank you

Amen

Susan Joy Nevile and Maurice Nevile

Confused

Luke 24:13-34

NARROW VISION CAN CONFUSE US, AND WE MISS WHAT MATTERS

For me, at the heart of the Emmaus story, and other Easter stories, is that Jesus does not leave his followers uncertain or confused. Well, he does call them 'foolish' and 'slow' (v. 25), but he does not leave them in that state. Jesus has risen from death, and as two of his followers are walking on the road, heading to Emmaus, not far from Jerusalem, he walks alongside and joins them, though they cannot recognise him. Jesus asks them what they are discussing as they walk along. They explain what has happened in the past days, of their hope that Jesus would be the one to redeem Israel, but that he had been tried and crucified, and now his body was gone. They are confused, they do not get it.

Jesus clarifies things for them, to alter their perspective. How does he do this, and how can it help us? I like to use the metaphor of blinkers, those eye covers used on some racehorses to stop them being distracted by keeping their focus fully narrowed and forwards. We tend to focus on ourselves, our needs, our feelings, what affects us, what matters to us, what suits us, what appeals to us. So it is like we are wearing blinkers, and sometimes they can confuse and make us miss seeing the bigger picture, what is around us, what is happening at the edges, what is in the distance, what is in the longer term, and what really matters for life. We focus on what we see now, what is happening now, and what is hurting now. Jesus can change this, altering our perspective, drawing us out and beyond the limits of our own areas of focus.

This is what happens for the two on the road. Jesus explains to them (v. 26), 'Did not the Messiah have to suffer these things and then enter his glory?', and beginning from Moses and the prophets, he elaborates on the scriptures concerning himself. He helped them to understand what happened, and what it means. They urge him to stay with them, and they eat together. As Jesus broke the bread, gave thanks, and began to share it, 'their eyes were opened' (v. 31) and they recognised him. Jesus removes their blinkers: they see him in a stranger, not in a temple, not during a discussion of the scriptures, but in the everyday act of sharing a meal. And they understand.

One Emmaus story message is that Christ is there around us and when we try to see him, we look differently: we look at the world differently, we look at others differently, and we look at ourselves differently. We can then widen, change, and clarify our understandings, and so not be confused. Seeing Christ means seeing more clearly. It enables us to see the bigger picture.

So, while it is important to feel and recognise the pain of Good Friday, there is more, there is Easter Sunday, there is God's love that is so powerful that death could not hold it down. Christ's crucifixion can capture the pains that we experience and encounter daily, and that echo throughout our lives; the struggles, the suffering, the unjust, the wrong actions of people, on which it is often too easy to focus, dwell and anger. We can come to believe that is all there is, that the world is black, that hearts are cold. Our confusion and cynicism can justify a lack of action, and compassion. We can believe that Good Friday is the story of Christ around us, in suffering, and stop there. But the risen Christ means that we can see beyond, to life, to light, and to love.

When I read the Emmaus story, I wonder at the followers' mindset. They had perhaps travelled to Jerusalem for the Passover, maybe they were part of the crowd calling Hosanna to the king, or they were riding with Christ, thinking that 'this is it', they were on the way, it was all happening! Then on the Friday came the humiliating death, the end of their hopes. But on Sunday the women came with the surprising news that the tomb was empty, they had seen angels, and the body was gone. Jesus was alive. It is little wonder they were confused. It is little wonder that they could not see beyond Good Friday, beyond their immediate disappointment and grief. Their minds were closed, until they met with Jesus and spoke to him. Then they could see, really see, as we can.

Confused

> **ARE YOU MISSING THE BIGGER PICTURE?**

God
in our narrow focus
on the here
on the now
we cannot see everything you see

we miss the distant
we miss the long term
we miss the bigger picture
and we become confused

open our eyes and minds to see
beyond pain
beyond grief
beyond ourselves
beyond the immediate
beyond disappointment
to what really matters
to the risen Christ
to life and light and love
Amen

Susan Joy Nevile and Maurice Nevile

Tumbled and tossed

Matthew 2, Acts 7

WE CAN FIND OUR FEET ON NEW GROUND

How do we respond to God's invitation to be tossed and tumbled, to have our understandings and lives turned upside down, as we follow in Christ's way? Here I will focus on Christmas and baptism. Often, when we tell the Christmas story we seem to stop at Matthew 2:12. The wise men have finished their journey, they have brought their gifts, they are kneeling in awe at this young one whose birth has changed forever the relationship between people and God. It is a tender moment, as the revelation of light has come. We can all heave a sigh of relief, pat ourselves on the back, and pack away the Christmas paraphernalia for another year. It is done.

But after we have feasted and celebrated, we re-gather to hear what happened next, and when we do hear, we wish we had not because what we hear is a story of violence, of horror, of oppression most foul. We hear of the slaughter of innocent babies (Matthew 2:13-18). It is as if a fierce blast of cold air blows in under the door, exposing our cracks, or perhaps it is as if a wave has swept us off our feet when we thought we were safely wading, and now it is tugging us out of our depth and into dangerous currents.

When we look around for relief, the texts for St Stephen's Day are not much better (Acts 7)! Here we have the story of a man who was brimming with God's grace and energy. Stephen was doing wonderful things among the people, unmistakable signs that God was among them. Those who spoke against him were no match for his wisdom and spirit. Stephen was, as we in the household of deacons like to remember, the first deacon. He was one of the seven set aside to take care of the widows and to distribute food to those who needed it, ministering to those on the edges, the outside, the vulnerable, the oft forgotten ones. This is where those who are called to the distinctive diaconate are sent, to follow Jesus' model of the servant leader. Stephen was also the first saint and martyr. For no sooner do we hear of the great things he was doing than we hear of his death, by stoning. He was bought to the temple court on trumped up charges, and in the face of his eloquence the courtroom was transformed into a lynch mob (see 'Standing, kneeling'). Again, we see how thin the veneer of civility and judicial order in society can be. These two stories, of the innocent boys of Bethlehem, and of Stephen, pull us free of the sentimental Christmas card images. As Joy Carroll Wallis points out, putting Herod back into Christmas reminds us that 'Jesus enters a world of real pain, of serious dysfunction, a world of brokenness and political oppression' (from 'Putting Herod Back into Christmas', at http://liturgy.co.nz/church-year/herod-christmas, accessed 22 November 2020). In the death of Stephen, we see that things had not changed. And we don't have to look very far to see this still happening today, when people, including babies and children with lives of great potential, drown in a bid for safety or freedom, or are killed and injured in bombings, or are brought up to fear and hate those who speak the truth.

Yet for all his faults, Herod saw something that we, in the comfort of our lives, and the familiarity of the Christmas story, can sometimes miss. Herod saw Jesus as a threat. The birth of this child threatened to undermine Herod's power. It threatened to sweep Herod off his feet, to turn his life upside down. In a similar way, those in power in the Jewish temple saw danger in these followers of Jesus, as possibly overturning the balance and way of life that kept them secure. And in this they saw the truth of God's message. As Joy Carroll Wallis continues:

> Jesus was born an outcast, a homeless person, a refugee, and finally he becomes a victim to the powers that be. Jesus is the perfect saviour for outcasts, refugees, and nobodies. That's how the church is described in scripture time and time again – not as the best and the brightest – but those who in their weakness become a sign for the world of the wisdom and power of God.

It is a message of reversals, of transformations, of turning understandings upside down. The poor are to be lifted up, the rulers are to be cast down, the blind shall see, the prisoners will be set free, those who mourn will be comforted, those wanting to lead must first serve, and anyone wanting to gain life must give up their life. We hear all this in Jesus' teaching, in the words of the prophets, in Mary's song (the *Magnificat*), and it is there also in John's invitation to come and be baptised. This is the invitation of baptism, which quite literally means drowning. The old dies, is swept away, revealing the new. Baptism is to be made a part of the new order of life, a part of God's family. It is a revolutionary act, a commitment to the kingdom – a kingdom which was grounded in pain and suffering, yet which brings the promise of joy and peace. As songwriter Peter Kearney puts it in the song 'John and Jesus':

Come on everyone to the river to drown
To be tumbled and tossed, turned upside down
Change your heart, come clear your mind
And find your feet on new ground.

(https://peterkearney.bandcamp.com/track/john-and-jesus, accessed 22/11/2020)

In baptism services, we use symbols to tell the story: we use *water*, like John's river Jordan, like the waters of creation, like the waters of the flood, like the waters of birth. Water tells us of death and life. *Oil* is a sign of anointing, of God's Spirit pouring out as it did on the great kings like David, on the day of Pentecost, and when Jesus was baptised and we hear God declare 'this is my beloved son'. Oil tells us of God's Spirit drawing us into his family. A *candle* is a reminder of God's first command, LET THERE BE LIGHT, of his promise to be a light, a guide for us on our journey, and is also a reminder of Jesus' presence as light for the world. A candle tells us of light breaking, and overcoming, the darkness. So, to celebrate a baptism is always a great opportunity to reflect on how we respond to the invitation to be swept off our feet, to be tumbled and tossed, to be turned upside down.

From Matthew and Acts, our focus texts present some quite different alternatives for response. Do we hold on to what we know, clutching like *Herod and the Temple authorities* to those things that safeguard our power, our self-image, the status quo, no matter what? Or, do we respond: like the *wise men*, the Magi, going home by a different route, forever altered by their experience, no longer at ease in the old dispensation?; like *Joseph*, the faithful one who listened, who believed and packed up his small family and took them to safety?; or like *Stephen*, the first deacon, servant in his community and first martyr, who died praying 'Lord, do not hold this sin against them'? (v. 60). Do we respond like a king, or like a servant?

> HOW ARE YOU TUMBLED AND TOSSED?
> HOW DO YOUR FEET FIND NEW GROUND?

God
you tumble us, you toss us
you turn us upside down

to be exalted we must be humble
to lead we must serve
to gain life we must die

as we follow you
sweep us off our feet
to find new ground
so that we can change
so that we can listen
so that we can believe
so that we can truly live

Amen

   Susan Joy Nevile and Maurice Nevile

(in part adapted from words of the Peter Kearney song 'John and Jesus')

Failing to act

Matthew 21:23-32

WE CAN CHANGE, AND ACT

Here I reflect on our willingness to see and act on the truth, to not just choose but follow through to action. In the passage from Matthew, Jesus tells the chief priests and elders of the temple what is known as the parable of the two sons. A father has two sons and asks one to go and work in the vineyard. The son says he will not, but later he changes his mind and goes. The father then asks the same of the second son. He says he will go, but then does not. Jesus asks which of the two sons did what the father wanted.

Does this story sound familiar? Our words and actions do not always match up. We fail to act. We can relate to the idea of saying one thing and doing another. Jesus uses this short story to call into question those who had questioned his authority. At the beginning of the passage, the chief priests and the elders had queried Jesus' right to act in the way he did. They are specifically referring to Jesus' cleansing of the temple. After he rode into Jerusalem, and the crowds welcomed him as the Messiah, Jesus went straight to the temple and overturned the money changers' tables, accusing them of making the temple into a den of thieves. Then Jesus returns the next day and starts teaching. So, the chief priests and the elders, who feel that *they* have the right to control the temple, and that *they* have the authority to teach, move in to attack Jesus' authority. Jesus stumps them with his question about John, and then tells the story here about the two sons and the choices they make.

The story is, therefore, also about recognising and responding to authority, to God's authority (see 'Authority'). Jesus was suggesting to the elders that they were like the second son. They could talk the talk but could not walk the walk. They knew all the rules but lacked the heart to bring the rules to life. Notice how Jesus rubs it in at the end with his comment about the tax collectors entering the kingdom of God before the chief priests. It is a bit like Jesus' message that the first shall be last, because, in terms of holiness, the elders and the chief priests certainly thought they were way ahead of the tax collectors. But actually, Jesus is saying 'no', the tax collectors have recognised and responded to the truth, and so they are closer to the kingdom.

This story fits well into our thinking about the kingdom of God (see 'Kingdom') because its essential idea is that the kingdom is about how we live. All our big ideas and words are meaningless if they do not go hand-in-hand with doing what God's law of love demands, and Jesus demonstrates this with a life of obedience to God. The cross is the proof that Jesus means what he says. The story with an unmerciful and unforgiving servant (see 'Forgiving') led us to compare ourselves to the characters and to reflect on what we are like with forgiveness. The story here certainly encourages us to think about how we respond when we are asked to carry out a task, when we are called to act. Are we like the *first* son and hate to be interrupted, to be told do something that needs doing? Do we suddenly find something 'important' to do, and somewhere important to be, when we are asked to do something we may not want to do? Or are we like the *second* son, saying 'yes' but just not really meaning it, and then not following through with action, maybe when we wished to keep the other person happy, quiet, off our back?

So, what sort of things interrupt our good intentions, what gets in the way of us acting? But the story also gives hope that we are not bound by our poor choices and failure to act. We can be like the first son, like the tax collectors who are able to see the truth, change and act. Our lives can come around to be the way God wants them to be, and the kingdom will grow closer.

> **WHAT STOPS YOU FROM ACTING?**

God
the cross is the proof
that Jesus means what he says...
but we often fail to act
we get busy
we get tired
we get scared
we get distracted
we get our priorities wrong...
we are sorry
we hope to change
we want to see the truth
and with you we know that we can
Amen

Susan Joy Nevile and Maurice Nevile

Facing giants

1 Samuel 17:1-51 (NIV)

WITH GOD, WE CAN DO EXTRAORDINARY THINGS

The story of David and Goliath reminds us that when we face the giants of our lives, we are not alone. We learn of how David, a boy representing the Israelite army, wearing no armour, and armed only with a slingshot, defeated the Philistine army's representative, Goliath, a huge man who was heavily armoured and armed. The odds were massively stacked against David. He was chosen by God, anointed by Samuel to be king, even though he was the youngest and least important son, the son who got stuck with tending the sheep. After rejecting the older brothers, God says to Samuel: 'People look at the outward appearance, but the Lord looks at the heart' (1 Samuel 16:7). God saw what potential David had, and was proved right. In his heart, David put his trust in God. David certainly did not get everything right, and as king he made some spectacular mistakes, but for these he was sorry, and he never lost sight of his love for God.

David's trust in God was quite different to that of the other characters we hear about in the story. The *Philistines* operated from a belief that power lies with those with the most might, the strongest muscles, the heaviest spears, the biggest swords, the finest armour. They put their trust in the power of Goliath. The *Israelites*, and King Saul, demonstrated by their action, or rather their inaction, that they too believed that power is located with might and weaponry. They were scared and overwhelmed by what seemed invincible odds. David certainly was not a fool – he knew what he was up against. But he also knew what God wanted him to do in his situation. For David, it was clear: how could he stand there and let this Philistine mock them, and in so doing mock God? He had to take on Goliath, and he knew that when he did so God would be with him. It was not his own strength that he was depending on, but God's. David faced his fears, he was true to himself, he did not give up, he knew his strengths, he knew what was just, and he had confidence in the power of God. David's is like many stories in the Bible of people doing extraordinary things, like Abraham, Esther, Jeremiah, Mary, Moses, Paul and Peter.

Our own giants, the challenges and difficulties and pains of life, can take many forms. We can know that feeling, in situations where we have no power, where power lies with others who are better positioned and equipped, are bigger, stronger, faster, older or younger, and who can defeat us in thought and argument, or just out-muscle or out-manoeuvre us somehow. We can feel overwhelmed, that we have no chance, that the odds are stacked against us, that it is totally unfair. But we are not without power, we always have the power to ask: how can God help me in this situation? What, or who, has God given me for support? How does God enable me to persevere? And we can always quietly ask ourselves how we are coping, how we can change things, and with whom can we share our struggle to ease the burden.

Jesus said that the smallest seed can grow into the largest

tree. To anyone troubled, struggling, hurting, confused, in conflict, or lost, an offer of help, an invitation, a smile, or even just someone being there, present alongside, can lift the spirits, empower, and allow hope to grow. Maybe it comes from simply knowing that we are not alone, and that God is always there with us, just as he was with David, helping him to do extraordinary things.

> WITH GOD, WHAT GIANT
> HAVE YOU DEFEATED?
> WITH GOD, WHAT EXTRAORDINARY THING
> HAVE YOU DONE?

God
when we face the giants of our life
remind us
that you are always beside us
that we can trust in your strength
that our hope can grow
and that with you we can do extraordinary things

Amen

Susan Joy Nevile and Maurice Nevile

Reaching out

Matthew 14:22-33 (NIV)

WE CAN ALWAYS REACH OUT FOR GOD'S HELP

At times, we can feel alone, and that we must rely on ourselves. Our story here reminds us that God reaches out to us and wants us to reach out to him. The story centres on water, so I will start there. But I will first note that it is interesting how where you are born, and especially where you are brought up, can affect the way you look at the world around you. I was born in Armidale, in inland country New South Wales, but I was brought up on the coast in Sydney. I grew up overlooking the harbour, I went to the beach most weekends, I took for granted using ferries as public transport, and I went sailing with my cousins. So, I was quite comfortable in and around water. In contrast, my mother was born and brought up in the Western Australian sheep belt, where the largest body of water was the dam down the hill. I suppose she could swim, but I have no memory of her ever doing so. My mother's attitude towards water is one of suspicion. To her, water is treacherous, just waiting to lure you into complacency before it attacks. Water is definitely not to be trusted.

When it comes to water, the mindset of the average Galilean about the time of Jesus was more like my mother's than mine. The Jews were not a great sailing nation, not like the Greeks or the Phoenicians who sailed all around the Mediterranean. Yes, there were fishermen who ventured out onto the lake, but these were a minority. The Jews viewed water, especially a large body of water, with great trepidation. In fact, to them, symbols of seas, oceans, or lakes, represented chaos, the uncontrollable forces of nature. In the story, the disciples are in a boat on the lake, quite some distance from shore, and being buffeted by winds and waves. Jesus walks out to them, on the water. The disciples think he is a ghost, and they are terrified, but Jesus assures them of who he is. Yet Peter is unconvinced and prompts Jesus to tell him to come and join him on the lake. So, Jesus says 'Come' (v. 29), and Peter gets out of the boat and begins walking on water to approach Jesus. But when Peter experiences the wind, he becomes afraid and begins to sink, crying out 'Lord, save me!' (v. 30).

Today, it can help to think about this whole story using symbols. The turbulent wind and water are chaos, or whatever makes us feel unsettled, unsure, out of control, possibly overwhelmed. For example, these might be rejection, isolation, fear, loneliness, loss, hurt, or change. The boat therefore can be symbolic of whatever makes us feel safe, like work, money in the bank, a roof over our heads, good health, or more social things like strong friendships, being accepted, having influence, knowing your direction, and feeling competent and successful. Feeling safe could come simply from experiencing whatever is familiar in our life, like the places and people and activities we know well.

How then do we understand what happens with Peter and Jesus? In momentary confidence Peter prompts Jesus to call him do something that does not make sense – in the middle of the rough weather to leave the boat and do something impossible! And Jesus calls him: 'Come'. Perhaps then God does not want us just to sit where we feel safe, where we are comfortable, where we are familiar. God asks us to take risks. Now I do not mean that God wants us to run with scissors, stand on an unstable ladder, or make random life decisions. It is not that kind of risk! What God calls for is different for different individuals. For some friends of mine, it meant leaving their jobs to move to Zambia to help people with food production. For another friend, it meant traveling to refugee centres to visit people so that they did not feel so alone. For someone else, it meant working at a local drop-in centre for the hungry and homeless people. For another it meant just standing up for a person that others put down.

But 'risk' does not have to be a form of service and care to others that takes us far from home, or at least out of our comfort zone. For me, it is standing up to talk in front of more than 300 people, when actually I am quite shy. For one of my sons, it was saying 'I believe in God', even when his school friends were telling him it was all rubbish. For my other son it was choosing not to play with the coolest kids in his year because he did not like some of the things they did. Taking a risk may mean just meeting new people for the chance of friendship, making a change of career, moving home, or taking on something new and creative.

Yet we still have not got to the end of the story. Jesus does not leave Peter floundering in the water but reaches out to him and takes him back to the boat. There Peter is truly safe, as Jesus calms the weather. So, we are not left alone to be overwhelmed, God is there ready to carry us, even when we let him down. When the waves threaten to swamp our boat, when the things that we find most scary are at their worst, we find that God is with us always, and that is what can calm the storm we find ourselves in. That is what can make us feel safe. As Jesus says as he reaches out to Peter, 'You of little faith … why did you doubt?' (v. 31). We are not alone. We can have faith that God will reach out to us, and in confidence we can reach out to God.

> YOU ARE NOT ALONE. CALL FOR GOD
> TO REACH OUT TO YOU

God
when we risk
when we try to walk on water
to come to you in faith
the wind is strong
the waves are high
we are afraid of the depths
we are far from the shore
and so, we call to you
'Lord, save us!'

thank you for hearing us
for reaching out to us
for holding us close
and for leading us back to safety

Amen

Susan Joy Nevile and Maurice Nevile

Shouting out!

Mark 10:46-52 (NIV)

JESUS! SON OF DAVID! I WANT... I NEED...

Imagine shouting out to Jesus for something you need. Here we begin with Bartimaeus, a blind beggar, sitting by the side of the road as Jesus passes, shouting out to gain Jesus' attention. Have you ever been in Bartimaeus' situation, in a crowd pushed to the back, where you could not see and experience something that was important to you? I remember it happened to me when I went to see my daughter in a school play. I could not see past the people I was sitting behind. Should I move, stand on the side or at the back? Should I try to swap seats with someone during the interval? I was too shy, too meek. I did not want my daughter to be embarrassed, and as a result I spent hours enjoying the show but not seeing much of my daughter perform, and so missing out on something very special.

But Bartimaeus was not going to miss out – he shouted more loudly! Remember that beggars were lowly, they did not draw attention to themselves, especially when someone important was around. So, everyone tried to shut him up: 'shush, you're an embarrassment'... 'shush, go away'. But Jesus stops and calls him over, drawing him into the spotlight. I am reminded of the unimportant being important – the first shall be last and the last shall be first (Matthew 20:16). Here is Jesus putting this into practice. And Jesus asks Bartimaeus, 'What do you want me to do for you?' Bartimaeus gets straight to the point! – 'I want to see' (v. 51).

Although physically blind, Bartimaeus actually already sees – with the eyes of faith – and *this* is what Jesus responds to: 'your faith has healed you' (v. 52). How do we know Bartimaeus has faith? How can *we* see it? We see it in his initial yelling out 'Jesus! Son of David! Have mercy on me!' (v. 47), in his persistence despite pressure to be silent and invisible, in his response to Jesus' call, and in knowing what to ask for, what his need really was. And interestingly, Bartimaeus does what another young man could not (see 'Riches') – he becomes a follower of Christ, not just one in the crowd.

Now imagine that *you* are in that large crowd, and that Jesus walks through the masses of people, and *you* shout out to him, and he stops, and he looks into *your* eyes, and he asks *you*: 'What do you want me to do for you?'. What would your response be? What is your need? How could Jesus help and heal you?

> **JESUS IS WALKING PAST, SHOUT OUT
> IN FAITH, TELL HIM YOUR NEED!**

Jesus, Son of David!
many people shout out to you
they are poor, they are sick
they are lost, they are hurt
they are alone, they are weary
they are scared, they are confused
and they are distressed
have mercy on them, and help us
to give them what they need

Jesus, Son of David!
we shout out to you also
in our need
have mercy on us, and help others
to give us what we need

Amen

Susan Joy Nevile and Maurice Nevile

The scream

Luke 7:11-17 (NIV)

JESUS SHOWS US HOW TO FEEL, AND HOW TO LOVE

I first struggled with this passage, a story from Luke in which Jesus raises a widow's only son, until finally I heard the *scream*. I am someone who is attuned to narrative, always looking for what is happening in a story, what it means, and I am always seeking to pick the ending of a movie (which makes my husband groan, because I am very often right). And Luke's story is simple. Jesus and his friends come to a small town, arriving during a funeral procession. There is a large crowd. Jesus has compassion, intervenes, raises the young man to life, the locals are extremely impressed, and news of Jesus spreads. The story is only told by Luke, and it felt to me distant, somehow unreal, and difficult to connect to.

So, I thought and thought about the mother, a widow, in the middle of burying her only son, and I remembered some of the people I have met in my hospice and hospital pastoral care work. I heard her scream, their scream, of shock and sadness, of loss and separation, of powerlessness and uncertainty, and of fear. I have regularly sat with those who are hurting, despairing, or are close to death, and also with their families. It occurred to me that their stories are never simple, distant, or unreal. They are complex, immediate, and

The scream

very very real. No matter if the dead is three hours old, three days old, three years old, or thirty-three years old, the mothers are torn apart. There are tears, there is groaning and shaking, and utter disbelief, and that is true for fathers, wives, husbands, children, brothers, sisters, lovers. Edvard Munch captures such a sense of 'scream' in his iconic painting.

A sense of this experience is shown too in a scene of the 1990s German movie *Run Lola Run (Lola Rennt)*. In a race against time, Lola finds herself in a crowded casino, at the roulette wheel, needing to win money to save the life of her beloved boyfriend. Confronted by his potential loss, Lola bets all she has. She stands, staring at the spinning wheel, leaning forward, with fists clenched ... and then she screams, a long and loud scream of hope and desperation, with every fibre of her body, with every ounce of her energy, with every particle of will she can muster. She screams for the ball to drop at the right number, to change destiny, to change their lives. People cower and cover their ears, and wine glasses shatter. And then, as the ball drops into place, the room is utterly silent. While Lola collects her winnings, everyone has stopped what they are doing, and they face her, standing still, in shock, in awe of the power, sensing the moment's significance for her. Affected by his own life destiny battles, this scene moves my husband to tears.

In my pastoral care work, such a scream may not be sounded, but nevertheless it echoes through the lives of the people I meet, as they sit by the bed of their unresponsive loved one, as they begin to process their diagnosis, as they stare into the reality of circumstances and care. And oddly, it is a scream that initially I did not hear in Luke's story. I had to fill it in, remembering that a burial would be held within twenty-four hours of death, that the woman's loss would be raw indeed, and remembering too that this is the second loss for this woman: first her husband, and now her only son. She has lost both the men who, in that time, would have been crucial for her support, status and wellbeing. Her world had been not only shaken; it had collapsed.

It is into this life ruin that Jesus and his friends enter, as only casual passers-by at the town gate. Yet we are told that 'When the Lord saw her, his heart went out to her' (v. 13). Jesus heard that scream of her world falling apart, and with compassion he acted. Our translation into English makes it sound a bit soft and chocolate boxy, but the Greek is more hard hitting. Luke uses a word which is far more visceral, conveying that Jesus' 'bowels turned over'. We would say he was 'gutted'. We know the feeling, when our stomach drops, feels like it is tied in knots, or ripped out. The word carries meaning of both physical pain and emotional distress. That is what Jesus felt for the widow he did not know.

Luke only uses that word in two other places, in the two great stories of compassion that Jesus told. One story is when the Samaritan saw a man lying by the side of the road, beaten, bruised, left to die, and so crossed over, bound the man's wounds, and brought him to safety. And the other story is when the father waited for his son, who had left home, wasted money, time, and self, only to return, and when catching a glimpse of that young man on the road runs to gather him in his arms. These two beloved stories use that same word to capture the depth of Jesus' feeling, not a superficial passing response, and they open for us both an understanding of God's compassion, and of our compassion for others.

The scream

In Luke's story we have Jesus enacting this for us. This is what Jesus does, this is what incarnation is all about. God indeed has visited his people. Luke, back in chapter 4, is clear when he sets out Jesus' agenda: the poor, the imprisoned, the blind, the downtrodden, will be set free. And later, in chapter 7 (v. 22), Jesus tells the followers of John, 'Go back and report to John what you have seen and heard: the blind receive sight, the lame walk, those who have leprosy are cleansed, the deaf hear, the dead are raised, and the good news is proclaimed to the poor'. Here we have it, the kingdom made real, God's love in action. Jesus sees and understands the need. Jesus gives comfort, and then reaches out to transform the situation, raising the man from death and restoring him to his mother and community. God, as some writers have put it, is making house calls.

And in this story, we are shown the model for our response, for we who are called to follow Jesus are called to be workers in the kingdom. We are called to see, to feel, to be gutted, to stand beside those who are most vulnerable, those whom the world sees as hopeless, needy, a burden. And in so doing, we can learn how to love. I am reminded of theologian Paul Gondreau, reflecting on his relationship with his son Dominic, living with disability, who states that:

> Dominic's special vocation in the world is to move people to love. We human beings are made to love, and we depend on examples to show us how to do this... Yes, I give much to my son, Dominic. But he gives me more, WAY more. I help him stand and walk, but he shows me how to love.

> In Catholic Moral Theology, http://catholicmoraltheology.com/a-special-vocation-to-show-people-how-to-love/, accessed 7 September 2020

> LISTEN CAREFULLY ...
> CAN YOU HEAR A SCREAM?

God
help us to hear the scream
the long loud scream
the desperate scream
of those in need
who have sadness
who have loss
who have pain
who have burdens
and who will for a change in destiny

help us to feel for them
and to follow Jesus' example
for how to love them

and God when we scream
help others to hear us
to feel for us
and to love us too

Amen

Susan Joy Nevile and Maurice Nevile

Burdened

Colossians 3:1-17 (NIV)

WE CAN CARRY WHAT MAKES OUR LIFE JOURNEY LIGHTER

As we journey in life, what we take with us, what we must carry, really matters. What we carry affects how we can move, what we can do, and even where we can go. It can burden us. With my school classes, I would demonstrate this by bringing in luggage I have used on holidays. I would show one bag that I had bought specifically because it was easy to carry and handle, and I compared it to the one I had previously used that went over my arm and kept getting twisted. With the older bag, I kept feeling that it was going to break because I had so much stuff in it, as one does for long travels. In fact, having too much with you on a trip soon becomes a real hassle. So, we need always to think what it is that we really want, and really need, what will be useful and helpful, and what instead will be a burden and slow us down. In life, as in travel, we need to be very careful about what we carry!

My demonstration for the school children would continue with a backpack heavy with stuff. I would struggle to lift it onto my back and ask the class to imagine if I had this on my back *all* the time, how difficult it would be to get around and to bend over, to eat lunch, etc. I would prompt some of the children to have a turn carrying it, or at least to try lifting it. And then, as they truly begin to grasp the effort, I suggest they need to check out what I have packed. Maybe I have overdone it? In their shock and horror, they find and remove a brick, and then many stones! The children wonder, out loud, why anyone in their right mind would want to carry this stuff around! I am reminded of the Burke and Wills expedition of 1860-61, to cross Australia from south to north, which left with a huge amount of equipment including enough food to last two years, a cedar-topped oak camp table with two chairs, and a Chinese gong!

In the letter to the Colossians, Paul details some 'earthly things' that burden us, just like the unnecessary brick and stones in my backpack. We need to put them aside if we are to set our hearts and minds on things above, where Christ is. For example, we do not need to 'carry with us' immorality, greed, evil desires, anger, malice, lying, and bad language. These do not help us, they slow us down, they prevent us doing what we are really able to do. And they can hurt us, and others. The good news is that when we follow Jesus, we do not need to carry these, we can put them right away. Instead, Paul outlines new attitudes and behaviours, that Jesus would have (vv. 12-15).

> ...as God's chosen people, holy and dearly loved, clothe yourselves with compassion, kindness, humility, gentleness and patience. Bear with each other and forgive one another if any of you has a grievance against someone. Forgive as the Lord forgave you. And over all these virtues put on love, which binds them all together in perfect unity. Let the peace of Christ rule in your hearts, since as members of one body you were called to peace. And be thankful.

This is beautiful writing: 'And over all these virtues put on love'. To continue the backpack metaphor, *these* are what we *can* carry, what we *need* to carry, because they are good for us, and good for others. It is these that will make our life journey lighter. But even more, by carrying these, in Christ, we lose our old self, and we put on a new self, as we are now living and journeying with God.

> **WHAT IS IN YOUR BACKPACK?**

God
on our walk with you
we carry the bricks and stones
of worldly life...

we get angry
we get greedy
we hurt others
we forget the truth
we forget to hope
and we forget where we are headed...

help us Lord
to drop these worldly bricks and stones
to carry instead what you give us
compassion
kindness
humility
gentleness
patience
forgiveness
and love
lots and lots of love
Amen

Susan Joy Nevile and Maurice Nevile

Scarred

John 20:11-23, Luke 24:13-48

Rachel Naomi Remen (2006) *Kitchen Table Wisdom: Stories that Heal*. Riverhead Books, New York.

OUT OF SCARS AND VULNERABILITY COMES RESURRECTION

Some scars are visible, and some are hidden, but I think every scar tells a story. The story might tell of wounding, pain, foolishness, mishap, adventure, or of courage, healing, and growth. The story might also tell of resurrection. We all have scars, but I wonder which of your scars would you be willing to show? And I wonder, what would your scars tell about you? I have got a very neat scar on my ankle, where they put a line in when I was a baby. I had picked up a gastro bug and was severely dehydrated. It looks a little long now, but I assume the tube was not really as big as the scar suggests and that the scar has stretched and grown with me over the years. To me, the scar is a reminder to be thankful for care. I also have one on the back of my head from when my sisters pushed me down the back stairs when I was little. That scar is a reminder about older siblings! I received a great burn scar as a teenager, from a gas heater, the type with bars across the top that used to be in schools. As a foolish young person, I wore my school uniform on the short side, and one winter's day I had been huddling with others in front of the heater. I was accidentally pushed onto it, and for years I carried the stripes on my thigh, as if I had been scratched by a big cat. That scar is a reminder of my vanity. Another scar on my upper chest is where they cut the growth out of my thyroid, after it threatened the life of my first child still in utero.

Those four are about the sum of my scars – and they are mostly hidden. Some people's scars are far more obvious. I had one friend who carried a raised, red scar on his face. It was always the first thing anyone noticed upon meeting him. He had some great stories about it – bar fights, fencing accidents, muggings: it took some time to get to the truth. Playing a game as a lad he had jumped through a window and caught his face on the latch. Actually, in itself, that tells quite a bit about him.

When it comes to scars, Jesus had some to impress. And in the texts here, as he appears to the disciples, it is Jesus who starts the offering of proof. In he comes – the one who is the way, the gate, the door – making his way past their locked door. He then greets the disciples with peace and shows them his hands and his side (John 20:19-23). It is then, when they see the scars, that we are told the disciples recognise Jesus, and they become excited. They start to understand what is happening. Jesus' wounds, the scars, bring that moment of clarity. With Mary, recognising Jesus comes with the saying of her name, and a moment of intimacy (vv. 11-18). Elsewhere, we know the fishermen recognise Jesus at the instruction to do things differently, to 'Throw your net on the right side of the boat' (John 21:6-7), and the consequent provision of fish, far more than they needed. This reveals the one who said he had come to give abundant life (John 10:10). Cleopas and his friend recognise Jesus with the blessing and breaking of the bread, from that reconnection with meals shared (Luke 24:13-35).

These moments of recognition do not seem to require proof, but Jesus seems to understand that his friends do need something more. Luke (24:38-39) tells us that Jesus, appearing to the disciples as a group, says, 'Why are you troubled, and why do doubts rise in your minds? Look at my hands and my feet. It is I myself! Touch me and see; a ghost does not have flesh and bones, as you see I have'. The actual marks of the crucifixion are not mentioned, but why else would Jesus proffer his hands and feet as a way of identifying himself? After the wild stories of hope from Mary and the women, it is not Jesus' presence, it is not even his words of 'peace'; it is the wounds that make the hope real. It seems that it is the scars of crucifixion that reveal who Christ is.

So, what is the story that *these* scars tell? The scars are obvious reminders of Jesus' anguish, especially for those who had actually seen crucifixions. For us they are fairly intellectual, we know in theory what they are like. But for Jesus' friends, the scars form vivid statements of torture, humiliation, grief, and isolation. Here stands one who knows what it is to endure suffering. And not just suffering: these scars speak of death. Looking at the wounds that one would normally see on a corpse leaves no room for wondering about what has happened. The risen Christ standing before them is the same Jesus who had suffered and died. In this, the scars say that death, the source of so much fear, so much anguish, so much pain, has been defeated. As Peter declares to all who would listen: 'God untied the death ropes and raised him up. Death was no match for him' (Acts 2:24, MSG). For just as he promised, Jesus had risen, the usual order is overthrown. No wonder the disciples take a while to get it, and to rejoice!

Yet it is important to see that the scars remain, because in this we see that the resurrection cannot, must not, undo the crucifixion. Grief, anger, pain, do remain. The resurrection does not wipe them out. It is not as if we can make these lines in our life story disappear, like plastering or painting over, or using the delete key. What the scars offer is a different perspective to despair: they offer the possibility of growth, the possibility of change, and they offer the way of resurrection and hope.

From experiences of her work in medicine, Rachel Naomi Remen (pp. 114-118), tells the story of a young man who, as part of his treatment, had drawn a broken vase, to represent his body. Two years later, she meets with him again, and shows him the picture, asking if he remembers it. He says yes, but that it is not really finished. With a yellow crayon, he then drew lines radiating from the large crack in the vase to the edge of the paper. When finished, he put his finger on the crack and said softly, 'This is where the light comes through'. Resurrection is seen in the places of damage, in the scars and the wounds of life. Resurrection is in the points where we are the most vulnerable. It is there that God can work. In the hard places where we struggle, with disappointment, disillusionment, powerlessness, illness, loss, those are places for resurrection – right here, and right now.

When Martha confronts Jesus with his failure to turn up and heal Lazarus (John 11:17-27), Jesus tells her that to believe in him is to be part of his resurrection life in the here and now. Believing in Jesus is not an intellectual assent, it is not about rational explanations or logical discussions. As Karoline Lewis explains, in the book of John, believing is 'always a verb, never a noun' (viawww.workingpreacher.org/preaching, accessed 26 September 2020). It is this belief that allows Jesus to send his friends, and us, into the world. Forgiveness, reconciliation, the healing of relationships, is to be our work. We are sent by Jesus, as he was sent by the Father – that same relationship. What flows from this belief, this relationship, is life: life that is cracked and changed, life that is covered with the scars of our healing, life that lets the light shine through.

> **WHAT STORIES DO YOUR SCARS TELL?**
> **WHICH SCARS CANNOT BE SEEN?**

God
we are wounded
we are damaged
we are broken
we are scarred

where we are vulnerable
where we struggle
where we hurt
where we die
let your light shine through the cracks
deep into our lives
so that we can rise again

Amen

Susan Joy Nevile and Maurice Nevile

Separated

Matthew 28 (NIV)

WITH EASTER, WE ARE NO LONGER SEPARATED FROM GOD

Often, we can feel separated from others, from the familiar, or from God, and we can come to fear separation. We can especially fear death as the ultimate form of separation, to become apart from the physical world as we know and live it. But at Easter, we remember and celebrate that death and separation have been transformed.

When I think of Easter and Christmas, in ministry life, in many ways Christmas seems easy. People are already looking forward to it, there is a sense of anticipation and celebration in the air, and an acceptance that it is a special time. It helps that many people have heard the story before. The images of stars, shepherds, wise men, a mother cradling a baby, are instantly recognisable and able to be connected to key parts of the story. Easter is a lot harder. What do we think of at Easter time? The first image is the cross, and that is an unwelcome reminder of death. Then we have images of bunnies, bilbies, chicks, chocolate eggs, and other chocolates, none of which is mentioned in the Bible. These are no immediate help to understand Easter.

Is there one word to sum up Easter's significance? There are a few likely contenders: love, sacrifice, salvation, resurrection and reconciliation. These are all fine, but a word that really sticks in my mind is *transformation*: Easter transforms our separation from God. To me, this word captures the sense that things are fundamentally changed, the point when something stops being one thing and becomes another thing, now able to do, and be, what is totally 'other'. So, maybe butterflies are a better representation, as they transform from a crawling caterpillar into a beautiful and gentle flying insect. We can quickly relate the period in the cocoon to Christ's time in the tomb, all wrapped up, hidden away, and with no hint of the spectacular change for the new life to emerge.

The Easter story has many transformations. First, Jesus is transformed, from death to life, from criminal to saviour, from a might-have-been to the real thing. Second, his tomb itself was transformed from a place of death, of silence, dark, stillness, to somewhere with voice, and bursting with light and life. Jesus' friends were transformed, from being broken-hearted, confused, lost, afraid, and despairing, to being full of joy and hope, with confidence and enthusiasm. They go out and tell others of Jesus. In fact, if they had not, we would not be celebrating the Easter story at all.

It is as if Christ's transformation is the centre, as if the rolled-away tomb stone is thrown into the lake, and from that come ripples and waves of change that move ever outward. As the angel says (v. 6), 'he has risen', not risen and far off, but risen and waiting. The ripples and waves from the stone become wider and wider, not only changing lives but transforming death itself from something to be feared, the ultimate in separation, into a doorway to new life.

And so, it is not just these examples of transformation,

but the whole story itself that transforms. The good news it tells has the profound ability to change lives, and it does so wherever it is told. Evil, darkness, and hate have not won. Death has been overturned. Goodness, light, life, and love have the victory. Just as God would not allow death to be the end for Jesus, so God will not allow it to be the end for us either. We know that nothing, not even death, has the power to separate us from God, or to put us beyond the reach of God's love. This challenges us not only to change how we think about death, but how we live, now, as not separated but always connected.

> **HOW ARE YOU CONNECTED TO GOD?**

God
Jesus transforms pain, suffering, even death
into amazing joy, of new life
and we are separated no more

let that joy fill us
to change us
to renew us
to transform us
into your people of light and hope

Amen

Susan Joy Nevile and Maurice Nevile

5 We change, we become

5. We change, we become

Getting ready

Luke 3:1-6, Mark 1:1-8

IN HOW WE LIVE, WE CAN BE READY FOR THE ONE WHO IS COMING

How can we live to be ready, ready for the one who is coming? When I was teaching infants classes, we once learned a catchy new Christmas song, and the chorus was remarkably simple: 'get ready, get ready, get ready, get ready, Jesus is coming soon! Oh yes'. In some senses, I feel it is somewhat ironic, as it is almost like a theme song for the shopping malls inciting us to go out and shop, to be ready for Christmas. At my place, the junk mail would pile up, screaming at me to go out and buy my way to Christmas.

But, of course, this is not what the song is on about, its meaning is much closer to John's words when he cries out 'get ready, the Lord is coming'. John must have been an incredible preacher because people flocked to hear him and to be baptised. Now sometimes baptism today may seem a little tame – a baby in a nice white dress, with some water trickled gently on the head. So, we may wonder why everyone got so worked up about it. Well, in John's time it was not like that, it was a dramatic public statement about your life. John was calling people to get ready for the arrival of the promised one: the one they had been waiting for, hoping for, was coming, and they needed to be prepared! How? – by repenting – that good old-fashioned church word, *repentance*. What does it mean?

Repenting means to stop what we are doing and to change the path we are on. I am reminded of how teachers or parents tell children to 'stop, look, listen!'. Repenting is like turning right around: baptism is the outward sign that you are prepared to do this. Baptism means drowning, it is all about death and new life. It is the death of the old you – your old habits, your old ways of thinking, your old ways of talking, your old ways of being – and committing yourself to a new way, to God's way. As I listen to the rain sometimes, I think how it captures the feel of that moment, as the old is washed away and the new is taken on. That is the kind of getting ready that the song, as simple as it is, is all about.

We cannot all regularly rush out and get baptised, but we can get ready. First, we can recognise in ourselves that we need to change, that we do not get it right all the time. Our words and our actions sometimes end up hurting people, by accident or intentionally. It is worth spending some time thinking about how we would like to change, the things we have done that we wish we could take back, the things that we didn't do and those that we wish we had done. That is the stopping point, the point when we look at ourselves. But then we also need to listen to what it is we could or should be doing, and then act on that.

It is not a coincidence that in Advent we have both John's call for repentance and the promise of peace. The peace of Advent has two sides to it. There is the peace we feel after we have been forgiven, when what we have done has been washed away. And there is the peace we bring to others when we are consciously trying to live differently.

> **HOW ARE YOU READY?**

God
help us to stop, to look, to turn around
and then to listen to your promise of peace
that we feel for ourselves
that we bring to others
so that we can change and get ready
for the one who is coming

Amen

Susan Joy Nevile and Maurice Nevile

Invited

Luke 14:15-23 (NIV)

**JUST AS GOD'S INVITATION CHANGES US,
WE CAN INVITE AND CHANGE OTHERS**

Who will be invited? I recall that when my children were young, always a few weeks before their birthday, we would have a conversation about who would come to their party. What usually would happen next is that the child would go and get a pencil, a bit of scrappy paper, and begin to make a list. They would try to balance out school friends, church friends, neighbourhood friends, and family, and then together we would start the negotiations about just who could actually come. For my children, an invitation really mattered, I think because they felt that it told someone 'you're special to me, I like being with you'. I know this is not unique to my family, the act of including others in the celebrations of life is important to most people. So that while we may not have ever hosted a wedding banquet, as in the story here from Luke, we can easily identify with what Jesus tells. We know what it is like to invite others, the excitement and effort to plan what will happen, what food or drink to serve, and we look forward to replies. We look forward to people being there with us at the significant and memorable moments in our life.

Jesus tells a parable of a man preparing a great banquet, and who invites many guests. But at the time of the banquet, one after another the invited guests offer reasons for why they cannot be there. The banquet host becomes angry and tells his servant to go into the town to bring in the poor and physically disadvantaged. When there is *still* more room for guests, he tells the servant to go *out* of town and search the nearby country: 'compel them to come in, so that my house will be full' (v. 23). It can be discouraging when person after person declines, but also when there is an event for which you have not been invited. And it is not just children who get disappointed, who feel overlooked, rejected, and excluded. It is not just children who can feel as if they are not good enough.

These common feelings give us an intuitive sense of Jesus' parable and help us to appreciate what he was explaining. Jesus tells it as an image of God's kingdom, and when we hear it this way it is an encouraging story. We tend to identify with those who are *brought* to the banquet, so it is a good news story: God invites all to his feast, to God's kingdom, and goes to great effort to ensure we get there. This is another picture of amazing grace, of God choosing to fill the celebration with those who had been forgotten, who are often left outside. Joy! It is easier to forget the invitations that did *not* come our way when we can remember that God invites and welcomes us to *the* most important party of all.

However, here there is also a challenge because the message does not stop there: the kingdom is not just about God, it is about us, about the choices we make, about how we live. Do we live to welcome others as God welcomes us? Do we include others as God includes us? Do we go beyond our comfort zone to engage with others? Imagine that you are organising a party, or some occasion or event. You can invite just five people. You might just be together at home, to have a barbecue, talk about books, play board games, watch a movie, or maybe you go out to a restaurant, go bowling, whatever! But you can only invite five people. Who would you ask?

You may think instantly of inviting your closest friends, or someone fun to be with, or who brings decent food and drink, or who gives great gifts, or who has been kind to you or asked you to their parties. That is often how our thinking works, because we want to maximise our good time. Have you thought of five people? Now think of someone you might *not* normally include, perhaps someone who does not usually get invited: they might be someone at your workplace, your church, your university/school, or in your sports team, or hobby/interest group, or maybe they are a neighbour, or a distant family member. In the past, you may have thought, 'Hmmm, not her, not him'. Now imagine actually inviting and including that person. How might it make them feel, to be invited and included and welcomed? Perhaps such acceptance could initiate a real change for them, impacting how they understand and feel about themselves, and can connect with others. Perhaps the invitation changes the relationship between you.

God's great invitation can likewise change us, and impact us for how we understand and feel about ourselves, as connected to others, as we are brought into new relationships through God. As invited guests to God's kingdom we are included and welcomed.

> YOU ARE INVITED:
> WHO WILL YOU NOW INVITE?

God of the great banquet
thank you for inviting us
and preparing a place for us

we accept your welcome
we accept the chance to change
we accept our new relationship with you

help us to invite and include others
so that we can sit together at your table
where all are welcome
where all are valued
where there is a place for everyone

Amen

Susan Joy Nevile and Maurice Nevile

Beginning

Isaiah 6:1-8 (GNT)

WE CAN BEGIN SOMETHING NEW WITH TRUST, AND GOD'S STRENGTH

There are times when we stand on the edge of something new. It could be a new job, a new project, a new home, a new relationship, a new school or level of education, or a major change in life circumstances. Each new year reminds me that there is something very precious about beginning – the sense of freshness and potential is wonderful. We have a sense of awe at birth and new life, waiting for bulbs to open, or even a sunrise. Even when just beginning a new book by a favourite author, there is the anticipation of what will unfold, of characters, settings, plot, of drama and surprise. When we begin travels there is hope and expectation of what will be seen and experienced, places we might go, activities we might do, people we might meet, foods we might try. If we are sporty or active, at the beginning of an event, the mind and body are ready to go, and we have plenty of energy. There is even something simply satisfying when opening a new tub of ice cream and making that very first scoop!

As a school chaplain and teacher, I remember how the new school year could feel like that to students: a different teacher, new classmates, new rooms, new books, new lessons, and excited thoughts of special occasions, camps, assemblies, performances, and playing sports. However, alongside there were also doubts and even anxieties, with the loss of what was familiar and routine and comfortable from the previous year, and with the effort to get in the groove all over again. Over the break it was great to just relax, and what if the new work is too hard? It could all be a bit overwhelming.

Let us think about Isaiah of the Old Testament. The story here comes at an important point in his life, and it can be helpful when we get ready to face something new. God calls Isaiah to be a prophet. As you read the passage, try imagining what is happening, and how Isaiah would be experiencing it. For example (vv. 6-7), 'Then one of the creatures flew down to me, carrying a burning coal that he had taken from the altar with a pair of tongs. He touched my lips with the burning coal and said, "This has touched your lips, and now your guilt is gone, and your sins are forgiven"'. Yes, that is quite an announcement of change.

It is a great story, but what does it tell us about starting something new? Isaiah is in the temple praying when he sees a vision of God – and to put it simply, it blows him away. Isaiah was a Jew, and so an especially important part of life for him was trying to be good, to be pure, because that was how he could come close to God. But when Isaiah gets a glimpse of God, he realises how impossible it is for him to do that. He realises just how much he has failed. God's response is to repair this. An angel comes with a burning coal, and Isaiah's sins, what he has done wrong, what separates him from God, are now gone. He can come close to God. And in coming close, Isaiah hears God. He is able to hear the cry from God's heart 'whom shall I send?', and Isaiah replies: 'I will go. Send me!' (v. 8).

Isaiah's attitude is striking. He does not say 'that's too hard', or 'what's in it for me?', or 'Oh God, I just want to stay with you', or 'I'm not ready' (see 'God's vision'). Isaiah *is* ready, to take on whatever it is that God has lined up for him, and not on his own strength, but on God's. Isaiah does not know all the details, but he trusts that God will empower and enable him. I am reminded of Frodo's courage and faith in J. R. R. Tolkein's *The Lord of the Rings: The Fellowship of the Ring*. While others quarrel, Frodo accepts the challenge to embark on the great and perilous quest, to carry the One Ring, the ring of power, saying 'I will take the Ring... though I do not know the way'.

When we begin something new, there can be substantial challenge, and we do not know exactly what will confront us, or how we will do what is required of us, or cope with what will happen. But we can be ready: ready to ask for help when we need it; ready to hear and respond; ready to lend a hand to those alongside us who need our help; and ready to accept God's forgiveness and call. With God's help and strength, we can say, with confidence, 'I am ready, I will, I can do it. God knows the way'.

> **WHAT ARE YOU BEGINNING?**
> **HOW CAN GOD SHOW YOU THE WAY?**

God of beginnings
we stand on the edge of the new
it is fresh, it is precious
it is exciting, it is awesome, it is wonderful

but we doubt
we fear failure
we are challenged
we think it is impossible
and we do not know the way

give us hope
give us strength
help us to trust
that we are ready
that you know the way
and that you will show it to us

Amen

Susan Joy Nevile and Maurice Nevile

Knowing yourself

Matthew 16:13-20 (NIV), Matthew 15:10-20

Karen Beaumont and David Catrow (2004) *I Like Myself!* Koala Books.

OUR WORDS ARE A MIRROR, REFLECTING WHO WE ARE

What really makes me, me? With my younger school classes I would use the picture book *I like myself!*. The main character, a young girl about 6 years old, discovers with enthusiasm, and in various ways, how to appreciate who she is. It begins with her balancing two balls on her head, saying, 'I like myself! I'm glad I'm me. There's no one else I'd rather be'. It is a cute book, but as for many children's books, it can raise an interesting question. If, like her, you like yourself because you are you, then how do you know who *you* are? How do we know we are getting a true picture of ourselves? It is easy to see who we are, on the *outside* – a mirror will show me the colour of my eyes (blue) or my hair (blond) and will show if I am having a bad hair day. But the story establishes that actually it does not matter what we are like on the outside.

What matters, what makes her her, is what is on the *inside*. And what makes her her is not muscle, or bone, or anything bodily. She is talking about something else. Some would say it was her mind, others her heart. But how do we know what that is like? We do not have a mirror that reflects our mind, or our heart, that shows what we are really like, that shows who we are. If you know the story (or movie) of Mary Poppins then you might agree that it would be great if, like her, we had something able to take the measure of a person. She has a tape to measure the two children, with Michael being 'extremely stubborn, and suspicious', and older sister Jane as 'rather inclined to giggle, doesn't put things away'. Mary then measures herself as 'practically perfect in every way'. How much easier that would be! But we do not have such a tool.

In fact, in the story here, Jesus asks his disciples about himself: 'Who do people say the Son of Man is?' (Matthew 16:13). He gets a few different answers, John the Baptist, Elijah, Jeremiah, or maybe he is one of the prophets. Then Jesus really gets to the point and asks them, 'But what about you? Who do you say I am?' (v. 15). And likely there is a stony silence. We can imagine the disciples looking into the distance and shuffling their feet. Simon answers 'You are the Messiah, the Son of the living God', and Jesus replies with, 'Blessed are you, Simon son of Jonah, for this was not revealed to you by flesh and blood, but by my Father in heaven' (v. 17). Simon saw Jesus for who he was.

Sometimes it is our close friends who know us the best, and so listening to them, or maybe our family, to what they say about us, is one way to know about ourselves. However, it is hard to imagine something for looking *inside* ourselves as quickly and easily as a mirror or Mary Poppins' tape measure can allow us to see ourselves from the outside.

So, here is another suggestion for knowing ourselves, again from the book of Matthew (15:10-20). Jesus was discussing what made people holy, what made them close to God, as the kind of person God wanted them to be. And Jesus was challenging the Jewish authorities who had created many rules about what made people pure (Matthew 15:10-14).

> Listen and understand. What goes into someone's mouth does not defile them, but what comes out of their mouth, that is what defiles them'. Then the disciples came to him and asked, 'Do you know that the Pharisees were offended when they heard this?' He replied, 'Every plant that my heavenly Father has not planted will be pulled up by the roots. Leave them; they are blind guides. If the blind lead the blind, both will fall into a pit'.

In other words, Jesus tells us that if we want a mirror to show us what we are like on the inside, we must stop and listen to ourselves: the words we say are that mirror. If the words coming out of our mouth are mostly angry, or negative, or about ourselves, that can give us a good idea of what we are like. We get a good idea also, and more worryingly, if our words are all targeted at others, finding fault, making them feel small, or causing hurt. Let us hope that when we stop and listen to what we are saying to others that we will find a reflection of ourselves to be proud of.

> **LISTEN TO YOUR WORDS:**
> **HOW DO YOU SEE YOURSELF?**

God
you see us
you know us
you love us
our mind
our heart
our every breath and bone

help us to see ourselves
to know ourselves
to love ourselves
so that what comes from us
truly reflects who we seek to be

Amen

Susan Joy Nevile and Maurice Nevile

Wearing armour

Ephesians 6:10-18 (NIV)

PRAYER IS PRACTISING TO WEAR AND USE GOD'S ARMOUR

It is an inevitable part of life that we regularly find ourselves in some kind of conflict, and often in more than one conflict simultaneously. We might struggle with other people, with circumstances and situations we find ourselves in, or with bigger issues in our community and society. In his letter to the Ephesians, Paul is concerned about struggling against the devil, against evil, against spiritual forces, against influences that are not from God. To outline the resources God gives us for protection, Paul takes up the metaphor of a soldier ready for battle. He extols us to put on 'the full armour of God', and it is an elaborate description! (vv. 10-18).

> Finally, be strong in the Lord and in his mighty power. Put on the full armour of God, so that you can take your stand against the devil's schemes. For our struggle is not against flesh and blood, but against the rulers, against the authorities, against the powers of this dark world and against the spiritual forces of evil in the heavenly realms. Therefore put on the full armour of God, so that when the day of evil comes, you may be able to stand your ground, and after you have done everything, to stand. Stand firm then, with the belt of truth buckled around your waist, with the breastplate of righteousness in place, and with your

feet fitted with the readiness that comes from the gospel of peace. In addition to all this, take up the shield of faith, with which you can extinguish all the flaming arrows of the evil one. Take the helmet of salvation and the sword of the Spirit, which is the word of God. And pray in the Spirit on all occasions with all kinds of prayers and requests. With this in mind, be alert and always keep on praying for all the Lord's people.

If we wear the armour, we can be 'strong in the Lord' and 'stand firm'. It is an encouraging and empowering message. When Paul wrote this letter, people were familiar with the picture he was drawing, but this is a pity because the main message lies in the armour of the day, and we don't have the same sense of a soldier carrying a large shield and heavy sword, and wearing a belt, breastplate, helmet, while repelling flaming arrows. So, the idea of becoming like such a soldier can be strange and less helpful to us. But what if we shift the picture to a context with which many of us are more familiar, like sport, and maybe from cricket? The picture of 'God's armour' could be something like a batsman ready to repel deadly fast bowling, with the gloves of truth, the chest guard of righteousness, the boots of peace, the pads of faith, the helmet and face protector of salvation, and, of course, the bat of the Spirit.

This image of a cricket batsman likely makes more immediate sense to us than an ancient soldier. We can better understand the danger of the bouncing ball seeking to cause us damage and get us out (evil, not from God), and we can better see the value of protection from pads (faith), chest guard (righteousness), and helmet (salvation), and we can see how boots (peace) can make our path and movement smoother. Gloves (truth) help us to hold the bat, and we know that without the bat (Spirit), we can never progress and triumph. All this equipment enables us to go all out for our team, to stay in there and persist, to succeed and reach our desired goals. With this alternative picture, we can more easily appreciate readiness for battle: how righteousness and faith protect against doubt and hardship; how living as a peacemaker makes us more ready to do God's will; how speaking the truth will hold us to the one who described himself as the truth; and that God's Spirit is essential to participate and achieve anything at all.

But very importantly, in Paul's message (v. 18), prayer was singled out. Prayer is the way to take up the whole armour of God – so what would prayer be in our picture of the cricketer ready to go into bat? Perhaps it would be good to think of prayer as training – without training there is little point in trying on all the equipment. The pads, the boots, the helmet all make more sense if we know what to do with them, and if we practise using them. Prayer helps us to know how to use our equipment – our armour. Prayer draws us closer to God by helping us to know that we are part of a team. We are not alone out there. Most importantly, prayer gives us strength – the Bible reminds us that when we try and use our own strength, we quickly run out of energy, but God's strength does not fail. If we want to be strong in God's mighty power, as Paul tells us at the beginning of the passage, then we can find strength in prayer.

> **HOW DOES GOD'S ARMOUR PROTECT YOU?**

God
we put on your armour
and with prayer we practise using it
so that we are strong
standing firm
alert and ready
to resist doubt
to speak truth
to make peace
to do your will
to walk with the Spirit
with your energy
with your power
with your triumph

Amen

Susan Joy Nevile and Maurice Nevile

Leader

Acts 1:1-11 (NIV)

GOD CALLS US TO LEAD IN CONTINUING HIS WORK

As his followers, Jesus calls on us to become leaders. Jesus has died, risen, appeared to the disciples over forty days, and here in the book of Acts we have the story of his ascension (v. 9): 'he was taken up before their very eyes, and a cloud hid him from their sight'. The points of this story that appeal to me concern the disciples, or really apostles, as we call them after Jesus' death. My husband believes that the apostles are in the story just to make us feel better, easier in our own understanding, because they are so dimwitted. At this moment, they have gone through three years with Jesus, listened to his teaching, watched the healings, seen him challenge authority, and had long in-depth discussions into the night. Yet they still seem not to understand what Jesus is talking about. They gather around Jesus, and ask, 'Lord, are you at this time going to restore the kingdom to Israel?' (v. 6).

The apostles seem to think that Jesus is going to overturn the Roman occupation of their land and become the King. They had got to Easter, lived through the devastation of the Friday and Christ's death, had the amazing news of the Sunday and Christ's rising, and rejoiced that he is with them again. Certainly, now he was different; he could move through locked doors, and disappear, but at least he is there, teaching them again. And still they get it wrong. We can imagine Jesus sighing deeply. But he does not give up on them! He corrects them and changes their perspective by saying that it is not for them to know, that effectively, 'Well, that's up to God'. Jesus tells them that what matters, now, is that they must carry on his work, right here, right now. In other words, they must finally develop, and grow up.

They must follow in Jesus' footsteps, but they must stop being 'followers' and start being leaders. They must begin to do the work that Jesus has been preparing them for, letting people know the good news, the gospel, that God loves them. Jesus promises them a helper who will enable them to do this. They are to wait in Jerusalem, and in a few days, they will be baptised with the gift of the Holy Spirit. And then he leaves them, and they stand there looking intently up to the sky as he goes. So, two angels appear before them and say, more or less, don't just stand there, get on with it: 'Why do you stand here looking into the sky? This same Jesus, who has been taken from you into heaven, will come back in the same way you have seen him go into heaven' (v. 11). It is a great scene to picture in your mind! The apostles head back to Jerusalem to wait.

Maybe my husband is right, about the disciples, they seem so often to miss the point, yet God sticks with them, and they go on to do all kinds of amazing deeds, as we see in the book of Acts, the Acts of the Apostles. I find it encouraging that God will not give up on us, and does not expect us always to understand and get it right, even as he calls us to be leaders in carrying on his work here, 'to the ends of the earth' (v. 8). But if we persevere, God will help us to do amazing things.

When I spoke on this topic to my school classes, we would light a special Christ candle, and at the end of class, to symbolise the end of Jesus' time on earth, we would blow it out. I would remind the students that there was little point in all standing together to watch the smoke dissipate, wondering what happened to it. Better that we could keep the candle lit always, to remember that Christ asks us to be the light for the world, and we are to get on with doing it!

HOW CAN YOU LEAD?

God
as your followers
help us to lead others
to look forwards, not upwards
to get moving, not stand still
to do your work
just as we are
right here
right now

Amen

Susan Joy Nevile and Maurice Nevile

Servant

Mark 1:16-20 (NIV), Matthew 20:20-28 (NIV)

Rachel Naomi Remen (2001) *My Grandfather's Blessings: Stories of Strength, Refuge, and Belonging.* Riverhead Books, New York.

GOD OFFERS AN ALTERNATIVE MODEL OF BEING: TO LIVE AS LIGHT, AND TO SERVE

The idea of being a servant often does not sit well in our individualistic, hedonistic, success-driven, commercialised culture. We often have a cringe reaction. Perhaps a variety of images pop up in our minds when we hear the word 'servant', of butlers and maids in stiff black clothes, or of African slaves in the American cotton fields. Maybe the word raises too many connotations of subservience, of having to obey and act without question, and of being exploited.

But the idea of servant is essential to the story of Christ's ministry and message, as we will see in this extended reflection. Let us start with Jesus calling the disciples. This poem, 'Follow, follow', by Stuart Barrie, captures Jesus' call to James and John that day by the lake:

> Never once, did he say,
> 'Worship me I am the one.'
> Adoration was not sought
> or ever needed by the Son.

All he wanted was the heart,
no chant or hollow plea.
The gift he asked? ... 'Release your grasp.
Relax, and follow me.'

Published in *Bare Feet and Buttercups: Resources for Ordinary Time* (2008)
Ruth Burgess. Wild Goose Publications, Glasgow.

I am not sure how you imagine the story in Mark, two men in a boat, sitting, talking, working, doing just what they did every day, mending their nets. We are not told much about James, other than what he was doing and that he had at least one brother, a father, and later we hear of his mother. We do not know if he got on with his family, if the fishing was particularly good or bad that day, if he was devoted to fishing or had always wondered about life beyond the Sea of Galilee. Mark just says, 'Without delay he called them, and they left their father Zebedee in the boat with the hired men and followed him' (v. 20).

Such a simple story, yet it has the power to invite us in, to capture us, to sweep us along in James' unfolding adventure. The capacity to enter the story is something I was lucky enough to be a part of when, as a school chaplain, I led 'Godly Play' lessons, a Montessori method of telling Bible stories. Godly Play is an invitation to engage with a sacred story, to listen, to wonder, and to play. The children gather and prepare themselves for listening. The story is told very simply with wooden figures, and then the leader gives the invitation to wonder, through a series of questions, like, 'I wonder what it would be like to meet Jesus for the first time', 'I wonder if Jesus asked others and they did not respond', 'I wonder what James thought would happen when he followed', 'I wonder what it means to follow Jesus', 'I wonder where you are in the story?'. In Godly Play, the questions are not answered directly, the children are free to wonder, and then to respond – perhaps through art, or construction, or re-enactment. Some children play with the whole story, some focus on tiny details, some make connections with other parts of their lives.

This is much the same as we ministers do when we preach. We 'play with' the story, entering in, perhaps finding our place within it, wondering, and trying to connect to the big picture, and at times focusing on the details. So, it is interesting to try and place ourselves in the story. At one level, it is easy for me, to say 'Yeah, I'm with James and the guys, I heard, I responded, I was ordained by the Bishop'. But I think again about one of the Godly Play questions I mentioned above, 'I wonder if Jesus asked others and they did not respond'. I think then of people we do not hear of directly, the possibility of meeting Jesus by the lakeside, being invited to follow, and then *not* responding. What drew me to that? It is simply that it is not a one-off call – Jesus invites us every day to follow him. I cannot sit back as if it is done: there are nets that I can be picking up again. There is more to this process of following.

There is always comfort to be found in the knowledge that James and the others did not really know what following was all about. We know with the power of 20/20 hindsight that James and the other disciples did not really have a clue. To be fair, James and John did not even get 'and I will make you fish for people', *they* just got a 'follow me' sense of urgency from the immediacy of Jesus' call. 'The time has come, the kingdom of God has come near. Repent and believe the good news!' (v. 15). The kingdom 'has come near', and we can *see* it, like a bright light showing us the way home, we can *hear* it, like the shepherds calling their sheep at the end of the day, and we can *taste* it, like salt on a sea breeze telling us we are nearly at the beach, or the *smell* of freshly baked bread telling us it is time to eat. And 'at once' they left their nets. This sense of urgency occurs repeatedly throughout Mark (over thirty times). Jesus is taking the initiative, calling them to follow, calling them to be partners in his work. He needed companions on the way.

The kingdom is not a solitary place, but a place of community. It is not a distant mystical place, but a social reality. We at times fail to grasp the social dimension of Jesus' message about the kingdom of God. It was not simply to restore our broken relationship with God. Much of Jesus' message had to do with healing the broken relationships among people who have been separated from each other. The problem for James and John is that they were not told exactly what this social reality entailed, well, not straight away. For a minister, the joy of the lectionary is that it gives you an answer on the same day – it took James three years to get there. Three years on and they are still following, this time down a dusty road on their way to Jerusalem.

In the book of Matthew, it is their mother who asks: where will my boys sit in your kingdom? In other tellings, the boys do it themselves. The result is much the same. Jesus, in true form, responds with a question: 'Are you able to drink the cup that I am about to drink?' (Matthew 20:22). That is, 'Can you follow me, even in this?' We remember that this passage comes directly after Jesus foretells his death and resurrection. Commentators speak of the cup as an image of death. We know, as we encounter this story, of the truth of Christ's foretelling, and that most of his earliest disciples, including James, are said to have been martyred.

Perhaps we wonder as we sit with this story, where *we* are placed within it. Can we say, 'Yes I can drink from this cup'? Are we able to answer this call with 'I will follow'? When James and John answer 'yes', if they understood what they were saying or not, Jesus affirms them, 'Yes, you will'. Jesus leaves it to God to sort out the rest. But the other followers are not happy. So, Jesus spells it out for them. You want to be a leader? Well, if you are following my leadership, it is all about being a servant. It is that wonderful upside-down perspective we get when the rug is pulled out from underneath our feet!... 'the first will be last', 'you must lose your life to gain it'. Jesus tells them: 'Whoever wants to become great among you must be your servant, and whoever wants to be first must be your slave – just as the Son of Man did not come to be served, but to serve, and to give his life as a ransom for many' (Matthew 20:26-28).

Having pulled the rug out from others, Jesus remains secure in who he is and what he is doing. Across the Gospels, all the descriptions that Jesus has given of himself – shepherd, bread, water, resurrection, vine, and light – are leading to this understanding: Jesus is the source of our life because he gave up his own life. They are descriptions of servanthood, ways of healing the broken relationships among people who have been separated from each other. They are ways of connecting, building community, of forging the kingdom.

Here is the heart of Jesus' call to us, to follow his way, to drink his cup – we are being offered an alternative model of being. It is not a question of abdicating responsibility when we follow his lead. It is not that we are being asked to do what we do not want to do. We are being challenged to want something different. It is not about us. It is not about us saving our lives. It is not about us guaranteeing our spot with Jesus in heaven. It is not about us at all. It is instead about Jesus, about who he is, about his way of the cross, his way of being in the world, not for himself but for the sake of others. Jesus found himself with the poor and the outcasts in life, and he found himself poor and outcast on a cross in death, because there, not where we get for ourselves but where we give of ourselves, Jesus says, is *true life* found: in the life of the servant.

This is another image of 'the servant', one that Jesus, as a devoted Jew, would have known, and undoubtedly used throughout his lifetime as he celebrated Hanukah. In the household menorah, there are places for nine candles, one for each of the eight nights of Hanukah, and one for the Shamash, or the servant candle. This is the candle that is lit first, the candle that serves the others, that brings light and enables others to find the light within them. Rachel Naomi Remen recounts her grandfather's explanation: in the first ever call that God made, 'Let there be light', he is speaking to us personally. God is telling us what is possible, for how we may choose to live, as light. God has not only given us the chance to carry the light – he has made it possible for us to kindle and strengthen the light in ourselves, and in one another by passing the light along.

> **HOW CAN YOU SERVE?**

God
you call us to be servants
but we often struggle to serve
to follow your way
to drink your cup

please help us to serve
as a light shining the way for others
just as you are the light for us

Amen

Susan Joy Nevile and Maurice Nevile

Sorry, reconciled

2 Corinthians 5

RECONCILIATION BRINGS HEALING

What is it to say sorry, to be sorry, and to be reconciled with others? In Australia, for many people 'Sorry Day' is especially significant. Sorry Day is part of the process of recognising what the Aboriginal and Torres Strait people have experienced and endured over the last 200 or so years of European presence. In particular, it recognises the devastation caused by the forced removal of Aboriginal children from their families. It has been described as a journey of healing, and this journey continues today. Sorry Day grew out of the realisation that reconciliation – bringing together two opposing sides, giving and receiving forgiveness, breaking down divisions – is crucial in a healthy life, for individuals and for communities.

So, 'reconciliation' has taken on special meaning concerning the relationship between indigenous peoples and the wider Australian society. Sorry Day provides an opportunity to move forward by not ignoring the past, as paradoxical as that sounds. It is a process whereby healing can come, by understanding, acknowledging, and admitting the problem, and the pain felt. This was the case for the South African Truth and Reconciliation Commission. As people's pain was revealed, as victim and perpetrator came face-to-face in the truth, the country was able to move on beyond the divisions and hurt brought by years of apartheid. That experience shows how, amid a problem, it is often important, even necessary, to stop, stand back, be still, and reflect, to then progress and initiate change and healing. This is true for the life of a country, a city, a community group, a workplace, a school, a family, a couple, a friendship. It is true of any relationship.

Sometimes, it can seem that wherever we look, especially in the media, that the things that divide people are growing stronger, relating to wealth, race, religion, nationality, residency status, and within the family and community. And when we take time to look at the range of hostile feelings and thoughts in our own hearts and minds, we will see the many little and big 'wars' of which we ourselves are part. Our 'enemy' could be a family member, a colleague, a neighbour, a friend, someone at church, a teacher, even a stranger. Anyone can become the 'other', 'them', and that is where reconciliation is needed. But when we accept the need for reconciliation, we must also reflect on how to do it, not only in terms of a national level but also in our own daily lives.

What examples of reconciliation do we have to go on? The greatest process of reconciliation ever recorded happened at Easter! God was reconciling the world to himself, in Christ, and we can learn much from Easter as an example for what to do. First, we can see that reconciliation is a hands-on process – it does not happen from a distance. God did not sit out there, hoping that things would get better. In Jesus, we see that God became fully human, became one of us. So, we cannot be reconciled to one another, or work for reconciliation, without close involvement, without action. Second, we can also certainly say that reconciliation is costly. Jesus was rejected and despised by many, he suffered pain and humiliation, and ultimately, he gave up his life. True reconciliation does not come cheap – perhaps for us the cost may be admitting that we were wrong, or it may be forgiving someone else. Finally, we can understand that if we are to succeed in reconciliation, we need a non-judgmental attitude. Henri Nouwen was a Dutch Catholic priest who shared his life with people with mental disabilities. He puts it like this:

> To the degree that we accept that through Christ we ourselves have been reconciled with God we can be messengers of reconciliation for others. Essential to the work of reconciliation is a nonjudgmental presence. We are not sent to the world to judge, to condemn, to evaluate, to classify, or to label. When we walk around as if we have to make up our mind about people and tell them what is wrong with them and how they should change, we will only create more division. Jesus says it clearly: 'Be compassionate just as your Father is compassionate. Do not judge; ... do not condemn; ... forgive' (Luke 6:36-37).
>
> (https://henrinouwen.org/meditation/a-nonjudgmental-presence/ accessed 26 September 2020).

The world around us seems to push us in the opposite direction. We are often warned to keep our distance, not to get involved. The general rule seems to be to go for the easiest and cheapest solution, and we are constantly offered opportunities to judge those around us, as so-called reality television shows so well. Yet this is not God's way. God calls us into action his way. We can all become involved in reconciliation, to take the risk of approaching someone we have argued with, maybe even hurt, and to say sorry. And we can take the time to ask for God's help to find and act on those situations in our life that cry out for reconciliation, and so begin a process of change and healing.

> ARE YOU SORRY?
> HOW CAN YOU BE RECONCILED?

God of reconciliation
for those times we let you down
when we were too busy, too tired, too lazy
when we did not stay awake
when we missed a chance
to hear your voice
to see the world your way
to help someone in need
we are sorry

forgive us, and help us
to stay awake always
with you, and for you
wherever you are
and whenever you appear
Amen

Susan Joy Nevile and Maurice Nevile

Getting excited!

Acts 2:1-13

GET EXCITED, FOR THE SPIRIT WORKING THROUGH US

A lovely thing about working with very young children is that you can see and share their enthusiasm for life. When you are young, everything is exciting, like the simple beauty of appreciating the changes of the season. For example, there is the joy of crunching in autumn leaves, the surprise of frost and the prospect of snow (at least where I live, in Canberra), the wonder of watching a butterfly emerge from its cocoon, and, at the beach, the challenge of sustaining a sandcastle against relentless waves. But to a young child, few things are as valued and precious as birthdays! At a birthday we celebrate that a person is alive, and we rejoice with them. With children, this often means a party, with friends bringing presents, and usually also cake, singing, balloons and streamers.

We would have those in my school chapel services at Pentecost too, because Pentecost is the celebration of the church's birth. As we reflect elsewhere (see 'Bearing fruit'), the Spirit of God is poured out on Jesus' friends, overwhelming them so that they are consumed by God's love, and the desire to share it with everyone. It must have been an incredible experience, both for Jesus' followers, and those who rushed into the street to see what was happening. Three thousand people were baptised that day. The disciples were not the only ones who felt the power of the Spirit!

Yet when we read about it, it can be hard to capture that excitement, hard to really understand and appreciate how the Spirit works. Often when I try to reflect on a Bible story, I find some art relating to it. Looking at others' creative interpretations of what happened can spark or deepen our own understanding. I am struck that in artworks Pentecost seems dominated by images of flame, and light, maybe because while we can feel the wind, it is awfully difficult to draw and paint. So, I like to think about the wind to understand the Spirit. With my school chapel services, I would demonstrate with balloons. I would hold up an uninflated balloon, and suggest it shows what we are like without the Spirit. I would then blow into it and hold it up, fully inflated, to show the difference. Then I would release it! Sometimes we would together do multiple balloons. It was an exciting if chaotic way to remind everyone that we often best see the wind by its effects on the things, and people, around it! And this is certainly also true of the Spirit. The Spirit brings life to people and situations that are otherwise lifeless, and it brings movement, and it brings change.

It would be great if it were as simple and easy to see that. I remember watching with my children the movie *Cheaper by the Dozen*. In one scene, the dad pretends he has a 'guilt detector' and he runs it over the heads of his children to identify the evil genius behind some earlier mischief (like Mary Poppins' measure of character; see 'Knowing yourself'). Maybe that is the kind of thing that we need, a detector that would tell us when a person, or a community, was being moved by the Spirit. It would clearly show us God's Spirit in action and help us to know whom to look up to, whose advice to follow, and whose vision for the future we could trust, and together work to fulfil. Well, we do not have a detector, but there is hope. Just as the wind can be seen by its effects, Paul (Galatians 5:22-23) describes the effects of the Spirit, its fruits as joy, peace, patience, kindness, generosity, faithfulness, gentleness and self-control.

Imagine if, like a massive wind, these effects of the Spirit roared through us, and through our communities. It would be exciting to see what a difference the Spirit could make, in us and in those around us.

> HOW DO YOU FEEL THE SPIRIT'S POWER?
> HOW DO YOU SEE THE SPIRIT'S EFFECTS?

God, we are getting excited!
the wind of the Spirit is with us
releasing us
moving us
giving us life
bringing change

we pray that its effects roar through us
and by our actions
through our communities too

Amen

Susan Joy Nevile and Maurice Nevile

Reshaped

Jeremiah 18 (MSG)

LIKE A POTTER WORKS CLAY, GOD CAN RESHAPE US

We do not have to look far to see that we are surrounded by troubles. All it takes is five minutes of the morning news to hear of pain, suffering, and hatred echoing around the world, close to us or far away. When we find ourselves having to live through troubled times, we want someone trustworthy to turn to, someone to help us to know what to think, how to carry on, how to pray. We want someone who has been through it, someone who knows what it is like to have their own world picked up and shaken, damaged, even destroyed. We can think about Jeremiah.

Jeremiah's life spanned one of the most troublesome times in Hebrew history, the years leading up to the fall of Jerusalem in 587 BCE, the destruction of the temple, followed by the Babylonian exile. Everything that could go wrong did go wrong! And Jeremiah was in the middle of it all, standing out, praying, preaching, suffering, striving, writing, and believing. He authored two books in the Bible. The first is named for him – the book of Jeremiah – and the second is the book of Lamentations.

Jeremiah was called by God to be a prophet, someone who unashamedly delivers God's commands and promises to his people – and that is a really tough task. A prophet has to remind people that God has something to say about every aspect of our lives, the way we feel and act in the privacy of our hearts and homes, the problems we face, the wars we fight, the way we make and spend our money, the people we hurt, and the people we help. Nothing is hidden from God. Prophets must wake people up so that they can see the way they are living. It is not an easy job, but it is also not a job that one can avoid if called (as Jonah found out; see 'Called'). Jeremiah was called when he was young, and he was given a clear instruction: 'Your job is to pull up and tear down, take apart and demolish. And then start over, building and planting' (Jeremiah 1:10).

This image of destruction followed by rebuilding is echoed in the potter's house. God tells Jeremiah to go to the potter's house, and there Jeremiah sees the potter working at his wheel. Jeremiah hears from God that just as the potter works his clay, God works on his people, shaping and reshaping their lives. Amid what seems like a dark and hopeless situation, God says 'I can reshape it'. A misshapen lopsided piece of clay can become something of beauty and purpose. Jeremiah's message is not only a warning but also a message of hope. This is true for individuals, that situations in our lives can be reshaped, for example that friendships can recover and grow even out of breakdown. And we can change the parts of who we are, the parts that we wish were not there, which end up hurting those around us, and ourselves, such as a ferocious temper, bad language, selfishness, envy, or quick judgment and criticism of others. All these and more can be reshaped. God will not give up, there is nothing so broken and ugly that God cannot reshape it, like the potter brings to reality the vision or dream for the clay.

Like the job of a prophet, change is often not an easy process. I once saw an interview with a man who had been a politician. He had been forced out of the parliament due to charges of corruption, and he had spent some time in prison. Many would see this as a personal catastrophe. He described it as a precious time in his life, a time when he was able to reassess what was important to him, who he was, and how he could change. He now acts as an advocate for poor and homeless people in his community. Out of personal failing and disaster came hope, both for him and for others. The hope that Jeremiah offers is not limited to individuals – communities and whole countries can be reshaped and transformed.

In recent years, and no doubt into the foreseeable future, we are confronted with the presence and power of terror in our world. In the face of terror, we need to be like Jeremiah and recognise the transformational power of hope. Although it can all seem too huge, that we cannot make a difference, we can start by reshaping ourselves, and our relationships, including our relationship with God. For living in hope, we can express our concerns through prayer to God, knowing that God will listen.

HOW IS GOD RESHAPING YOU?

God
like a potter works clay
to create beauty and purpose
you constantly reshape us
and our lives

you hold in your hands
our every hurt
our every loss
our every fear
our every fault
our every battle
and with our hope and prayer
you can transform them
so that we can make a difference to our world

Amen

Susan Joy Nevile and Maurice Nevile

Transformed

Matthew 11:2-11 (NIV)

IF WE LOOK, WE WILL SEE SIGNS OF TRANSFORMATION

For many people, a general rule of life is to believe what they can see. Have you ever gone to the Easter/Royal show and bought show bags? Today, it seems that show bags are filled with cheap plastic toys that break as soon as you get them home. It was not like that when I was a child – when you went to the show back then you did not buy 'show bags' you bought 'sample bags'. Originally, they were free, and over time and they cost just a nominal amount, I remember them at 40 cents each. The reason they were called 'sample bags' was because the manufacturers thought that by giving you a sample of their products, you could try them, and so later might go out and buy them. Not a bad idea, and if you go shopping these days, you can see it still happening, for example at the fruit markets where some fruit is cut up and you are welcome to try it. And when you buy clothes or shoes, you get to try them on first, to see what they look like, to experience what it would be like to have and wear them. In a way, it reminds us of the proverb 'seeing is believing'. If you actually see yourself wearing the jeans, then you can better believe that they are worth buying!

In Matthew 11:2-11, we see that poor old John was not seeing very much. He had earlier drawn in the crowds with 'Prepare the way! Get ready the one is coming'. Now it is later in Jesus' ministry. John is stuck in prison, hearing rumours, after all Jesus was not acting like the Messiah... and the doubts have set in: maybe Jesus is not the one, maybe I was wrong, maybe the Messiah is still to come. So, John sends his followers to ask Jesus 'Are you the one...?' (v. 3).

Jesus replies very simply, 'Go back and report to John what you hear and see' (v. 4). It is a wonderfully simple instruction, and it is grounded in reality, in what has been happening. Jesus had been traveling around preaching that the kingdom of God is near, telling people what they must do to be a part of it. But he had not only been talking, he had also been doing – and with just a touch of literary style he adds a reference to the Jewish prophets, Isaiah 35. The blind can see, the lame can walk, the lepers are healed, the deaf can hear and the dead have been raised to life. Jesus says listen to me, watch me, then make up your own mind. Jesus does not try to prove he was the Messiah by conventional human means – he does not compose a well-argued logical answer, there are no large-scale political rallies, there are no TV commercials, there are no armies to overthrow the Romans, there are not even any self-serving dramatic displays of power. He does not throw lightning bolts at the Pharisees.

Instead, Jesus told stories, he shared meals, he offered healing, and he showed people a new way to live. In this way, he demonstrated the way that God was keeping his promise. These were signs of promise that we hear in Isaiah, the promise of transformation, the deserts will bloom, the blind will see, and the deaf will hear.

Now we may think, 'Lucky them, they could hear the stories, they could eat the meals, they could experience the healing, they could see what Jesus was doing, no wonder they believed. It is much harder for us'. But I believe there *are* signs for us to see – *signs of transformation*. Sometimes we see these signs on TV – such as the overwhelming response of communities after natural disasters – I remember in one instance the support agencies even said, 'Thank you, no more please, we have enough!'. Or we see signs when business people, politicians, and scientists get together to discuss climate change and how we should be treating our natural resources. For me, many signs of transformation also come from the stories I hear and see of people's lives, sometimes from close to home, of people opening their lives by running soup kitchens for people living on the street, or sometimes from further away, from the work and contribution of overseas aid projects. Some signs of transformation came to me in the school community where I was chaplain, when I heard of students making a special effort with someone who is hard to like. Other stories arise from the hospice and hospital communities, when family members bond together and transform their relationships in their care for a loved one who is injured, ill, or dying.

Or we may see signs of transformation in ourselves, in how we are transformed. Perhaps we are amazed at how well we take on a new challenge, persevere at something truly daunting, recover from a setback, keep our temper in a difficult situation, or are able to forgive someone who has hurt us. All these are signs of transformation, of hope, of peace and of joy, and once we start looking, we will see them more and more.

> **LOOK *around* YOU: WHAT SIGNS OF TRANSFORMATION DO YOU SEE?**
> **LOOK *within* YOU: WHAT SIGNS OF TRANSFORMATION DO YOU SEE?**

God of change
you promise transformation

help us to see its signs *around* us
in people's stories
of love
of kindness
of patience
of perseverance
of relationship

help us to see its signs *within* us
in our own stories
of hope
of change
of faith
of joy
of forgiveness

with transformation we can know
a new way to live
Amen

Susan Joy Nevile and Maurice Nevile

Living with faith

Hebrews 11 (GNT)

FAITH IS ACTIVE AND CONSTANTLY LIVED FOR ALL TO SEE

In the 1980s, George Michael had a hit singing that he had 'gotta have faith', but what is it to have faith, what does it look like, and how is faith something that we can live?

The book of Hebrews tells us of faith, and has the reputation of being a bit tricky, so one of the best places to start is to remember that it began as a letter, from an experienced Christian to a community of believers. It was written to a group of people who were being persecuted and hurt because they believed in Jesus; and perhaps out of fear they had grown passive in their faith. The writer did not want them to give up and so needed to give a message that would encourage the listeners to keep on going, to reach the goal they longed for, to hold on, to keep the faith. The writer of Hebrews was not saying that life would be easy, or that what they feared would not happen, but that with faith it is possible to continue, and even to overcome.

Indeed, chapter 11 of Hebrews is a roll call of people in the Jewish scriptures who stood out because of their faith, starting with Abel, Noah, Abraham, Isaac, Jacob, Joseph, Moses, Rahab, Gideon, Samson, David, Samuel and the prophets. These were the Big Names, the heroes of the Jewish people. Verses 8-18 focus on Abraham, whom God called when he was 75 years old. God made some extremely specific promises to Abraham and his wife Sarah. Through this aged and childless couple, a great nation would arise which would bless all people on the earth. What is more, God would give Sarah and Abraham a land of their own. But they would have to leave their own home and rely on God to lead them to this unknown place. This, for both Jews and Early Christians, was *the* great example of faith. Everyone wanted to have faith like Abraham. No doubt, this letter was a motivational winner for its first listeners because looking at heroes is a great way to reflect on what it means to keep the faith. But for us, today, Abraham just does not cut it as a role model.

So, I thought of a relatively more contemporary hero: Indiana Jones. In the climactic late scene of the movie *Indiana Jones and the Last Crusade*, Indiana must make a leap of faith to cross a rocky chasm. There is no bridge – no visible means of crossing. At first sight he says it is impossible, but with his dying father nearby saying, 'You must... believe', Indiana takes some deep breaths, calms himself, and makes a large step off the edge and into the nothingness. It turns out that there *is* a bridge, but it is does not emerge, it cannot emerge, *until* he steps off. It is in Indiana's use of faith that faith's usefulness is revealed. Only *as* he steps, and *because* he steps, does the bridge materialise and appear to support him, and so keep him from falling into the abyss. When Indiana steps, his faith makes sense. It is a powerful and memorable scene!

We all have faith, even if we are not usually conscious of it. But faith in what? Well, in the physical world, we have faith that the walls will keep the roof up, the chair will continue to hold our weight, the cup handle will not break away, and on the road that other cars will stop at the red light, that the truck will pass safely by, that our car will drive as it should. And I have faith that when I type and save these words, the computer will store them! We act as if the things around us will perform just as we expect. Indeed, we must do so, to live our lives in an ordinary way. We cannot constantly act in doubt and check everything.

What then can we learn from both Abraham and Sarah, and Indiana Jones? Well, for a start, we must be continually reminded of what we believe, because it is not always easy to keep our belief alive and active. Often, we find a battle between our faith and our moods and feelings, especially with strong emotions like fear. We may be afraid – afraid of what will happen, of what we are able to do, of what others will say and do, of what might or might not happen. This is true no matter in what we have faith. Indiana Jones was not distracted by his fear, or of what he 'knew': he could see no bridge, there was no bridge on which to step. Indiana held on to what he believed that he could trust. To hold on to our faith when things are tough, are uncertain, we need always to recognise the voice of emotions and remind ourselves of what is true. This is what the writer of Hebrews wanted the listeners to recognise. To 'have faith' is 'to be sure of the things we hope for, to be certain of the things we cannot see' (Hebrews 11:1).

Having faith does not mean that we always get it right. In fact, the more we learn about many of the people on the roll in Hebrews, the more we know that their lives were not spotless: Abraham told lies about his wife; Moses did not make it to the promised land because he had disobeyed God; Rahab was a prostitute; Samson gave in to Delilah and blabbered about the secret of his amazing strength; and David, the great king, was rather keen on another man's wife. Yet these people are held up as examples, and one reason why is that they did not give up – they got it wrong, but they did not let that stop them. They held on to what was important, and at the end they triumphed, just as Indiana Jones did.

Finally, the heroes of Hebrews 11, and Indiana Jones, each had to make a leap of faith, because faith does not really make sense until it is used. The promises that faith holds are not reached by agreeing to them, and then putting them on the shelf – they are reached by acting on them. Abraham was promised a homeland for his descendants, but this is meaningless if he does not pack up and move; the bridge did not appear until Indiana stepped into where it could be.

When I think on this Hebrews text, the most powerful part for me comes at the end: all those people were still living by faith when they died. What hits me is the idea of faith as something that is constantly lived and rooted in community – faith is not a remote idea or a distant and safe philosophy, something to think on, for some day. Instead, faith is something active that we enact, daily, always and for all to see. When life's journey is hard, with faith we can hold on to what we know to be true, and so move on from doubts, hesitations, discouragement, obstacles, mistakes, and pain, to make not one leap of faith, but many!

> **IS THERE A CHASM BEFORE YOU?**
> **HOW CAN YOU STEP OUT IN FAITH?**

God
sometimes we must step
into nothingness
knowing that our faith
will make sense
will be of use
will save us
only when we do

help us to make that step
to live our faith actively
today, tomorrow, and always
always, always
Amen

Susan Joy Nevile and Maurice Nevile

Finding true life

Mark 8:27-38 (NIV)

WE FIND TRUE LIFE WHERE WE GIVE OF OURSELVES

There is disagreement about when Mark's Gospel was written, who wrote it, and for whom it was written, but most commentators agree in identifying two interrelated themes: who is Jesus? and what does discipleship entail? The passage here from the book of Mark hits the jackpot! We have Jesus and his closest friends discussing who he is, and what it means to be his follower. Jesus warms them up by first asking who others say he is, and then he moves in with the key question: 'But who do you say I am?' (v. 29). And Peter, after all the time spent with Jesus – after seeing him walk on water, heal the sick, feed the thousands – has what appears to be a moment of clear insight when he replies, 'You are the Messiah' (v. 29). Wow! If Peter was on a TV game show, the lights would flash, balloons would fall from the ceiling, the crowd would cheer, and he would take home the grand prize – the car, the holiday, the cash, whatever. It was the right answer! Well, at least on the surface. And often that is where we stop, with worldly wisdom and with being happy with what sounds right. If it feels good, do it. You deserve it. Why wait? The world bombards us with surface answers to our questions, with surface responses to our needs.

But Jesus continues, he goes deeper, he pushes the disciples, he starts to explain, to teach what his understanding of being the Messiah is. It is like he says, 'So you think you know who I am, do you really want to know what it means to be the Messiah? It is like this...' For a start, Jesus uses the title Son of Man. The title Messiah, the anointed one, had connotations of a kind of kingship, of power and prestige. But instead of identifying himself with that form of royalty, Jesus here identifies himself with the people, with everyone. Then he spells it out – being the Messiah means suffering, rejection, death, and resurrection.

We have got to love Peter because he certainly was not shy. He rebukes Jesus, and we can just see him with his arm around Jesus' shoulders saying, 'No, no, no, you can't say that'. Peter clearly had a good understanding of worldly wisdom. He knew that no one would follow a leader who predicted his own suffering and defeat. These kinds of words would overturn all the good work that had been done. People want a strong, masterful successful leader. In Peter's understanding, that is what the Messiah would be. That is what is needed.

I wonder how often we are like Peter in this, operating with a fixed idea, maybe even using the right words, but with an understanding that flows from our own needs or experiences, rather than from God's wisdom. When we talk of God's inclusive love, who do we imagine it actually includes? The poor, the homeless, the in-laws, the mentally ill, an addict, a criminal, a refugee?... or really just someone mostly like us? When we speak of God as a loving parent, do we have a picture in our minds of a father with a white beard? When we imagine taking up our cross, do we think only of the daily struggles that everyone lives with?

To avoid confusion, just as he spelt out what it means to be the Messiah, Jesus also spells out what it means to be one of his disciples. He effectively says forget about your life as you know it now, pick up your cross and follow me. It sounds clear enough, but these instructions to deny yourself and take up your cross have resulted in a great deal of confusion. Is it simply a matter of not doing what you want to do – for a while, perhaps during Lent? Is it saying to yourself that 'I need to hate myself, or at least constantly put myself down in front of others'? Is it putting up with abusive relationships, exploitative working conditions, poverty, or ongoing physical harm and pain? No, I find it hard to believe that the one who said 'I have come to bring life in its fullness', in abundance, would be advocating that we accept such hurting and life-denying states and situations.

Instead, we are being offered an alternative model of being, shown in Jesus' death on the cross, giving his life for us. That is where true life is found. Only when we can say who Jesus is, as the one who suffers and dies on the cross, can we begin to understand that. Only then, when we live our lives as the people of the cross, following that same road and giving of ourselves for the people around us, do we find the life to which Jesus calls us.

> **WHO IS JESUS TO YOU?**

God
in Jesus you call us to true life
in its fullness, in its abundance
and offered freely

help us to hear your call, to find true life
not in what we receive, and have
but in what we give, of ourselves
living as people of the cross

Amen

Susan Joy Nevile and Maurice Nevile

I am

John 6:25-59 (NIV), 2 Samuel 11, 12 (NIV)

Walter Brueggemann (1984) *The Message of the Psalms: A Theological Commentary.* Augsburg Pub.

John Goldingay (2000) *Men Behaving Badly,* Paternoster Press.

I AM... SOMEONE WHO NEEDS GOD

In my school chaplaincy and teaching, I would often use the 'I am' game, within a unit of work that explored who Jesus was. We would begin with the students, mid primary school age, standing around me in a circle. I would point to a child randomly and ask, 'Who are you?' They would have to answer with a statement about themselves, starting with 'I am': 'I am the youngest in my family', 'I am a chocolate lover', 'I am a book reader', 'I am very stubborn', etc. It got harder as the game progressed because they were not allowed to say something that was untrue, they were not allowed to repeat something already said, and they could not hesitate. Also, they did not know when I would pick them (sometimes twice in a row). One by one they would be eliminated. They became highly creative in saying who they were, expressing different aspects of their character!

I would then tell the class that now they were detectives investigating a notorious criminal of the past. We had to examine what others said of this criminal, we even looked at various mug shots that had been painted of him over the years, and I told the class it was very important to see *what he said of himself*. The problem was, I said, that he often spoke in a kind of a code which we would have to work out. He used picture language. The game led into a discussion of Jesus' 'I am' statements found in John's Gospel: I am the direction maker, the tear wiper, the name knower, the way opener, the sap channel, the dark destroyer, the stomach filler. But you might better recognise some of these ones: I am the true vine; I am the way; I am the resurrection; I am the good shepherd; I am the gate; I am the light for the world; I am the bread of life.

Jesus would have been great to play the 'I am' game with, but I doubt we could have caught him out. He knew who he was, and he took delight in showing that to people, in both his actions and in his words. In this final and extended reflection, we step into the gospel story just as Jesus has fed the five thousand, and walked on water to his disciples, telling them 'It is I; don't be afraid' (v. 20). These signs are not merely miracles, they are actions that have the potential for revealing God and to generate belief. Jesus knows who he is and what he is doing: 'I am the bread of life. Whoever comes to me will never go hungry, and whoever believes in me will never be thirsty' (v. 35). Jesus connects the deep needs of those he encounters with the gift of meeting that need, in God. Jesus confronted people with the presence of God, demonstrating God's power over nature, over life, over suffering, over evil. *In* Jesus' presence, people were brought face-to-face with who they are, and *by* his presence they were offered wholeness. No, I would never have caught Jesus in the game. He is the life-giver.

But let us imagine David playing the 'I am' game: 'I am the youngest in my family; I am a shepherd; I am a giant killer; I am a musician; I am a warrior; I am a faithful friend; I am the king'... I wonder how long it would have taken David to get to... 'I am an adulterer; I am a murderer; I am lost'. So, when Nathan asks David, 'Who are you?', he goes by another route (2 Samuel 12). Like Jesus, Nathan uses the power of story. He draws David into a simpler world of right and wrong. The rich man takes the beloved lamb of the poor man. This is something David understands, he bursts into righteous anger as he pronounces judgment: 'As surely as the Lord lives, the man who did this must die! He must pay for that lamb four times over, because he did such a thing and had no pity.' (vv. 5-6). And there Nathan has him: 'You are the man!' (v. 7). How has David come to this point? For all those other 'I am' statements are true, and to really appreciate what is happening in this conversation (2 Samuel 12) we really need the back story. This is David, the one chosen by God, not because of how he looked on the outside, but because of his heart. This is David, who with a sling, some river stones, and faith, defeated a giant. This is David, who is protected by God through battle and from Saul. This is David, who has received a promise from God that his house and kingdom will endure ... to which his humble response is, 'Who am I... that you have brought me this far?' (2 Samuel 7:18).

Yet 2 Samuel chapter 11 reads like a bad episode of an American television soap opera, like those classics *Dallas* or *Days of Our Lives*. There is indolence, as David remains in Jerusalem even though it is spring and the season for war; lust, as David gazes at the unknown woman; adultery, as David takes her; corruption, as David tries to cover it up; and ultimately, there is murder. 'Who am I' indeed. David has lost sight, or forgotten who he is, especially who he is in relationship with God. In earlier chapters of Samuel, we hear David consulting with God in his decisions: 'Shall I go up to one of the towns of Judah?' he asked. The Lord said, 'Go up.' David asked, 'Where shall I go?' 'To Hebron,' the Lord answered.' (2 Samuel 2:1). But now David has become the king, he has grown used to making his own decisions, and to having and manipulating power. When we read chapter 11, two things stand in strong contrast to each other: one is the number of times we hear of David sending people. For example, he sends Joab off to war, he sends for Bathsheba, he sends for Uriah and then sends him to his death. David uses kingly power. Also standing out is the complete absence of the Lord. The sin of David is not ultimately about sex and murder, it is, as Walter Brueggemann (p. 102) claims, the sin of pride, of living one's life without reference to Yahweh and to Yahweh's commandments. This is shown by the Lord's absence, right up to the last sentence (2 Samuel 11:27): 'But the thing David had done displeased the Lord'. God may have been absent from the narrative, pushed into the background, forgotten, but God was not absent from the story.

And at the start of Samuel chapter 12, we hear 'The Lord sent Nathan' (v. 1). David thought he was in control, but no, think again, it is time for the prophet to speak to the king. Truth speaks to power. Who are you? This is the new role of prophets, to confront the people who hold institutional power. As John Goldingay explains, in his book *Men Behaving Badly*, prophets are the means by which God gets a word in edgeways when people in official positions are inhibited, by their positions, from hearing and knowing what God is saying. I love this image of 'God getting a word in edgeways', of cutting across those things that hold God's word back.

It makes me wonder, how are we called to be a part of this: how, when, where, must we speak truth to power? In some ways, for me, this is a comfortable question, as in the past I have written protest letters, and taken part in marches and rallies. Those are familiar ways of being and acting. It is harder and less comfortable when I think of the need to confront on a more personal level, for example in my workplaces, when those in authority act unjustly, or without consideration or compassion.

And it is harder again when I am forced to turn the question over. As I approached my ordination, I could not avoid the realities of being a leader in the church. Uncomfortable as I am with the thought of wielding power, it is present in the words I say, the actions I take, the decisions I make – how do I use the power and authority that I have? What might Nathan say to me? As a deacon? As a pastoral carer? As a minister? As a wife? As a mother? When I have power, do I use it to dominate, manipulate, or control? Sometimes it is hard to tell, and know, and sometimes the temptation is very subtle.

We may use power because we want to help, to advise, to fix. That is how it was when I was a hospice pastoral carer – in the rawness, and the vulnerability of that place, people are open to control, albeit well-meaning. Those in power, due to their expertise, their job-title, their position on staff, who are making decisions, advising, and consoling, need constantly to be deeply aware of the influence they can have on others' lives, in every decision, action, even word.

But that is not the final question this story raises – for me at least – because, like it or not, I do have power, and the Lord will send 'Nathans' into my life. How will I respond?

For David's response, despite all he had done, and out in the wilds of his 'lostness', is true to his heart. When confronted, David does not dodge, or deny or bully. I wonder if there is relief as he accepts responsibility: 'I have sinned against the Lord' (2 Samuel 12:13), in effect, 'I have let Yahweh down'. Some thinkers tie Psalm 51 directly to this moment in David's story, and it can give insight into the point of renewal in a deeply disoriented life (Psalm 51:1-2, NIV)

> Have mercy on me, O God,
> according to your unfailing love;
> according to your great compassion
> blot out my transgressions.
> Wash away all my iniquity
> and cleanse me from my sin.

If nothing else, Psalm 51 gives us the words to use when we come ourselves to that point of self-knowledge: who am I? I am someone who needs God. So, 'Create in me a pure heart, O God, and renew a steadfast spirit within me' (Psalm 51:10, NIV). We can turn to God knowing that Jesus came, proclaiming the kingdom of God, bringing light, fulfilment, connection, wholeness, Jesus as the direction maker, tear wiper, name knower, way opener, sap channel, dark destroyer, stomach filler. My hope for us all is not only that we will act as Nathan in this world, speaking truth in difficult places, but also that when God sends 'Nathans' into our own lives, confronting and challenging us, we can hear, and turn to the life giver, the true vine, the way, the resurrection, the good shepherd, the gate, the light for the world, the bread of life.

> **WHO ARE YOU? 'I AM... ... ...'**

God
you are present, always present
you are the great I am

we need your light
we need your life
we need your love

in you we are found
in you we are whole
in you we are true

confront us, challenge us
have mercy on us
as we walk in faith with you
life giver, true vine
way, resurrection
good shepherd, gate
light for the world
bread of life

Amen

Susan Joy Nevile and Maurice Nevile

Sources

Bible versions

GNT: Good News Translation

MSG: The Message

NIV: New International Version

NIRV: New International Reader's Version

Other sources

Batchelor, Mary (1985) *Mary Batchelor's Everyday Book*. Lion Hudson, Hertsfordshire, England.

Beaumont, Karen, and Catrow, David (2004) *I Like Myself!* Koala Books, Mascot, NSW.

Bidegain, Ana Maria (2004), in Persaud, Christopher H. K., *Famous People Speak About Jesus: A Compendium of Expressions of Praise and Reverence*. Xlibris, Bloomington, IN., USA.

Brueggemann, Walter (1984), *The Message of the Psalms: A Theological Commentary*. Augsburg Publishing House.

Goldingay, John (2000), *Men Behaving Badly*. Paternoster Press, Carlisle.

Haugen, Gary (1999), *Good News about Injustice: A Witness of Courage in a Hurting World*. World Vision, USA.

Lachenmeyer, Nathaniel (2005) *Broken Beaks*. Michelle Anderson Publishing, Melbourne.

Lewis, C. S. (1971) *Prince Caspian*. Penguin Books, Harmondsworth. First published 1951.

Lewis, C. S. (1980) *The Magician's Nephew*. Fontana Lions, London. First published 1955.

Nouwen, Henri J. M. (1994) *The Return of the Prodigal Son: A Story of Homecoming*. Darton, Longman, and Todd, London.

Remen, Rachel Naomi (2001) *My Grandfather's Blessings: Stories of Strength, Refuge, and Belonging*. Riverhead Books, New York.

Remen, Rachel Naomi (2006) *Kitchen Table Wisdom: Stories that Heal*. Riverhead Books, New York.

Schulz, Charles M. (1963) *Security is a Thumb and a Blanket*. Paul Hamlyn, London.

Schulz, Charles M. (1964a) *Christmas is Together-time*. Paul Hamlyn, London.

Schulz, Charles M. (1964b) *I Need All the Friends I Can Get*. Determined Productions, San Francisco.

Summers, Susan, Morris, Jackie (1998) *The Fourth Wise Man. Based on the Story by Henry Van Dyke*. Dial Books for Young Readers, New York.

Watts, Bernadette (1997) *Shoemaker Martin*. Adapted and illustrated from original story by Leo Tolstoy. North-South Books, New York.

Williams, Terry Tempest (2000) *Leap*. Pantheon Books, New York.

www.ingramcontent.com/pod-product-compliance
Lightning Source LLC
Chambersburg PA
CBHW010244010526
44107CB00063B/2674